COMPLETE ENLIGHTENMENT

COMPLETE ENLIGHTENMENT

Translation and Commentary

on

The Sutra of Complete Enlightenment

Ch'an Master Sheng-yen

Acknowledgements:
Managing Editor/Translator: Venerable Guo-gu Bhikshu
Translators: Pei-gwang Dowiat, Ming-yee Wang, Paul Kennedy
Editorial Advisor: Peter Gregory
Editor: Chris Marano, Lindley Hanlon
Editorial Assistants: Lisa Commager, Susan Curran,
Ernest Heau, Xiujue Zhu
Production: Trish Ing
Cover Design: Chih-chin Lee

☙

We are grateful to Mr. Chin-shiang Lin for his generous donation in support
of this project through the Lin Pan Cultural and Educational Foundation.

First Edition 1997

Library of Congress Catalogue Number 94-74086
ISBN 0-9609854-7-6

Printed in the United States of America on recycled paper

Contents

Foreword

In the true teaching of Lord Buddha, Complete Enlightenment is made of incomplete enlightenments. This means that in the heart of your daily mindful actions, thoughts, and speech, Complete Enlightenment is already there, and you should not strive to look for Complete Enlightenment anywhere else.

Suppose you are on the road between Boston and New York. Looking in one direction is Boston; looking in the other direction is New York. If you want to go to Boston, you should turn in the direction of Boston. Once you have turned in the direction of Boston, Boston is already in you. But if you turn in the direction of New York, Boston is lost. Lost, but it is still there for you, if you knew how to turn around. Every point of the road contains Boston. And any point of the road contains New York. Complete Enlightenment and Complete Ignorance are exactly the same. They contain each other.

In our practice, we listen to the Dharma, we participate in Dharma discussions to deepen our understanding, and we find ways to apply the Dharma in our daily life: sitting, standing, walking, eating, drinking, cleaning, cooking . . . . *The Sutra of Complete Enlightenment* is a Dharma discussion between the Buddha and several great bodhisattvas in the presence of a large Sangha. If you know how to be there and how to listen, you will be able to actually participate in it. It is still going on. And if you do well, you will not get caught in words (like *samadhi*, *samapatti*, and *dhyana!*), sentences, and ideas. Many people just enjoy ideas, even great ideas, and are not able to put them into practice. This is something the Buddha does not want us to do.

We should also not be caught in the idea whether such or such sutra was truly spoken directly by the Buddha or by one of his disciples, right in the time of the Buddha or hundreds of years later. If a disciple of the Buddha practices well, and gets the true insight, then his or her words will be the same as the words of the Buddha. If you bear this in mind, you will learn and profit greatly from this well-known sutra.

Ch'an Master Sheng-yen is a great teacher and I have great confidence in his scholarship and wisdom. I feel privileged to be his friend, and admire what he has been doing for the Buddhadharma in the East as well as in the West. These few lines, written as the foreword to this book, are a wholehearted dedication to that friendship. Please enjoy this beautiful translation of the sutra and also the valuable commentaries and instructions offered by this great and rare teacher.

Thich Nhat Hanh
Plum Village
December 6, 1996

Introduction

The Sutra of Complete Enlightenment is an extremely important text in the history of Chinese Buddhism. It was held in high regard by followers of the Hua-yen tradition (a sect based on the teachings of the *Avatamsaka Sutra*). Today it is also highly respected by Ch'an and Zen practitioners.

Within the Indian Tathagatagarbha system of Mahayana Buddhism, there are numerous representative texts such as the *Ratnagotravibhaga* (*Uttaratantra*) *Sastra*, the *Tathagatagarbha Sutra*, and the *Srimala Sutra*, which developed with great clarity the Tathagatagarbha system of thought. However, Chinese Mahayana Buddhists rarely rely on these texts. Instead, they have adhered almost exclusively to *The Sutra of Complete Enlightenment*, *The Surangama Sutra*, and *The Awakening of Mahayana Faith Sastra*. Therefore, in order to understand the special flavor of Chinese Buddhism, one must begin with a study of these texts.

According to available information, there have been two translations of *The Sutra of Complete Enlightenment* from Sanskrit into Chinese. The first translation was completed in 647 by a mysterious individual named Luoho tanjian. We know he was Indian, but the name does not correspond to any known Indian translator. The second translation was by another Indian, Buddhatrata, in 693. His translation is the one commonly used.

Buddhatrata's Chinese translation of this sutra appears in one volume. However, numerous exegetical works on *The Sutra of Complete Enlightenment* have been written, the most famous being

The Great Exegesis on the Sutra of Complete Enlightenment (Yuan jue jing da shu chao), written in 26 fascicles by the prominent Hua-yen and Ch'an master, Zongmi (780-841). Before his commentary, however, there were already four others in existence. To this date, there are dozens of exegeses and commentaries available. However, even now, when people write commentaries on *The Sutra of Complete Enlightenment*, they often ignore all exegeses but Master Zongmi's.

Master Zongmi also compiled a ritual manual entitled *A Manual of Procedures for the Cultivation and Realization of Ritual Practice (Yuan jue jing dao chang xiu zheng yi)*, based on the eleventh chapter of *The Sutra of Complete Enlightenment*, where the Buddha taught specific methods of practice for fixed time periods: 120 days, 100 days, and 80 days.

Why does *The Sutra of Complete Enlightenment* hold such an important position in Chinese Buddhism? For one thing, we cannot overlook the impact that Master Zongmi has had on Buddhism. Master Zongmi was highly respected as both a great scholar and a great practitioner. Therefore, his particular emphasis on *The Sutra of Complete Enlightenment* strongly influenced successive generations of Chinese Buddhists. Master Zongmi is the Fifth Patriarch of the Hua-yen sect and a patriarch of the southern Ho-tse Ch'an lineage, which can be traced to Shenhui (684-758), a disciple of the Sixth Patriarch, Huineng (638-713). The lineage proceeds: Huineng—Shenhui—Zhiru—Weizhong—Daoyuan—Zongmi.

In the Tang dynasty (618-907), Prime Minister Peixiu (787?-860) wrote a preface to *The Sutra of Complete Enlightenment* and mentioned Master Zongmi's connection with the sutra. According to the preface, one day Master Zongmi was participating in a ritual in which monks chanted *The Sutra of Complete Enlightenment*. As they chanted, Master Zongmi was greatly touched. Tears flowed down his face and he had an experience similar to enlightenment. After relating the experience to his master, his master told him to devote his studies and practice to the sutra. From that point on until the end of his life, Master Zongmi took up the task of expounding and propagating *The Sutra of Complete Enlightenment*.

After Master Zongmi, the Hua-yen sect was absorbed by the Ch'an school which primarily followed the teachings and lineage of

Huineng. In fact, by the time of the Song dynasty (960-1279), virtually all sub-lineages of Ch'an, namely the Five Houses and the Seven Sects, branched out from the southern tradition of Huineng. Because of Master Zongmi's connection to the southern tradition, the Ch'an school in turn was influenced by *The Sutra of Complete Enlightenment.*

However, people have long questioned the authenticity of *The Sutra of Complete Enlightenment.* When sutras were compiled and catalogued during the Tang dynasty, people had reservations about the translator of *The Sutra of Complete Enlightenment* and the date of its translation. Even the title is peculiar. In the Chinese title, the word "sutra" appears twice. A translation of the complete title of it from the Chinese is *Mahavaipulya-purnabuddha-sutra-prasannartha-sutra.* Modern scholars have yet to satisfactorily resolve these ambiguities. In fact, two other texts, *The Surangama Sutra* and *The Awakening of Mahayana Faith Sastra,* have been scrutinized for similar reasons. Nevertheless, these three texts have had a tremendous impact on Chinese Buddhism.

Over the centuries, scholars may have had doubts about the translation of *The Sutra of Complete Enlightenment*, but, at least among Chinese Buddhists, no one doubts the profound importance of its teachings. The sutra is filled with beautifully written passages and useful instruction. According to Master Zongmi, *The Sutra of Complete Enlightenment* includes both the gradual and sudden teachings of the Mahayana tradition and both the incipient as well as the ultimate Buddhist teachings. Therefore, people of all backgrounds can benefit from this sutra.

The Sutra of Complete Enlightenment often speaks of the Complete Enlightenment practitioners can attain through its teachings. In the first chapter, the Buddha points out that Complete Enlightenment can give rise to purity, true suchness, bodhi, nirvana, and the paramitas. It also mentions that all Buddhas attained Buddhahood because they practiced methods of Complete Enlightenment. Again, in the seventh and eighth chapters, the Buddha teaches three methods of practice: *samatha, samapatti,* and *dhyana.* Ch'an practitioners usually regard these as gradual methods of practice, but in the context of this sutra, they are presented as sudden methods of practice. *The Sutra of Complete Enlightenment* also uses many (at least twenty-three) analogies as well as ordinary language to convey its profound ideas. Its power of expression is yet another reason why *The Sutra of Complete Enlightenment* is so revered.

This commentary on *The Sutra of Complete Enlightenment* is based on a series of lectures delivered at the Ch'an Center in New York City to the general public. These lectures covered a period of four years (from 1982 to 1985). Had I spoken on a regular basis, the lecture series might have been completed sooner, but I was often away from New York, either on lecture tours or in Taiwan.

I chose to speak on this sutra for a simple reason. *The Sutra of Complete Enlightenment*, along with the two other texts I previously mentioned, are of great significance in Chinese Buddhism and the Ch'an school. Before this sutra, I lectured on *The Awakening of Mahayana Faith Sastra*, and after I finished with *The Sutra of Complete Enlightenment*, I went on to speak on *The Surangama Sutra*.

I do not profess that *The Sutra of Complete Enlightenment* contains the highest teachings of the Buddha. I simply use the concepts and methods of practice taught in this sutra to guide practitioners, especially to guide them on the ways in which they can incorporate Buddhism in their daily lives.

The flavor of this book is somewhat different from my previous English publications. Most of my other books are based either on lectures given during retreats or during special classes for serious Ch'an practitioners, and so emphasize methods and concepts of practice as well as guidance in cultivating a Ch'an attitude. The series of lectures on *The Sutra of Complete Enlightenment* also included such guidance, but in this case, emphasis was placed on providing the Ch'an view of life, how one can practice the teachings of *The Sutra of Complete Enlightenment* in daily life, and the benefits one may derive from it.

My commentary is based entirely on what I have learned and experienced from Buddhadharma. For this reason, I could exercise greater flexibility in my lectures than scholars who followed the commentaries of previous masters and patriarchs. I did not limit myself to the conventional format of traditional Chinese Buddhist commentaries. Sometimes I dealt briefly with only the main points of a section. At other times, I spoke at length on a single sentence. Also, I chose not to comment on the section on the Bodhisattva of Sound Discernment, as I feel it comprises largely repetitious variations of the three practices of *samatha*, *samapatti* and dhyana. To comment on this section would entail meticulous explanations of these practices which would not be suitable for a general audience. Moreover, there is a danger in presenting methods of practice in printed form. General readers may start to use these methods without the guidance of a master and experience negative results. However, the chapter on the Bodhisattva of Sound Discernment is included in the English translation of the sutra.

If readers are interested in knowing more about *The Sutra of Complete Enlightenment*, it is recommended that they read the original text and *The Great Exegesis of the Sutra of Complete Enlightenment* by Master Zongmi in Chinese. I only know of one other English translation, by Charles Luk. Also, for those who are interested, there is a book written by Professor Peter Gregory entitled *Tsung-mi and the Sinification of Buddhism* which explains more fully on the connection between Master Zongmi and *The Sutra of Complete Enlightenment.*

For the benefit of the Sunday lecture audience, I referred to Charles Luk's translation when I lectured. His translation proved to be enormously beneficial for this purpose, and for that I am deeply grateful. For this book, however, we originally planned on using the translation of Pei-gwang Dowiat, a task she willingly accepted. I am thankful for her arduous efforts. In 1995 I gave the whole manuscript to my attendant monk, Guo-gu Shi, for review. He carefully read the original Chinese sutra with the English translation and saw the need to delay the publication date and rework the manuscript. After some consideration, I asked him to retranslate the sutra and polish up the commentary. Having read through different commentaries on the sutra for several months, he spent three months retranslating the sutra. Most of the Chinese commentaries he relied on were by Master Zongmi and Master Tixian of the T'ien T'ai sect. He also listened to a set of audio tapes of my earlier commentaries on this sutra given in Taiwan to my monastic disciples ten years ago. These commentaries were short but deeper and more concise. Guo-gu Shi also relied on these to make the commentary in this book more complete.

Translating an ancient text, especially an ancient Chinese text, is a great and difficult endeavor since the classical Chinese language has many nuances and connotations. So much effort went into the translation because during the course of my lectures on the sutra, I found the older translation either insufficient for my purposes or in conflict with some of my interpretations. I also feel that it is necessary to bring to Westerners an English translation of this sutra that bears the flavor and visual quality of the original language without losing the essential meaning.

Since I prefer to speak Chinese for lectures, my words were interpreted and translated on the spot predominantly by Ming-yee Wang. Occasionally Paul Kennedy and Pei-gwang Dowiat filled in. Many people helped to transcribe the tapes of the lectures, then Chris Marano spent two years editing and putting together the book from the transcriptions. Afterwards, Ming-yee Wang carefully scrutinized the edited version of the lectures and made the appropriate corrections. Ming-yee has an outstanding memory and very often remembered what I had said years earlier. Guo-gu Shi took up the task of final editing, working closely with assistant editors to clarify and fine tune the whole manuscript, and working with book designers for final production.

Lastly, I thank Chih-ching Lee for the cover design, Trish Ing for the interior design and her assistance in the production of this book, as well as all others who contributed to the creation and publication of this book.

May all beings be free from suffering and accomplish Complete Enlightenment.

Master Sheng-yen
Ch'an Meditation Center
Summer 1996

Translator's Foreword

First, I wish to thank Pei-gwang Dowiat for providing the first translation of *The Sutra of Complete Enlightenment.* Her translation has not only given me firm ground to work on, it has also inspired me to refine and sharpen my own understanding of the concepts involved and the ideas expounded in the sutra. I also wish to extend my thanks to Professor Peter Gregory who kindly took time from his busy schedule at the University of Illinois to read my translation and give valuable suggestions, as we shared each other's understanding and interpretation of certain difficult passages. I also consulted parts of a translation of the sutra by Charles Muller. The range of viewpoints and skill presented among other translators and scholars led me to deeper reflections on and investigation of the meaning of the sutra, which I believe contributed to the quality of this final translation.

Above all, I am grateful to Shifu, Master Sheng-yen, for the teachings I have received from him since I was a boy, whose life and work continuously give spiritual inspiration and insight to me and to people throughout the world. I am also grateful to him and honored that he had the faith in me to entrust me with the responsibility of translating this sutra and editing his commentary on the sutra.

I tried to follow three principles to insure that the translation of the sutra is literal, accurate and poetic. Reasonable and sensible as these principles were, I sometimes found that they conflicted with each other, and that I had to make compromises. For example, the classical Chinese language is rich and evocative in meaning, often visual and poetic in style. In most cases the wording, especially of this sutra, is extremely condensed and to the point; it is intended for those well-read and experienced in Buddhist theory and practice. Sometimes it is concise to the point of being telegraphic, almost telepathic! A literal translation in English would have been virtually unreadable, let alone comprehensible. Therefore, the translation is supplemented with additional words in brackets. I tried to keep interpolated material to a minimum, without explaining the meaning of the text, in order to preserve as much as possible the powerful, laconic style of this sutra. Those sections of the sutra that are technical and difficult for the reader to follow I have explained in the endnotes and glossary. As usual, Master Sheng-yen has skillfully explained and related them to daily situations in his commentary.

Where the subject matter is difficult to understand or when a passage can be interpreted in more than one way, I tried to be as precise as possible in choosing terminology that in my understanding best conveys the intended meaning. Although Chinese terms cannot be translated to the same English word throughout, I tried, as a rule, to maintain an internal consistency in terminology, while, at other times, I chose an alternate translation to bring out different nuances of the same word, so that readers would gain a wider perspective on the rich meanings the language signifies. With the exception of proper names, all foreign words not included in the Webster's unabridged dictionary have been italicized. I have also adopted the *pinyin* romanization system for all Chinese terms, but kept the names of Buddhist schools in their familiar Wade-Giles forms.

This volume can be read in several ways. One can begin reading and studying the running translation of the sutra or, for those less familiar with the traditional terminology of Buddhist writing, one may wish to read the gathas first, printed at the end of each section of the sutra. The gathas are concise, poetic summaries of the main points raised in the longer dialogues between the

Buddha and his bodhisattva disciples which constitute the main body of the sutra. Or, one can proceed directly to Master Sheng-yen's commentary on each section of the sutra which is reprinted along with the commentary. Alternatively, of course, one can read the book from beginning to end, consulting the endnotes at the end of the sutra and the glossary of terms at the end of the book. Experienced or serious practitioners will want to reread many passages, as questions answered in the sutra arise in their own practice. Or, they may wish to refer to the index to answer specific questions on their practice or to explore specific topics of Buddhist inquiry. The sutra serves as a stimulating introduction to the Buddhist universe, and the commentary reveals the world of Ch'an practice for students of religion and other thinkers. The sutra is a challenging course of study for all contemplatives, not just in the Buddhist but in all sacred traditions.

The experience of translating this sutra has been an enriching and special process of deepening my own practice of Ch'an. In order to capture the essential meaning conveyed, while retaining the flavor of the original, I have had to refine my own understanding of the sutra. This refinement led me to redo different sections as I came to appreciate deeper levels of meaning. In the course of the several months spent in translating this text, I worked long hours reading, listening to, and contemplating commentaries by Masters Zongmi, Tixian, and Sheng-yen. These resources were indispensable in helping me to arrive at a proper understanding of the sutra. During this intense period of study and practice, I was completely immersed in the sutra day and night. I paid particular attention to those sections in which the Buddha expounds on the practice wherein all is seen as illusory; on the great differences between actualization and attainment among sentient beings, bodhisattvas, and Buddhas; on the four inverted views of self, person, sentient beings, and life; and on the four potential faults of a teacher and practitioner that hinder the correct view of the nature of practice and mind. The process of translation not only opened my mind to a deeper insight and appreciation of the sutra, but also mirrored and clarified my own practice. More importantly, the sutra challenged and revealed the flaws in my practice. For this, I feel deeply fortunate and grateful to the Dharma.

The Sutra of Complete Enlightenment is a revelation, not exposition. The questions posed to the Buddha in this sutra flow forth from the compassionate heart-minds of the twelve bodhisattvas. These questions reflect not only the obscurities in our own lives and practice but unfold the nature of our true condition. An authentic glimpse of the riches of the sutra and the commentary will allow us to participate or as the sutra puts it, "roam and play," in the wisdom minds of countless Buddhas and Buddhist masters from the past, present, and future in all traditions.

I humbly offer my endeavors in translating and managing the publishing of this book to the continuance of Buddhadharma in all places. Also, may all those who come in contact with *Complete Enlightenment* become the great cause for the benefit and happiness of infinite numbers of living beings.

Ven. Guo-gu Bhikshu
Ch'an Meditation Center
New York
October 1996

The Sutra of Complete Enlightenment

Translated from the Chinese of Buddhatrata

by

Ven. Guo-gu Bhikshu

The Sutra
of
Complete Enlightenment

Thus have I heard. At one time the Bhagavan entered the Samadhi of the Great Illuminating Storehouse of Spiritual Penetration.[1] This is the samadhi in which all Tathagatas brightly and majestically abide. It is the ground of the pure enlightenment of all sentient beings.

[The Bhagavan's] body and mind were in the state of quiescent-extinction,[2] where past, present, and future are intrinsically equal and identical,[3] and his completeness filled all ten directions, and was in accord with everything without duality. From within this condition of non-duality, he caused various Pure Lands to appear.

[The Bhagavan] was accompanied by one hundred thousand great bodhisattvas and *mahasattvas*. Chief among them were Bodhisattva Manjusri, Bodhisattva Samantabhadra, Bodhisattva of Universal Vision, Bodhisattva Vajragarbha, Bodhisattva Maitreya, Bodhisattva of Pure Wisdom, Bodhisattva at Ease in Majestic Virtue, Bodhisattva of Sound Discernment, Bodhisattva Cleansed of All Karmic Obstructions, Bodhisattva of Universal Enlightenment, Bodhisattva of Complete Enlightenment, and Bodhisattva Foremost in Virtue and Goodness. Together with their retinues, they all entered samadhi, abiding in the Tathagata's Dharma assembly of impartial equality.

Bodhisattva Manjusri

Thereupon Bodhisattva Manjusri rose from his seat in the midst of the assembly, prostrated himself at the feet of the Buddha, circled the Buddha three times clockwise, knelt down, joined his palms,[4] and said: "O World Honored One of great compassion! Please expound to the multitude who have come to this assembly the Tathagata's Dharma practice of the original-arising purity of the causal ground.[5] Please also expound to us how bodhisattvas may initiate this state of pure mind within the Mahayana and leave all illness. [Pray teach us] so that sentient beings in the future Dharma Ending Age who aspire to the Mahayana will not fall into errone-ous views." Having said these words, he prostrated himself on the ground. He made the same request three times, each time repeating the same procedure.

At that time the World Honored One said to Bodhisattva Manjusri: "Excellent, excellent! Virtuous man, for the benefit of the multitude of bodhisattvas you have asked about the Tathagata's Dharma practice of the causal ground. For the benefit of all sentient beings in the Dharma Ending Age who aspire to Mahayana, you asked how they can attain correct abiding and not fall into errone-ous views. Listen attentively now. I shall explain it to you."

Hearing this, Bodhisattva Manjusri was filled with joy and listened silently along with the assembly.

"Virtuous man, the Supreme Dharma King possesses the method of the great dharani[6] called Complete Enlightenment,[7] out of which emanates pure true suchness, bodhi and nirvana, as well as the paramitas to teach bodhisattvas. The original-arising [purity] of the causal ground of all Tathagatas relies on the complete illumina-tion of [intrinsic] enlightenment, which is pure [in essence] and permanently free from ignorance.[8] Only then do the [Tathagatas] accomplish the Buddha Path.

"What is ignorance? Virtuous man, since beginningless time, all sentient beings have had all sorts of delusions, like a disoriented person who has lost his sense of direction. They mistake the four great elements[9] as the attributes of their bodies, and the conditioned impressions[10] of the six sense objects as the attributes of their minds. They are like a man with an illness of the eyes who sees an [illusory] flower in the sky, or a second moon.

"Virtuous man, there is in reality no flower in the sky, yet the sick man mistakenly clings to it. Because of his mistaken clinging, he is not only deluded about the intrinsic nature of the empty space, but also confused about the arising of the flower. Because of this false existence [to which he clings], he remains in the turning wheel of birth and death. Hence this is called ignorance.

"Virtuous man, this ignorance has no real substance. It is like a person in a dream. Though the person exists in the dream, when [the dreamer] awakens, there is nothing that can be grasped. Like an [illusory] flower in the sky that vanishes into empty space, one cannot say that there is a fixed place from which it vanishes. Why? Because there is no place from which it arises! Amidst the unarisen, all sentient beings deludedly perceive birth and extinction. Hence this is called the turning wheel of birth and death.

"Virtuous man, one who practices Complete Enlightenment of the causal ground of the Tathagata realizes that [birth and extinction] are like an illusory flower in the sky. Thus there is no continuance of birth and death and no body or mind that is subject to birth and death. This nonexistence of [birth and death and body and mind] is so not as a consequence of contrived effort. It is so by its intrinsic nature.

"The awareness [of their nonexistence] is like empty space. That which is aware of the empty space is like the appearance of the illusory flower. However, one cannot say that the nature of this awareness is nonexistent. Eliminating both existence and nonexistence is in accordance with pure enlightenment.

"Why is it so? Because the nature of empty space is ever unmoving. Likewise, there is neither arising nor perishing within the Tathagatagarbha.[11] It is free from conceptual knowledge and views. Like the nature of *dharmadhatu*, which is ultimate, wholly complete, and pervades all ten directions, such is the Dharma practice [of the Tathagata] of the causal ground.

"Because of this [intrinsic completeness], bodhisattvas within the Mahayana may give rise to pure bodhi-mind. If sentient beings in the Dharma Ending Age practice accordingly, they will not fall into erroneous views."

At that time, the World Honored One, wishing to clarify his meaning, proclaimed these gathas:

Manjusri, you should know
that all Tathagatas,
from their original-arising causal ground,
use wisdom to enlighten
and penetrate ignorance.
Realizing that ignorance is like
a flower in the sky,
they are thus liberated from the continuance
[of birth and death].
Like a person [seen] in a dream who
cannot be found when [the dreamer] awakens,
awareness is like empty space.
It is impartial and equal, and ever unmoving.
When enlightenment pervades all ten directions,
the Buddha Path is accomplished.
There is no place where illusions vanish,
and there is no attainment
in accomplishing the Buddha Path,
for the intrinsic nature is already wholly complete.
By this, bodhisattvas
can give rise to the bodhi-mind.
Sentient beings in the Dharma Ending Age
through this practice will avoid erroneous views.

Bodhisattva Samantabhadra

Then Bodhisattva Samantabhadra rose from his seat in the midst of the assembly, prostrated himself at the feet of the Buddha, circled the Buddha three times clockwise, knelt down, joined his palms, and said: "O World Honored One of great compassion! For the multitude of bodhisattvas in the assembly, as well as for all sentient beings who cultivate Mahayana in the Dharma Ending Age, please explain how they should practice having heard about this pure realm of Complete Enlightenment.

"World Honored One, if these sentient beings come to understand illusion, then body and mind are also illusory. How can they then use illusion to remedy illusion? If all illusory characteristics were exhausted and extinguished, then there would be no mind. Who is it that practices? Why, then, do you say that practice is illusory?

"If sentient beings originally had no need to practice, then they would remain confined to illusory projections amidst birth and death and never discern the state [in which all is seen to be] like an illusion. How could they be liberated from illusory conceptualization? For the sake of all sentient beings in the Dharma Ending Age, please explain the expedient method of gradual cultivation of practice in order that sentient beings may permanently leave the state of illusion." Having said these words, he prostrated himself on the ground. He made the same request three times, each time repeating the same procedure.

At that time the World Honored One said to Bodhisattva Samantabhadra: "Excellent, excellent! Virtuous man, for the benefit of the multitude of bodhisattvas and sentient beings in the Dharma Ending Age, you have asked about the expedient, gradual stages of the bodhisattva's practice of the samadhi in which all is seen to be like an illusion, and which frees sentient beings from illusion. Listen attentively now. I shall explain it to you."

Hearing this, Bodhisattva Samantabhadra was filled with joy and listened silently along with the assembly.

"Virtuous man, all illusory projections of sentient beings arise from the wondrous mind of the Tathagata's Complete Enlightenment, just like flowers in the sky which come into existence from out of the sky. When the illusory flower vanishes, the nature of the sky is not marred. Likewise, the illusory mind of sentient beings relies on illusory [cultivation] for its extinction. When all illusions are extinguished, the enlightened mind remains unmoved. Speaking of enlightenment in contrast to illusion is itself an illusion. To say that enlightenment exists is to not have left illusion yet. [However], to say that enlightenment does not exist is also no different. There-fore, the extinction of illusion is called the unmoving [mind of enlightenment].

Virtuous man, all bodhisattvas and sentient beings in the Dharma Ending Age should separate [themselves] from all illusory projections and deluded realms. [However], when one clings firmly to the mind that separates [from all illusory projections and deluded realms], this mind [should also be taken as] an illusion, and one should separate oneself from it. Because this separation is an illu-sion, it should also be separated. One should then be free from even this 'separating from the illusion of separation!' When there re-mains nothing to be separated from, all illusions are eliminated. It is like rubbing two pieces of wood together to obtain fire. When the fire ignites and the wood completely burns, the ashes fly away and the smoke vanishes. Using illusion to remedy illusion is just like this. Yet even though illusions are exhausted, one does not enter annihilation.

"Virtuous man, to know illusion is to depart from it; there is no [need to] contrive expedient means! To depart from illusion is to be enlightened; there are no gradual steps! All bodhisattvas and sentient beings in the Dharma Ending Age who practice accord-ingly will permanently leave illusions behind."

At that time, the World Honored One, wishing to clarify his meaning, proclaimed these gathas:

Samantabhadra, you should know
that the beginningless illusory ignorance
of all sentient beings
is grounded on the Tathagata's
mind of Complete Enlightenment.
Like a flower in empty space,
its appearance relies on the sky.
When the illusory flower vanishes,
the empty space remains in its original unmoving state.
Illusion depends on enlightenment for its arising.
With the extinction of illusion,
enlightenment is wholly perfect,
for the enlightened mind is ever unmoving.
All bodhisattvas and sentient beings
in the Dharma Ending Age
should forever leave illusions far behind
until all illusions are extinguished.
It is like producing fire with wood,
when the wood is burned out,
the fire is also extinguished.
Enlightenment has no gradual steps;
the same applies to expedient means.

Bodhisattva of Universal Vision

Then the Bodhisattva of Universal Vision rose from his seat in the midst of the assembly, prostrated himself at the feet of the Buddha, circled the Buddha three times clockwise, knelt down, joined his palms, and said: "O World Honored One of great compassion! For the sake of the multitude of bodhisattvas in this assembly and all sentient beings in the Dharma Ending Age, please expound on the gradual stages of the bodhisattva's practice. How should one contemplate? What should one abide in and uphold? What expedient methods should one devise to guide unenlightened sentient beings, to universally enable them to reach enlightenment?

"World Honored One, if these sentient beings do not have the correct expedient methods and contemplation, they will be confused when they hear you expound this samadhi [in which all is seen to be an illusion] and will be unable to awaken to Complete Enlightenment. Would you be compassionate enough to expound the provisional expedient methods for our benefit and for sentient beings in the Dharma Ending Age?" Having said these words, he prostrated himself on the ground. He made the same request three times, each time repeating the same procedure.

At that time the World Honored One said to the Bodhisattva of Universal Vision: "Excellent, excellent! Virtuous man, for the benefit of the multitude of bodhisattvas and sentient beings in the Dharma Ending Age, you have asked the Tathagata about the gradual stages of cultivation, what contemplation one should abide in and uphold, as well as the various expedient methods one should use. Listen attentively now. I shall explain them to you."

Hearing this, the Bodhisattva of Universal Vision was filled with joy and listened silently along with the assembly.

"Virtuous man, newly initiated bodhisattvas and sentient beings in the Dharma Ending Age seeking the Tathagata's pure mind of Complete Enlightenment should hold the right thought of separating from myriad illusions. First, they should rely on the *samatha* practice of the Tathagatas and strictly observe the precepts. They should reside peacefully among an assembly of practitioners and sit in meditation in a quiet room.

"They should always be mindful that the body is a union of the four elements. Things such as hair, nails, teeth, skin, flesh, tendons, bones, marrow and brain all belong to the element of earth. Spittle, mucus, pus, blood, saliva, sweat, phlegm, tears, semen, urine, and excrement all belong to the element of water. Warmth belongs to the element of fire. Motion belongs to the element of wind. When the four elements are separated from one another, where is this illusory body? Thus one knows that the physical body ultimately has no substance and owes its appearance to the union [of the four elements]. In reality it is not different from an illusory projection.

"Due to the provisional union of the four conditions [of vision, hearing, perception, and awareness], the illusory six sense faculties come to exist. The inward and outward combination of the six sense faculties and the four elements [of earth, water, fire, and wind] gives rise to the illusory existence of conditioned energy. [In this process], there 'seems to be' something which is cognizant. This is provisionally called 'mind.'[12]

"Virtuous man, this illusory mind cannot exist without the six sense objects [of sight, sound, smell, taste, touch, thought]. When the four elements disperse, the six sense objects cannot be found. Once the elements and the sense objects disperse and are extinguished, ultimately there is no cognizant mind to be seen.

"Virtuous man, when the illusory bodies of sentient beings become extinguished, the illusory minds also become extinguished. When the illusory minds become extinguished, the illusory sense objects also become extinguished. When the illusory sense objects become extinguished, the illusory extinguishing also becomes extinguished. When the illusory extinguishing becomes extinguished, that which is not illusory is not extinguished. It is like polishing a mirror. When the defilements are wiped off, brightness appears.

"Virtuous man, you should know that both body and mind
are illusory defilements. When these appearances of defilement are
permanently extinguished, purity will pervade all ten directions.

"Virtuous man, for instance, the pure mani jewel reflects the
five colors as they appear before it, yet the ignorant see the mani as
actually possessing the five colors. Virtuous man, although the pure
nature of Complete Enlightenment likewise manifests as body and
mind, [people] respond in accordance with their capacities, yet the
ignorant speak of the pure Complete Enlightenment as having
intrinsic characteristics of body and mind. For this reason, they are
unable to depart from illusion. Therefore, I say that body and mind
are illusory defilements. It is in terms of separating from illusory
defilements that bodhisattvas are defined. When defilements are
thoroughly removed, their corresponding [cognition] is [com-
pletely] eliminated. Since there is nothing corresponding to defilement, there is also no 'one' there to designate.

"Virtuous man, if bodhisattvas as well as sentient beings in the
Dharma Ending Age realize the awakening of the extinction of
illusory appearances, at that time, unlimited purity and infinite
emptiness will be revealed and manifested in their enlightenment.
Because the enlightenment is complete and illuminating, it reveals
the mind in its purity. Because the mind is pure, objects of vision
are pure. Because vision is pure, the eye faculty is pure. Because
that faculty is pure, the visual consciousness is pure. Because the
consciousness is pure, hearing is pure. Because hearing is pure, the
faculty of hearing is pure. Because that faculty is pure, the consciousness is pure. Because the consciousness is pure, perception is
pure. The same holds true for the nose, tongue, body, and mind.

"Virtuous man, because the sense faculties are pure, the
objects of sight are pure. Because the objects of sight are pure, the
objects of sound are pure. The same holds in the cases of smell,
taste, touch, and thought.

"Virtuous man, because the six sense objects are pure, the
earth element is pure. Because the earth element is pure, the water
element is pure. The same holds for the elements of fire and wind.

"Virtuous man, because the four elements are pure, the twelve
entrances, the eighteen realms, and the twenty-five existences are

pure. Because these are pure, the ten powers, the four kinds of fearlessness, the four unhindered wisdoms, the eighteen exclusive attributes of the Buddha, and the thirty-seven aids to enlightenment are all pure.[13] The same holds for the purity of everything all the way up to the eighty-four thousand dharani doors.

"Virtuous man, because the nature of Absolute Reality is pure, one's body is pure. Because one's body is pure, a multitude of bodies are pure. Because a multitude of bodies are pure, likewise sentient beings in all ten directions are completely enlightened and pure.

"Virtuous man, because one world is pure, a multitude of worlds are pure. Because a multitude of worlds are pure, all things completely exhausting empty space in the past, present, and future are impartially equal, pure, and unmoving.

"Virtuous man, since empty space is equal, identical, and unmoving as such, you should know that the nature of enlightenment is also equal, identical, and unmoving. Since the four elements are unmoving, you should know that the nature of enlightenment is also equal, identical, and unmoving. Since [everything] up to the eighty-four thousand dharani doors are equal, identical, and unmoving, you should know that the nature of enlightenment is also equal, identical, and unmoving.

"Virtuous man, as the nature of enlightenment is pervasive and full, pure, and unmoving, being perfect and boundless, you should know that the six sense faculties also fully pervade the *dharmadhatu*. Because the sense faculties are pervasive and full, you should know that the six sense objects also fully pervade the *dharmadhatu*. Because the sense objects are pervasive and full, you should know that the four elements also fully pervade the *dharmadhatu*. So it is with everything up to all the dharani doors, which also fully pervade the *dharmadhatu*.

"Virtuous man, because the nature of wondrous enlightenment pervades everything fully, the nature of the sense faculties and the sense objects is indestructible and clear. Because the sense faculties and the sense objects are indestructible, [everything] up to all the dharani doors is indestructible and clear. It is like hundreds of thousands of lamps illuminating a room: their illumination pervades fully and is indestructible and clear.

"Virtuous man, since his enlightenment is fully accomplished, you should know that a bodhisattva neither is bound by dharmas nor seeks to be free from dharmas. He neither detests birth and death nor clings to nirvana; neither reveres those who uphold the precepts nor condemns those who violate them; neither esteems experienced practitioners nor slights beginners. Why? Because all [sentient beings] are enlightened. It is like clear vision that is completely aware of what is in front: when this clarity is perfect, it has no likes or dislikes. Why? Because the essence of this clarity is non-dual and itself has no likes or dislikes.

"Virtuous man, these bodhisattvas and sentient beings in the Dharma Ending Age who have gained accomplishments through cultivating the mind have neither cultivated nor accomplished anything. Complete Enlightenment is universally illuminating in quiescent-extinction without duality. Hundreds of thousands of millions of *asamkyas* of Buddha worlds, as innumerable as the grains of sand of the Ganges, are like flowers in the sky, randomly arising and perishing. They are neither identical to nor separate [from the nature of Complete Enlightenment]. Since there is no bondage or liberation, one begins to realize that sentient beings have intrinsically accomplished Buddhahood, and that birth and death and nirvana are like yesterday's dream.

"Virtuous man, because birth and death and nirvana are like yesterday's dream, you should know that they neither arise nor perish, neither come nor go. That which is actualized is neither gained nor lost, neither grasped nor discarded. One who truly actualizes [enlightenment] does not contrive, stop, allow things to be as they are, nor annihilate [vexations]. In the midst of the actualization, there is neither a subject nor an object. Ultimately there is neither actualization nor one who actualizes! The nature of all dharmas is equal and indestructible.

"Virtuous man, bodhisattvas should thus practice, thus [progress through] these gradual stages, thus contemplate, thus abide in and uphold, thus use expedient methods, and thus become enlightened. In seeking this Dharma, they will not be confused and perplexed."

At that time, the World Honored One, wishing to clarify his meaning, proclaimed these gathas:

Universal Vision, you should know
that the minds and bodies of
all sentient beings are illusory.
The body is the union of the four elements.
The nature[14] of mind is reducible
to the [six] sensory objects.
When the four elements are separated
from one another, who is the unifier?
If one practices gradual
cultivation like this, all will be pure.
[The nature of Complete Enlightenment]
is unmoving and pervades the *dharmadhatu*.
There is no contrivance, stopping,
allowing things to be as they are,
annihilation, nor is there one
who actualizes [enlightenment].
All Buddha worlds are like
flowers in the sky.
Past, present, and future are
all impartially equal.
Ultimately there is no coming or going.
The newly initiated bodhisattvas
and sentient beings in
the Dharma Ending Age,
in their quest to enter the Buddha Path,
should thus cultivate themselves.

Bodhisattva Vajragarbha

Then Bodhisattva Vajragarbha rose from his seat in the midst of the assembly, prostrated himself at the feet of the Buddha, circled the Buddha three times clockwise, knelt down, joined his palms, and said: "O World Honored One of great compassion! You have wonderfully expounded to bodhisattvas the great dharani of the Tathagata's pure Complete Enlightenment, the Dharma practice of the causal ground, and the expedient methods of gradual cultivation, so that sentient beings may unveil their obstructions. Because of your compassionate teaching, all in the assembly have cleared away illusory illnesses [of the eye] and their wisdom-eyes have become pure.

"World Honored One, if sentient beings have intrinsically accomplished Buddhahood, how can there be so much ignorance? If all sentient beings originally have ignorance, why does the Tathagata say that they have intrinsically accomplished Buddhahood? If sentient beings in all ten directions intrinsically accomplished the Buddha Path and afterwards gave rise to ignorance, then when will the Tathagata give rise to vexations again? Please do not forsake your unrestricted great compassion, but disclose the secret treasury for the benefit of the multitude of bodhisattvas, so that when all the sentient beings in the Dharma Ending Age who hear of this Dharma door to the ultimate meaning of this sutra will permanently sever doubts and regrets." Having said these words, he prostrated himself on the ground. He made the same request three times, each time repeating the same procedure.

At that time the World Honored One said to Bodhisattva Vajragarbha: "Excellent, excellent! Virtuous man, for the benefit of the multitude of bodhisattvas and sentient beings in the Dharma Ending Age, you have asked the Tathagata about the very secret and profound ultimate expedient methods, which are the highest teaching for bodhisattvas and the ultimate truth in the Mahayana. These methods are capable of causing practicing and beginning bodhisattvas in all ten directions and all sentient beings in the Dharma Ending Age to obtain [the stage of] resolute faith[15] and permanently sever doubts and regrets. Listen attentively now. I shall explain it to you."

Hearing this, Bodhisattva Vajragarbha was filled with joy and listened silently along with the assembly.

"Virtuous man, all worlds begin and end, are born and perish, have a before and after, exist and do not exist, coalesce and disperse, arise and cease. Thoughts follow one another in succession, going and coming in a ceaseless circle. With all sorts of grasping and rejecting, these [changing processes] are all cyclic existences. If one were to discern Complete Enlightenment while still in cyclic existence, then this nature of Complete Enlightenment would have the same [nature] as the turning flow [of cyclic existence]! If one wished to be free from cyclic existence, then there would be no place where [Complete Enlightenment] could exist. For instance, when one moves one's eyes, still water appears to have waves; when one fixes one's gaze, a circling flame appears to be a wheel of fire. The fact that moving clouds make it seem as if the moon were moving and a sailing boat makes one feel as if the shore were moving also exhibits the same principle.

"Virtuous man, while the motion is going on, it is impossible for those things to be still. How much more would this be so if one were to discern the Complete Enlightenment of the Buddha with the defiled mind of birth and death, which has never been pure; how could it not [appear to] be in motion?[16] For this reason, you gave rise to these three doubts.

"Virtuous man, for example, because of an illusory illness [of the eye], a flower is falsely seen in an empty sky. When the illusory illness [of the eye] is eliminated, one does not say: 'Now that this illness is eliminated, when will other illnesses arise?' Why? Because the illness[17] and the flower[18] are not in opposition. Likewise, when the flower vanishes into the empty sky, one does not say: 'When will flowers appear in the sky again?' Why? Because the sky originally has no flowers! There is no such thing as appearing and vanishing. Birth and death and nirvana are like the appearing and vanishing [flowers in the sky], while the perfect illumination of wondrous enlightenment is free from flowers or illnesses.

"Virtuous man, you should know that the empty sky does not temporarily exist and then temporarily not exist. How much more so in the case of the Tathagata who is in accordance with Complete Enlightenment, which is comparable to the equal intrinsic nature of empty space.

"Virtuous man, it is like smelting gold ore. The gold does not exist because of the smelting. As it has become [perfect] gold, it will not become ore again. Even after an inexhaustible period of time, the nature of the gold will not deteriorate. Therefore, one should not say that gold is not intrinsically perfect in itself. Likewise, the same holds true with Tathagata's Complete Enlightenment.

"Virtuous man, the wondrous and completely enlightened mind of all Tathagatas is originally without bodhi or nirvana; it has nothing to do with accomplishing Buddhahood or not accomplishing Buddhahood, illusory cyclic existence or non-cyclic existence.

"Virtuous man, even the sravakas, who have perfected the state where [the karmic activities of] body, mind, and speech are entirely severed, are still unable to enter the nirvana that is personally experienced and manifested [by the Tathagata]. How can one possibly use one's conceptual mind to measure the realm of the Tathagata's Complete Enlightenment? It is comparable to using the light of a firefly to scorch Mount Sumeru; one would never be able to burn it! He who attempts to enter the Tathagata's ocean of great quiescent-extinction by using the cyclic mind and giving rise to cyclic views will never succeed. Therefore, I say that all bodhisattvas and sentient beings in the Dharma Ending Age should first sever the root of beginningless cyclic existence.

"Virtuous man, contrived conceptualizations come from the existence of a mind, which is a conditioned [conglomeration of] the six sense objects. The conditioned impressions of deluded thoughts are not the true essence of mind; rather, they are like flowers in the sky. The discernment of the realm of Buddhahood with such conceptualization is comparable to the production of empty fruit by the empty flower. One merely revolves in this entanglement of deluded thoughts and gains no result.

"Virtuous man, deluded groundless thinking and cunning views cannot accomplish the expedient methods of Complete Enlightenment. Discriminations such as these are not correct."

At that time, the World Honored One, wishing to clarify his meaning, proclaimed these gathas:

Vajragarbha, you should know
that the quiescent and extinct
nature of the Tathagata
never had a beginning or end.
To conceptualize this with the cyclic mind
results in rotations in cyclic [existence].
One will then remain in cyclic existence
unable to enter the ocean of the Buddha.
Like smelting gold ore,
the gold does not exist
as the result of smelting.
Though it regains the original golden [quality],
it is perfected only after
[the process of] smelting.
Once it becomes true gold,
it cannot become ore again.
Birth and death and nirvana,
ordinary beings and all Buddhas,
are but appearances of flowers in the sky.
Conceptualizations are illusory projections.
How much more so are such questions asked
with an illusory mind?
If one can put an end to this [illusory] mind,
Complete Enlightenment can be sought.

Bodhisattva Maitreya

Then Bodhisattva Maitreya rose from his seat in the midst of the assembly, prostrated himself at the feet of the Buddha, circled the Buddha three times clockwise, knelt down, joined his palms, and said: "O World Honored One of great compassion! You have opened wide the secret treasure for bodhisattvas and have caused the great assembly to deeply awaken from cyclic existence and distinguish between the erroneous and the correct. Your teaching is capable of bestowing the Fearless Eye of the Path to sentient beings in the Dharma Ending Age, causing them to give rise to resolute faith in the great nirvana, and never again to flow within the realm of the turning wheel [of samsara] or hold cyclic views.

"World Honored One, if bodhisattvas and sentient beings in the Dharma Ending Age desire to sail on the Tathagata's ocean of great quiescent-extinction, how should they sever the roots of cyclic existence? In the various cyclic existences, how many types of capacities are there? What are the different kinds of cultivation of Buddha's bodhi? When [bodhisattvas] enter the world of passions, how many expedient methods should they devise to deliver sentient beings? Pray do not forsake your great compassion in saving the world, but cause all practicing bodhisattvas and sentient beings in the Dharma Ending Age to cleanse their wisdom-eyes and illumine their mirror-like minds. May they be completely awakened to the Tathagata's unsurpassed knowledge and vision." Having said these words, he prostrated himself on the ground. He made the same request three times, each time repeating the same procedure.

At that time the World Honored One said to Bodhisattva Maitreya: "Excellent, excellent! Virtuous man, for the benefit of the multitude of bodhisattvas and sentient beings in the Dharma Ending Age, you have asked the Tathagata about the most profound, secret, subtle, and wondrous truth so that bodhisattvas' wisdom-eyes may become pure, so that all sentient beings in the Dharma Ending Age may permanently sever themselves from cyclic existence, so that their minds may awaken to Absolute Reality, and so that they may possess the patient endurance of the unborn [wisdom]. Listen attentively now. I shall explain it to you."

Hearing this, Bodhisattva Maitreya was filled with joy and listened silently along with the assembly.

"Virtuous man, all sentient beings [experience illusory] cyclic existence due to all kinds of affection, love, craving, and desire[19] since beginningless time. The different types of births in the world — be they from egg, womb, humidity, or by transformation — are created by sexual desire[20]. You should know that attached love is the root of cyclic existence. Because there are all sorts of desirable [objects] that enhance and augment the activity[21] of attached love, birth and death proceed in unending succession.

"Desire arises because of attached love. The existence of life comes from desire. Sentient beings' love of their lives [in turn] relies on desire as a base. Therefore, love and desire are the cause, love of life is the consequence. Because the objects of desire [vary], like and dislike arise. If the object goes against one's grasping mind, one gives rise to hatred and jealousy and commits evil karmic deeds. As a result, one is reborn in hell or as a hungry ghost.

"Realizing that desire is detestable, if one desires to leave behind karmic paths and abandons evil and delights in doing good, one is reborn in the realms of gods or humans. If, further, one knows that attachment is detestable, and thus abandons attachment and delights in renunciation, one still stirs up the root of attachment. This results in increased worldly meritorious fruit, which, being samsaric, does not lead to accomplishing the holy path. Therefore, if sentient beings wish to be liberated from birth and death and to avoid cyclic existence, they should first sever craving and desire, and eliminate their attached love.

"Virtuous man, the transformation and manifestation of bodhisattvas [in various forms] in the world are not based on attachment. Out of their compassion, they cause sentient beings to abandon attachment by provisionally taking on all kinds of craving and desire so they can enter birth and death. If sentient beings in the Dharma Ending Age can abandon desire, eliminate love and hatred, permanently sever cyclic existence, and diligently pursue the Tathagata's state of Complete Enlightenment with a pure mind, they will attain awakening.

"Virtuous man, due to the inherent desire in all sentient beings, ignorance flourishes and increases. Thus [sentient beings] manifest five distinct natures. According to the two obstructions, their hindrances may appear to be deep or shallow. What are the two obstructions? The first is the obstruction of principle,[22] which hinders right views. The second is the obstruction of phenomena,[23] which perpetuates birth and death.

"What are the five distinct natures?[24] Virtuous man, sentient beings who have not eliminated and extinguished these two obstructions are called 'those who have not attained Buddhahood.' Sentient beings who have permanently abandoned craving and desire and have eliminated the obstruction of phenomena, but not the obstruction of principle, can only be enlightened as sravakas or pratyekabuddhas. They are unable to manifest and abide in the realm of bodhisattvas.

"Virtuous man, if sentient beings in the Dharma Ending Age desire to sail on the Tathagata's great ocean of Complete Enlightenment, they should first vow to practice with diligence and sever the two obstructions. When these two obstructions have been subdued, they will be able to awaken to the realm of bodhisattvas. If the obstructions of principle and phenomena are permanently severed, they will enter into the subtle and wondrous Complete Enlightenment of the Tathagatas and consummate bodhi and great nirvana.

"Virtuous man, all sentient beings [intrinsically] actualize Complete Enlightenment. If they meet a good teacher and can rely on his Dharma practice of the causal ground, [their karmic roots for attainments] will be either gradual or sudden. However, if they come across the Tathagata's unsurpassable bodhi and engage in the correct path of practice, they will attain Buddhahood whether they are of great or small [karmic] roots. If sentient beings, though they seek a good teacher, meet one with erroneous views, they will not gain correct awakening. These people are called ones of outer path nature. This fault is due to the teacher and not to sentient beings.

"The above are the five distinct natures of sentient beings.

"Virtuous man, with great compassionate expedient methods, a bodhisattva enters the world to expand and mature [the minds of] the unenlightened. He manifests in various forms, amidst favorable or adverse situations so that he may work together with sentient beings in order to guide them to Buddhahood. In so doing, he relies entirely on the power of his pure vows made since beginningless time.

"If sentient beings in the Dharma Ending Age can arouse the supreme thought of [awakening to] great Complete Enlightenment, they should make the pure great vow of bodhisattvas, declaring: 'May I, from now on, abide in Buddha's Complete Enlightenment, and may I, in my search for a good teacher, not meet outer paths and practitioners of the Two Vehicles.²⁵' With their practice based on this vow, they will gradually sever all hindrances. When all hindrances are exhausted, their vows will be fulfilled. They will then ascend the pure Dharma hall of liberation and actualize the wondrous, august citadel of great Complete Enlightenment.

At that time, the World Honored One, wishing to clarify his meaning, proclaimed these gathas:
Maitreya, you should know
that sentient beings
cannot attain great liberation
because of their craving and desire,
which cause them to fall into
the cycle of birth and death.
If they can sever like and dislike,
along with greed, anger, and delusion,
regardless of their difference in nature,
they will all accomplish the Buddha Path.
The two obstructions will also be permanently severed.
After correct awakening is attained
by meeting a good teacher,
one accords with the bodhisattva vow
and abides in the great nirvana.
All bodhisattvas in the ten directions,
relying on the great compassionate vow,

manifest the appearance of entering birth and death.
Practitioners now and
sentient beings in the Dharma Ending Age,
should diligently sever all attached views.
Then they will return to
great Complete Enlightenment.

Bodhisattva of Pure Wisdom

Then the Bodhisattva of Pure Wisdom rose from his seat in the midst of the assembly, prostrated himself at the feet of the Buddha, circled the Buddha three times clockwise, knelt down, joined his palms, and said: "O World Honored One of great compassion! You have broadly expounded to us inconceivable things which we have never seen or heard before. Because of your excellent guidance, our bodies and minds are now at ease and we have gained great benefit. For the sake of all practitioners of the Dharma who have come here, please expound again the nature of the Dharma King's complete and fulfilling enlightenment. What are differences in the actualization and attainment between all sentient beings, bodhisattvas, and the World Honored Tathagata? [Pray teach us] so that sentient beings in the Dharma Ending Age, upon hearing this holy teaching, may follow and conform to it, be awakened, and gradually enter [the realm of Buddhahood]." Having said these words, he prostrated himself on the ground. He made the same request three times, each time repeating the same procedure.

At that time the World Honored One said to the Bodhisattva of Pure Wisdom: "Excellent, excellent! Virtuous man, for the benefit of sentient beings in the Dharma Ending Age, you have asked the Tathagata about the distinct progressive stages [of practice]. Listen attentively now. I shall explain them to you."

Hearing this, the Bodhisattva of Pure Wisdom was filled with joy and listened silently along with the assembly.

"Virtuous man, the intrinsic nature of Complete Enlightenment is devoid of distinct natures [as described before], yet all different natures are endowed with this nature [of Complete Enlightenment], which can accord and give rise to various natures.[26] [Since these two natures are non-dual], there is neither attainment nor actualization. In Absolute Reality, there are indeed no bodhisattvas or sentient beings. Why? Because bodhisattvas and sentient beings are illusory projections. When illusory projections are extinguished, there exists no one who attains or actualizes. For example, eyes cannot see themselves. Likewise, this nature is intrinsically impartial and equal, yet there is no 'one' who is equal.

"Because sentient beings are confused, they are unable to eliminate and extinguish all illusory projections. Because of the illusory efforts and activities of those who extinguish and those who do not extinguish [vexations],[27] there manifest distinctions. If one can attain accordance with the Tathagata's quiescent-extinction, there is in reality neither quiescent-extinction nor the one who experiences it.

"Virtuous man, all sentient beings since beginningless time have deludedly conceived 'self' and that which grasps on to the self; never have they known the succession of arising and perishing thoughts![28] Therefore, they give rise to love and hatred and indulge in the five desires.[29]

"If they meet a good teacher who guides them to awaken to the nature of pure Complete Enlightenment and to recognize these arising and perishing [thoughts], they will understand that it is the very nature of such rising [thoughts] that causes toils and anxieties in their lives.

"If, further, a man permanently severs all toil and anxiety, he will realize the *dharmadhatu* in its purity. However, his understanding of purity may become his obstruction and he will not attain freedom and ease regarding Complete Enlightenment. This is called 'the ordinary man's accordance with the nature of enlightenment.'[30]

"Virtuous man, all bodhisattvas realize that this very understanding is a hindrance. Although they sever themselves from this hindrance of understanding, they still abide in this realization. The realization of hindrance is yet another hindrance. Therefore they do not have freedom and ease. This is called 'the bodhisattva before the stage of the first *bhumi*'s accordance with the nature of enlightenment.'[31]

"Virtuous man, 'attaining' illumination and realization[32] is a hindrance. Thus a great bodhisattva is constantly in realization without abidance, where the illumination and the illuminator simultaneously become quiescent and vanish. For instance, if a man beheads himself, there exists no executioner after the head has been severed. It is the same with eliminating various hindrances with a mind of hindrance: when the hindrances have been eliminated, there is no eliminator. The teachings of the sutras are like the finger that points to the moon. When one sees the moon, one realizes that the finger is not the moon. Likewise, the various teachings of all Tathagatas in instructing bodhisattvas are also like this. This is called 'the bodhisattva above the stage of the first *bhumi*'s accordance with the nature of enlightenment.'[33]

"Virtuous man, all hindrances are themselves [the nature of] ultimate enlightenment. Having a [correct] thought or losing it is not different from liberation. Conglomeration and dispersion of dharmas are both called nirvana. Wisdom and stupidity are equally prajna. The Dharma accomplished by bodhisattvas and that by outer path practitioners are both bodhi. Ignorance and true suchness are not different realms. [The threefold discipline of] *sila*, samadhi, and prajna[34] and [the three poisons of] greed, anger, and delusion are all pure activities. Sentient beings and the world they live in are of one Dharma-nature. Hells and heavens are all Pure Lands. Regardless of [their distinct] natures, all sentient beings have [intrinsically] accomplished the Buddha Path. All vexations are ultimate liberation. [The Tathagata's] ocean of wisdom which encompasses the whole *dharmadhatu* clearly illuminates all phenomena as empty space. This is called 'the Tathagata's accordance with the nature of enlightenment.'

"Virtuous man, all bodhisattvas and sentient beings in the Dharma Ending Age should at no time give rise to deluded thoughts! [Yet], when their deluded minds arise, they should not extinguish them. In the midst of deluded concepts, they should not add discriminations. Amidst non-discrimination, they should not distinguish true reality. If sentient beings, upon hearing this Dharma method, believe in, understand, accept, and uphold it and do not generate alarm and fear, they are 'in accordance with the nature of enlightenment.'

"Virtuous man, you should know that these sentient beings have made offerings to hundreds of thousands of millions of

Buddhas and great bodhisattvas as innumerable as the grains of sand of the Ganges, and have planted the roots of all merits. I say that such people will accomplish the [Buddha's] Wisdom of All Aspects."[35]

At that time, the World Honored One, wishing to clarify his meaning, proclaimed these gathas:

Pure Wisdom, you should know
that the nature of perfect bodhi
is without attainment or actualization.
It is without bodhisattvas or sentient beings.
However, when there is enlightenment
and unenlightenment,
there are distinct progressive stages.
Sentient beings are obstructed by understanding.
Bodhisattvas [before the first *bhumi*]
have not left behind realization.
[Once] they enter the first *bhumi*
there is permanent quiescent-extinction
with no abidance in any form.
Great enlightenment, being complete,
is called 'pervasive accordance.'
If sentient beings in the Dharma Ending Age
do not give rise to deluded thoughts,
the Buddha says that they are
bodhisattvas in this very lifetime.
Having made offerings to countless Buddhas
as innumerable as the sands of the Ganges,
their merits are perfected.
Though expedients are many,
all are called in accordance with wisdom.

Bodhisattva at Ease in Majestic Virtue

Then the Bodhisattva at Ease in Majestic Virtue rose from his seat in the midst of the assembly, prostrated himself at the feet of the Buddha, circled the Buddha three times clockwise, knelt down, joined his palms, and said: "O World Honored One of great compassion! For our sake you have extensively clarified the different ways of according with the nature of enlightenment and caused the enlightened minds of the multitude of bodhisattvas to be illuminated. Hearing your perfect voice, we have gained great benefit without cultivation.

"World Honored One, a great city has four gates. People coming from different directions have more than one entrance. Likewise, all bodhisattvas who embellish the Buddha Lands and attain bodhi do so by means of more than one single expedient method. Please, World Honored One, broadly expound to us all the expedient methods and stages as well as how many types of practitioners there are, so that bodhisattvas in this assembly and sentient beings in the Dharma Ending Age who aspire to the Mahayana may quickly attain enlightenment, and roam and play in the Tathagata's ocean of great quiescent-extinction." Having said these words, he prostrated himself on the ground. He made the same request three times, each time repeating the same procedure.

At that time the World Honored One said to the Bodhisattva at Ease in Majestic Virtue: "Excellent, excellent! Virtuous man, for the benefit of the multitude of bodhisattvas and sentient beings in the Dharma Ending Age, you have asked the Tathagata about such expedient methods. Listen attentively now. I shall explain it to you."

Hearing this, the Bodhisattva at Ease in Majestic Virtue was filled with joy and listened silently along with the assembly.

"Virtuous man, unsurpassable wondrous enlightenment pervades all ten directions. From it arise the Tathagatas and all dharmas, which are equal and identical to one another and of the same substance. [Likewise], the various methods of cultivation are, in reality, not different [from one another]. Though there are countless expedient methods for becoming attuned to the nature of enlightenment, if one categorizes them according to their different natures, there are three kinds.

"Virtuous man, if, after awakening to pure Complete Enlightenment, bodhisattvas with pure enlightened minds engage in the cultivation of stillness, they will cleanse and settle all thoughts. Becoming aware of the agitation and restlessness of consciousness, they will cause their wisdom of stillness to manifest. Their bodies and minds, [which will be realized as adventitious] guests and dust[36] will be permanently extinguished.[37] Inwardly they will experience lightness and ease[38] in quiescence and stillness. Because of this quiescence and stillness, the minds of all Tathagatas in all ten directions will be revealed like reflections in a mirror. This expedient is called *samatha*.

"Virtuous man, if, after awakening to pure Complete Enlightenment, bodhisattvas with pure enlightened minds realize the nature of mind and realize that the six sense faculties and sense objects are illusory projections, they will then generate illusion as a means to eliminate illusion. Causing transformations and manifestations among illusions, they will enlighten illusory sentient beings. By generating illusions, they will experience lightness and ease in great compassion. All bodhisattvas who practice in such a manner will advance gradually. That which contemplates illusion is different from illusion itself. Nevertheless, contemplating illusion is itself an illusion. When all illusions are permanently left behind, the wondrous cultivation completed by such bodhisattvas may be compared to the sprouting of seeds from soil. This expedient is called *samapatti*.

"Virtuous man, if, after awakening to pure Complete Enlightenment, bodhisattvas with pure, enlightened minds grasp on to neither illusory projections nor states of stillness, they will understand thoroughly that both body and mind are hindrances. [Awakening from] ignorance, their [minds] will be illuminated. Without depending on all sorts of hindrances, they will permanently transcend the realms of hindrance and non-hindrance and make full use of the world as well as the body and mind. They will manifest in the phenomenal world [without any obstructions], just as the sound of a musical instrument can travel beyond [the body of the instrument]. Vexations and nirvana will not hinder each other. Inwardly, they will experience lightness and ease in quiescent-extinction. They will accord with the realm of quiescent-extinction in wondrous enlightenment, which is beyond the reach of body and mind and the reach of self and others. All sentient beings and all life are only drifting thoughts. This expedient method is called dhyana.

"Virtuous man, these three Dharma methods are intimately in accordance with Complete Enlightenment. Tathagatas in all ten directions accomplish Buddhahood through these means. The myriad expedient methods used by bodhisattvas in all ten directions, whether similar or different, depend on these three activities. At the perfect actualization of these practices, one accomplishes Complete Enlightenment.

"Virtuous man, if in his practice on the holy path, a person teaches, delivers, and succeeds in guiding hundreds of thousands of millions of people into arhatship and pratyekabuddhahood, he cannot be compared with someone who, upon hearing these Dharma methods of the unhindered Complete Enlightenment, practices accordingly for even an instant."

At that time, the World Honored One, wishing to clarify his meaning, proclaimed these gathas:

Majestic Virtue, you should know
that the unsurpassable mind of
great enlightenment is intrinsically non-dual.
Even though the various expedients
that accord with it
are limitless in number,
the teachings of the Tathagata are
altogether three in kind.

Quiescent and still in *samatha*,
[the mind] is like a mirror
reflecting myriad images.
Samapatti, wherein all is seen as an illusion,
is like a bud growing gradually.
Dhyana is quiescent-extinction,
[yet, its functions are] like the sound
of a musical instrument.
These three wondrous Dharma methods
are all in accordance with enlightenment.
The Tathagatas in all ten directions
and the great bodhisattvas
achieve Buddhahood through them.
Perfect actualization of these three
is called ultimate nirvana.

Bodhisattva of Sound Discernment

Then the Bodhisattva of Sound Discernment rose from his seat in the midst of the assembly, prostrated himself at the feet of the Buddha, circled the Buddha three times clockwise, knelt down, joined his palms, and said: "O World Honored One of great compassion! Such Dharma methods are rare indeed. World Honored One, how many approaches are there in the bodhisattva's cultivation of these [three] expedient methods toward the gate of Complete Enlightenment? For the sake of this assembly and the sentient beings in the Dharma Ending Age, please expediently teach us so that we may be awakened to Absolute Reality." Having said these words, he prostrated himself on the ground. He made the same request three times, each time repeating the same procedure.

At that time the World Honored One said to the Bodhisattva of Sound Discernment: "Excellent, excellent! Virtuous man, for the benefit of the assembly and sentient beings in the Dharma Ending Age, you have asked the Tathagata about such practices. Listen attentively now. I shall explain it to you."

Hearing this, the Bodhisattva of Sound Discernment was filled with joy and listened silently along with the assembly.

"Virtuous man, being pure, the Complete Enlightenment of all Tathagatas is originally without cultivation and cultivator. All bodhisattvas and sentient beings in the Dharma Ending Age, while unenlightened, rely on illusory effort in their cultivation. Thus there are twenty-five kinds of pure samadhis.

"If bodhisattvas engage only in utter stillness, through the power of stillness, they can permanently sever vexations and accomplish the ultimate. Without arising from their seats, they enter nirvana. These bodhisattvas solely practice *samatha*.

"If bodhisattvas engage only in contemplating [all things as being like an] illusion, through the power of the Buddhas they can transform and manifest things in the world into all sorts of functions and fulfill all their pure, wondrous practices as bodhisattvas. While maintaining dharani, they do not lose mindfulness in quiescence, nor do they lose wisdom derived from stillness. These bodhisattvas solely practice *samapatti*.[39]

"If bodhisattvas engage only in extinguishing illusions without getting involved in functions, they will singly sever all vexations. When vexations are completely severed they will actualize Absolute Reality. These bodhisattvas solely practice dhyana.

"If bodhisattvas first engage in utter stillness and then, with the wisdom mind begotten by stillness, clearly illuminate all illusions and perform bodhisattva deeds, they practice *samatha* first, followed by *samapatti*.

"If bodhisattvas, with the wisdom begotten by stillness, fully actualize the nature of utter stillness and then sever vexations and transcend birth and death permanently, they practice *samatha* first, followed by dhyana.

"If bodhisattvas, with the wisdom begotten by quiescence and stillness, manifest the power of illusions and create all sorts of transformations and manifestations for the purpose of liberating sentient beings, after which they sever vexations and enter quiescent-extinction, they practice *samatha* first, followed by *samapatti*, ending in dhyana.

"If bodhisattvas, with the power of utter stillness, sever vexations and then perform the wondrous pure practices of a bodhisattva to liberate sentient beings, they practice *samatha* first, followed by dhyana and ending in *samapatti*.

"If bodhisattvas, with the power of utter stillness, sever the vexations in the mind, liberate sentient beings and establish the world, they practice *samatha* first, followed by both *samapatti* and dhyana.

"If bodhisattvas, with the power of utter stillness as a support, generate transformations and manifestations, and then sever vexations, they practice both *samatha* and *samapatti* first, followed by dhyana.

"If bodhisattvas, with the power of utter stillness as a support, attain quiescent-extinction, then give rise to functions in manifesting in and transforming the world, they practice both *samatha* and dhyana first, followed by *samapatti*.

"If bodhisattvas, with the power of transformations and manifestations to accord with all sorts of [sentient beings], then attain utter stillness, they practice *samapatti* first, followed by *samatha*.

"If bodhisattvas, with the power of transformations and manifestations, create various realms, then attain quiescent-extinction, they practice *samapatti* first, followed by dhyana.

"If bodhisattvas, with the power of transformations and manifestations, first perform Buddha works, then peacefully abide in quiescence and stillness, and then sever vexations, they practice *samapatti* first, followed by *samatha*, ending in dhyana.

"If bodhisattvas, with the power of transformations and manifestations, perform [bodhisattva] functions without hindrances, then sever vexations and peacefully abide in utter stillness, they practice *samapatti* first, followed by dhyana, ending in *samatha*.

"If bodhisattvas, with the power of transformations and manifestations, expediently perform [bodhisattva] functions, then accord with utter stillness as well as quiescent-extinction, they practice *samapatti* first, followed by both *samatha* and dhyana.

"If bodhisattvas, with the power of transformations and manifestations, give rise to [bodhisattva] functions to engage in utter stillness, then sever vexations, they practice both *samapatti* and *samatha* first, followed by dhyana.

"If bodhisattvas, with the power of transformations and manifestations as a support, cultivate quiescent-extinction, then abide in the pure, uncontrived stillness, they practice both *samapatti* and dhyana first, followed by *samatha*.

"If bodhisattvas, with the power of quiescent-extinction, give rise to utter stillness and abide in purity, they practice dhyana first, followed by *samatha*.

"If bodhisattvas, with the power of quiescent-extinction, give rise to [bodhisattva] functions, yet accord with both quiescence and functions in all circumstances, they practice dhyana first, followed by *samapatti*.

"If bodhisattvas, with the power of quiescent-extinction, abide in the contemplation of stillness amidst the distinct nature of all phenomena, then give rise to transformations and manifestations, they practice dhyana first, followed by *samatha*, ending in *samapatti*.

"If bodhisattvas, with the power of quiescent-extinction, from the uncontrived intrinsic nature [of all dharmas] give rise to the function of manifesting pure realms, then return to the contemplation of stillness, they practice dhyana first, followed by *samapatti*, ending in *samatha*.

"If bodhisattvas, with the power of quiescent-extinction, with various purities abide in stillness, yet give rise to transformations and manifestations, they practice dhyana first, followed by both *samatha* and *samapatti*.

"If bodhisattvas, with the power of quiescent-extinction as a support, engaging in utter stillness, then give rise to transformations and manifestations, they practice both dhyana and *samatha* first, followed by *samapatti*.

"If bodhisattvas, with the power of quiescent-extinction as a support, engaging in performing transformations and manifestations, then give rise to utter stillness and pure luminous wisdom, they practice both dhyana and *samapatti*, followed by *samatha*.

"If bodhisattvas, with the wisdom of Complete Enlightenment, perfectly harmonize all [dualities] and never depart from the nature of enlightenment[40] in relating to the diverse [dharma] natures[41] or phenomena,[42] they are perfect in the threefold practice of according with the intrinsic nature of pure [samadhi].

"Virtuous man, these are called the twenty-five practices of bodhisattvas. All bodhisattvas practice in this way. If bodhisattvas and sentient beings in the Dharma Ending Age wish to rely on these practices, they should uphold practices of purity,[43] quietly contemplate and wholeheartedly repent. At the end of twenty-one days, after placing a numbered tally for each of the twenty-five methods, they should wholeheartedly pray [and seek divination] by picking a tally at random. The number picked will indicate whether the method is gradual or sudden. However, a single thought of doubt or regret will cause them to fail in accomplishment."

At that time, the World Honored One, wishing to clarify his meaning, proclaimed these gathas:

> Sound Discernment, you should know
> that the unhindered, pure wisdom
> of all bodhisattvas arises from samadhi:
> the so-called *samatha*,
> *samapatti*, and dhyana.
> The gradual or sudden practice
> of this threefold Dharma
> has twenty-five variations.
> All Tathagatas in the ten directions
> and the practitioners in the past, present, and future
> achieve bodhi through this Dharma,
> with the only exceptions being
> those of sudden enlightenment
> and those who do not follow the Dharma.
> All bodhisattvas and sentient beings
> in the Dharma Ending Age
> should ever practice diligently
> in accordance with these methods.
> Relying on the Buddha's power of great compassion,
> they will before long attain nirvana.

Bodhisattva Cleansed of All Karmic Obstructions

Then the Bodhisattva Cleansed of All Karmic Obstructions rose from his seat in the midst of the assembly, prostrated himself at the feet of the Buddha, circled the Buddha three times clockwise, knelt down, joined his palms, and said: "O World Honored One of great compassion! You have broadly expounded to us such inconceivable things as the practices of all Tathagatas of the causal ground, and have caused the assembly to gain what they have never had before. Having seen the Buddha's arduous toil through kalpas as innumerable as the grains of sand of the Ganges, and his efforts in practice unfold as if they were in but an instant of a thought, we bodhisattvas feel deeply fortunate and joyous.

"World Honored One, if the intrinsic nature of this enlightened mind is pure, what caused it to be defiled, making sentient beings deluded, perplexed and unable to enter it? Pray let the Tathagata thoroughly expound and reveal to us the nature of dharmas so that this assembly and sentient beings in the Dharma Ending Age may use [your teaching] as a guiding vision in the future." Having said these words, he prostrated himself on the ground. He made the same request three times, each time repeating the same procedure.

At that time the World Honored One said to the Bodhisattva Cleansed of All Karmic Obstructions: "Excellent, excellent! Virtuous man, for the benefit of this assembly and sentient beings in the Dharma Ending Age, you have asked the Tathagata about such expedient methods. Listen attentively now, I shall explain it to you."

Hearing this, the Bodhisattva Cleansed of All Karmic Obstructions was filled with joy, and listened silently along with the assembly.

"Virtuous man, since beginningless time all sentient beings have been deludedly conceiving and clinging to the existence of self, person, sentient being, and life. They take these four inverted views as the essence of a real self, thereby giving rise to dual states of like and dislike. [Thus], based on one delusion, they further cling to other delusions. These two delusions rely on each other, giving rise to the illusory paths of karma. Because of illusory karma, sentient beings deludedly perceive the turning flow [of cyclic existence]. Those who detest the turning flow [of cyclic existence] deludedly perceive nirvana, and hence are unable to enter [the realm of] pure enlightenment. It is not enlightenment that thwarts their entering; rather, it is the idea that 'there is one who can enter.' Therefore, whether their thoughts are agitated or have ceased, they cannot be other than confused and perplexed.

"Why is this? Because the original-arising ignorance has been [falsely perceived as] one's own master since beginningless time, therefore all sentient beings are unable to give rise to the wisdom-eye. The nature of their bodies and minds is nothing but ignorance. [This ignorance which does not eliminate itself may be illustrated] by the example of the man who does not take his own life. Therefore, you should know that people get along with those who like them and resent those who contradict them. Because like and dislike nurture ignorance, sentient beings always fail in their pursuit of the Path.

"Virtuous man, what is the sign[44] of the self? It is that which is experienced in the minds of sentient beings. Virtuous man, for instance, when a man's body is well coordinated and healthy, he forgets about its existence. However, when his four limbs are sluggish and his body unhealthy and unregulated, then with the slightest treatment of acupuncture and moxa he will become aware of the existence of the self again. Therefore, the self manifests when experience is felt. Virtuous man, even if this man's mind experienced the realm of the Tathagata and clearly perceived pure nirvana, it would be but the phenomenon of the self.

"Virtuous man, what is the sign of the person? It is that which is experienced in the minds of sentient beings. Virtuous man, he who awakens to the self no longer identifies with the self. This awakening, which is beyond all experience, is the mark of the person. Virtuous man, both what is awakened to and the awakening are not the self. Thus, even if this man's mind were perfectly awakened to nirvana, it would be but the self [because] as long as there is even the slightest trace of awakening or striving in the mind to realize the principle,[45] it would be the sign of the person.

"Virtuous man, what is the sign of sentient beings? It is the experience which is beyond self-awakening and it is that which is awakened to in the minds of sentient beings. Virtuous man, if for example a man says, 'I am a sentient being,' we know that what he speaks of as 'sentient being' refers neither to himself nor another person. Why is he not referring to his self? Since this self is sentient being, it is not limited to his self. Since this self is sentient being, therefore it is not another person's self. Virtuous man, the experiences and awakenings of sentient beings are all [traces of] the self and the person. In the awakening beyond the traces of the self and person, if one retained the awareness of having realized[46] something, it would be called the sign of sentient beings.

"Virtuous man, what is the sign of life? It is the mind of sentient beings that illuminates purity, in which they are aware of what they have realized. Karmic [consciousness] and wisdom cannot perceive themselves. This is comparable to the root of life. Virtuous man, when the mind is able to illuminate and perceive enlightenment, it is but a defilement, because both perceiver and perceived are not apart from defilement. After ice melts in hot water, there is no ice to be aware of its melting. The perception of the existence of the self enlightening itself is also like this.

"Virtuous man, if sentient beings in the Dharma Ending Age do not understand these four characteristics [of the self], even after cultivating the Path diligently for many kalpas, [it is still] called practicing with attachments[47] and they will not be able to accomplish the fruition of sainthood. Therefore, this is called [cultivating] the True Dharma in the Dharma Ending Age. Why? Because they mistake the various aspects of the self for nirvana, and regard their experiences and awakenings as accomplishments. This is comparable to a man who mistakes a thief for his own son. His wealth and treasure will never increase. Why? Because if one grasps onto the self, one will also grasp onto nirvana. For him, the root of grasping onto the self is [merely] suppressed and [seemingly] there is the appearance of nirvana. If there is one who hates the self, one will also have hatred for birth and death. Not knowing that grasping is the real [source of] birth and death, hatred for birth and death is [also] not liberation.

"How does one recognize the Dharma of non-liberation? Virtuous man, if sentient beings in the Dharma Ending Age, while cultivating bodhi, have partial actualization [of Complete Enlightenment] and think they are already pure, then they have not exhausted the root of the trace of the self. If someone praises his Dharma, it gives rise to joy in his mind and he wants to liberate the praiser. If someone criticizes his achievement, that gives rise to hatred in his mind. Thus one can tell that his attachment to the phenomenon of the self is strong and firm. [This self] is hidden in the storehouse consciousness.[48] It wanders in the sense faculties and has never ceased to exist.

"Virtuous man, these practitioners, because they do not eliminate the phenomenon of the self, cannot enter [the realm of] pure enlightenment. Virtuous man, if one truly actualizes the emptiness of the self, there will be no one there who can slander the self. When there is a self who expounds the Dharma, the self has not been severed. The same holds true for sentient beings and life.

"Virtuous man, sentient beings in the Dharma Ending Age speak of illness [in their practice] as the Dharma. They are pitiable people. Though diligent in their practice, they only increase their illness and are consequently unable to enter the [realm of] pure enlightenment.

"Virtuous man, because sentient beings in the Dharma Ending Age are not clear about these four signs [of the self] when they take the Tathagata's understanding and conduct to be their own practice, they will never reach accomplishment. Some claim that they have had actualizations though they have not; some claim that they have had realizations though they have not. When they see others more advanced than themselves, they become jealous. Because these people have not severed their grasping onto the self, they are unable to enter the [realm of] pure enlightenment.

"Virtuous man, sentient beings in the Dharma Ending Age who wish to accomplish the Path should not seek awakening through increasing their knowledge by listening [to the Dharma]. This will only further strengthen their view of the self. Instead, they should strive to diligently subdue their vexations! They should generate great courage to attain what they have not attained and sever what they have not severed. In all circumstances, they should not give rise to craving, hatred, attached love, arrogance, flattery, crookedness, envy, and jealousy. Then, the affection and grasping between the self and others will be extinguished. [When they can do this], the Buddha says that they will gradually reach accomplishment. Furthermore, they should seek good teachers so that they will not fall into erroneous views. However, if they give rise to hatred and love in their minds while seeking [a good teacher], they will be unable to enter the ocean of pure enlightenment.

At that time, the World Honored One, wishing to clarify his meaning, proclaimed these gathas:

Cleansed of All Karmic Obstructions,
you should know that sentient beings,
because of their attachment to and love of self,
have been bound in the illusory turning flow
[of cyclic existence] since beginningless time.
Without severing the four signs [of the self],
bodhi will not be attained.
With the mind harboring love and hatred,
and thoughts carrying flattery and crookedness,
one is full of confusion and perplexity,
and cannot enter the citadel of enlightenment.
To return to the realm of enlightenment,
desire, anger, and delusion must first be eliminated.
When attachment to the dharma [of nirvana][49]
no longer exists in the mind,
one can gradually reach accomplishment.
This body is originally non-existent

so how can love and hatred arise?
A practitioner should also seek a good teacher
so as not to fall into erroneous views.
If hatred and love arise in the quest,
he will not accomplish [enlightenment].

Bodhisattva of
Universal Enlightenment

Then the Bodhisattva of Universal Enlightenment rose from his seat in the midst of the assembly, prostrated himself at the feet of the Buddha, circled the Buddha three times clockwise, knelt down, joined his palms, and said: "O World Honored One of great compassion! You have with no hesitation explained the faults in practice so that this great assembly [of bodhisattvas] has gained what it never had before. Their minds are thoroughly at peace and they have gained a great, secure, and steadfast [teaching as a guiding vision for their practice].[50]

"World Honored One, sentient beings in the Dharma Ending Age will gradually be further away from the days of the Buddha. The sages and saints will seldom appear, while the heretical teachings will increase and flourish. What kind of people, then, should sentient beings seek to follow? What kind of Dharma should they rely on? What line of conduct should they adopt? Of what faults [in practice] should they rid themselves? How should they arouse the [bodhi] mind so that the blind multitude can avoid falling into erroneous views?" Having said these words, he fully prostrated himself on the ground. He made the same request three times, each time repeating the same procedure.

At that time the World Honored One said to the Bodhisattva of Universal Enlightenment: "Excellent, excellent! Virtuous man, you have asked the Tathagata about such methods of practice which are able to impart to all sentient beings, in the Dharma Ending Age, the Fearless Eye of the Path so that they will be able to accomplish the holy path. Listen attentively now. I shall explain it to you."

Hearing this, the Bodhisattva of Universal Enlightenment was filled with joy and listened silently along with the assembly.

"Virtuous man, sentient beings in the Dharma Ending Age who wish to arouse the great mind should search for a good teacher. Those who wish to practice should look for one who has correct views in all aspects. Such a teacher's mind does not abide in characteristics. He has no attachment to the realms of sravakas and pratyekabuddhas. Though [expediently] manifesting worldly afflictions, his mind is always pure. Though displaying misdeeds, he praises the practice of purity and does not lead sentient beings into undisciplined conduct and demeanor. If sentient beings seek out such a teacher, they will accomplish unexcelled perfect enlightenment.[51]

"If sentient beings in the Dharma Ending Age meet such a teacher, they should make offerings to him even at the expense of their lives, not to mention their food, wealth, spouse, children, and retinue. Such a teacher always reveals purity in the four modes of conduct.[52] Even if he shows misdeeds and excesses, disciples should not give rise to pride and contempt in their minds. If these disciples do not entertain evil thoughts of their teacher, they will ultimately be able to accomplish correct enlightenment. Their mind-flowers will blossom and illumine all Pure Lands in the ten directions.

"Virtuous man, the wondrous Dharma that is actualized by this good teacher should be free from four kinds of faults. What are these four faults?

"The first is the fault of contrivance. If a man says: 'I exert myself in all kinds of practices based on my intrinsic [pure] mind in order to seek Complete Enlightenment,' this is a fault, because the nature of Complete Enlightenment is not 'attained' by contrivance.

"The second is the fault of allowing things to be as they are. If a man says: 'I neither wish to sever birth and death nor seek nirvana. There are no conceptions of samsara and nirvana as truly arising or perishing. I allow everything to take its course with the various natures of dharmas in my quest for Complete Enlightenment,' this is a fault, because the nature of Complete Enlightenment does not come about through accepting things as they are.

"The third is the fault of stopping. If a man says: 'In my quest for Complete Enlightenment, if I permanently stop my mind from having any thoughts, then I will attain the quiescence and equality of the nature of all [dharmas],' this is a fault, because the nature of Complete Enlightenment does not conform with the stopping of thoughts.

"The fourth is the fault of annihilation. If a man says: 'In my quest for Complete Enlightenment, if I permanently annihilate all vexations, then my body and mind, not to mention the illusory realms of sense faculties and dust, will ultimately be emptiness and utter nothingness. Everything will be [in the state of] eternal quiescence,' this is a fault, because the nature of Complete Enlightenment is not annihilation.

"One who is free from these four faults will know purity. To discern these faults is to have the right discernment. To have other discernments than these is called erroneous discernment.

"Virtuous man, sentient beings in the Dharma Ending Age who wish to cultivate themselves should, to the end of their lives, make offerings to virtuous friends and serve good teachers. When a good teacher approaches them, they should sever arrogance and pride. When the teacher leaves them, they should sever hatred and resentment. Be it a favorable or adverse condition that [a teacher] brings them, they should regard it as empty space. They should fully realize that their own bodies and minds are ultimately identical with all sentient beings', and are the same in essence, without difference. If they practice in this way, they will enter the [realm of] Complete Enlightenment.

"Virtuous man, when sentient beings in the Dharma Ending Age are unable to accomplish the Path, it is due to the seeds of love and hatred towards themselves and others since beginningless time. Thus they are not liberated. If a man regards his foes as he would his parents, without duality, then all faults will be eliminated. Within all dharmas, self, others, love, and hatred will also be eliminated.

"Virtuous man, sentient beings in their quest for Complete Enlightenment in the Dharma Ending Age should give rise to the bodhi-mind, saying: 'I will lead all sentient beings throughout boundless space into ultimate Complete Enlightenment. In [the realm of] Complete Enlightenment, there is no realizer of enlightenment, and [the signs of] self, others, and all characteristics are left behind.' Giving rise to such a mind, they will not fall into erroneous views."

At that time, the World Honored One, wishing to clarify his meaning, proclaimed these gathas:

Universal Enlightenment, you should know
that sentient beings in the Dharma Ending Age
who wish to seek a good teacher
should find one with correct views
whose mind is far away from the Two Vehicles.
The Dharma [he actualizes] should be free
from the four faults of
contrivance, stopping, allowing things
to be as they are, and annihilation.
Approached by the teacher, they should
not be arrogant and proud.
Left by the teacher, they should not be resentful.
When witnessing different conditions
displayed by the teacher,
they should regard them as precious rare occurrences,
like a Buddha appearing in the world.
[They should] break not the rules of discipline and demeanor
and keep the precepts forever pure,
lead all sentient beings into
the ultimate Complete Enlightenment,
be free from the signs of the self,
person, sentient beings, and life.
When relying on correct wisdom,
they will transcend erroneous views,
actualize enlightenment and enter *parinirvana*.

Bodhisattva of Complete Enlightenment

Then the Bodhisattva of Complete Enlightenment rose from his seat in the midst of the assembly, prostrated himself at the feet of the Buddha, circled the Buddha three times clockwise, knelt down, joined his palms, and said: "O World Honored One of great compassion! You have broadly expounded expedient methods for attaining pure enlightenment so that sentient beings in the Dharma Ending Age may receive great benefit. World Honored One, we have already awakened. Yet after the nirvana of the Buddha, how should sentient beings in the Dharma Ending Age who are not awakened dwell in retreats to cultivate this pure realm of Complete Enlightenment? Which of the three kinds of pure contemplation are foremost within the [cultivation of] Complete Enlightenment? May the great Compassionate One bestow great benefit upon this assembly and sentient beings in the Dharma Ending Age." Having said these words, he prostrated himself on the ground. He made the same request three times, each time repeating the same procedure.

At that time the World Honored One said to the Bodhisattva of Complete Enlightenment: "Excellent, excellent! Virtuous man, you have asked the Tathagata about such expedient methods for the sake of bringing great benefit to sentient beings. Listen attentively now. I shall explain them to you."

Hearing this, the Bodhisattva of Complete Enlightenment was filled with joy and listened silently along with the assembly.

"Virtuous man, whether during the time of the Buddha's stay in the world, after his nirvana, or in the declining period of the Dharma, sentient beings with Mahayana nature who have faith in the Buddha's mysterious mind of great Complete Enlightenment and who wish to cultivate themselves should, if they live in a monastic community with other practitioners and are occupied by various involvements, examine themselves and engage in contemplation as much as circumstances permit in accordance with what I have already taught.

"If they are not occupied by various involvements, they should set up a place for practice and fix a time limit: 120 days for a long period, 100 for a medium period and 80 for a short period. Then they should dwell peacefully in this pure place. If the Buddha is present, they should hold correct contemplation of him. If the Buddha has entered nirvana, they should install his image, generate right mindfulness, and gaze at him as if he were still living in the world. They should adorn [the sanctuary] with banners and make offerings of flowers and within the first twenty-one days make obeisance to the Buddhas in all ten directions with utmost sincere repentance. Thus they will experience auspicious signs and obtain lightness and ease [of the mind]. After these twenty-one days, their minds should be well collected.

"If the retreat period overlaps with the three-month summer retreat [of sravakas], they should adhere to and abide with the retreat of a pure bodhisattva instead. Their minds should stay away from the [ways of] sravakas, and they do not have to be involved with the community at large. On the first day of the retreat, they should say this in front of the Buddha: 'I, bhikshu or bhikshuni, upasaka or upasika so-and-so, in the bodhisattva vehicle, will cultivate the practice of quiescent-extinction and together enter [with other bodhisattvas] into the pure abode of Absolute Reality. I will take the great Complete Enlightenment as my monastery. My body and mind will peacefully abide in the Wisdom of Equality.[53] The intrinsic nature of nirvana is without bondage. Without depending on the sravakas, I now respectfully pray that I can abide for three months with the Tathagatas and great bodhisattvas in all ten directions. For the great cause of cultivating the unsurpassed wondrous enlightenment of a bodhisattva, I will not be with the community at large.'

"Virtuous man, this is called the retreat manifested by the bodhisattva. At the end of the three kinds of periods of retreat,[54] he is free to go unhindered. Virtuous man, if practitioners in the

Dharma Ending Age go into retreats on the Bodhisattva Path, they should not accept [as authentic] any experience which they have not heard [from the Tathagata].

"Virtuous man, if sentient beings practice *samatha*, they should first engage in perfect stillness by not giving rise to conceptualization. Having reached the extreme of stillness, enlightenment will come about. Such stillness [acquired] in the beginning [of practice] pervades a universe from one's body, as does enlightenment. Virtuous man, when enlightenment pervades a universe, a single thought produced by any living being in this universe can be perceived by these practitioners. When their enlightenment pervades hundreds of thousands of universes, the same condition prevails. They should not accept [as authentic] any experience that they have not heard [from the Tathagata].

"Virtuous man, if sentient beings practice *samapatti*, they should first be mindful of the Tathagatas in all ten directions and the bodhisattvas in all worlds. Relying on various methods, they will diligently cultivate samadhi in gradual steps, bearing hardship. They should make great vows [to save sentient beings] and thus ripen their seeds [of Complete Enlightenment]. They should not accept [as authentic] any experience that they have not heard [from the Tathagata].

"Virtuous man, if sentient beings practice dhyana, they should begin with methods of counting.[55] [Gradually] they will be clearly aware of the arising, abiding, and ceasing of each thought, as well as the state before the arising of a thought, the state after the arising of a thought, and the scope and number of these thoughts. Further on, they will be aware of every thought, whether walking, standing, sitting or lying down. By gradually advancing still further, they will be able to discern a drop of rain in hundreds of thousands of worlds as if seeing, with their own eyes, an object used by them. [Again], they should not accept [as authentic] any experience that they have not heard [from the Tathagata].

"These are the foremost expedient methods in practicing the three contemplation techniques. If sentient beings thoroughly practice and master all three of them with diligence and perseverance, it will be called, 'Tathagata appearing in the world.' In the future Dharma Ending Age, if sentient beings with dull capacities who wish to cultivate the Path are unable to gain accomplishment due to their karmic obstructions, they should zealously repent and always remain hopeful. They should first sever their hatred, attachment, envy, jealousy, flattery, and crookedness, and pursue the unsurpassable mind.[56] As to the three kinds of pure contemplation, they should practice one of them. If they fail in one, they should try another. They should steadily strive to attain realization without giving up."

At that time, the World Honored One, wishing to clarify his meaning, proclaimed these gathas:

Complete Enlightenment, you should know
that all sentient beings
seeking to tread on the unsurpassed Path
should first enter a retreat.
They should repent their beginningless
karmic obstructions for twenty-one days
and then engage in right contemplation.
Experiences that they have not heard [from the Tathagata]
should not be accepted [as authentic].
In *samatha* one practices perfect stillness.
In *samapatti* one upholds right mindfulness.
In dhyana one begins with clear counting.
These are the three pure contemplations.
Those who practice them with diligence
are called "Buddhas appearing in the world."
Those with dull capacities who are not accomplished
should repent zealously of all the misdeeds
they have created since beginningless time.
When all obstructions are extinguished,
the realm of Buddhahood appears.

Bodhisattva Foremost in Virtue and Goodness

Then the Bodhisattva Foremost in Virtue and Goodness rose from his seat in the midst of the assembly, prostrated himself at the feet of the Buddha, circled the Buddha three times clockwise, knelt down, joined his palms, and said: "O World Honored One of great compassion! You have broadly revealed to us and sentient beings in the Dharma Ending Age such inconceivable things. World Honored One, what should this Mahayana teaching be named? How should one receive and observe it? When sentient beings practice it, what merit will they gain? How should we protect those who keep and recite this sutra? What will the extent of the benefit be if one spreads this teaching?" Having said these words, he prostrated himself on the ground. He made the same request three times, each time repeating the same procedure.

At that time the World Honored One said to the Bodhisattva Foremost in Virtue and Goodness: "Excellent, excellent! Virtuous man, for the benefit of the multitude of bodhisattvas and sentient beings in the Dharma Ending Age, you have asked the Tathagata the name and merit of this teaching. Listen attentively now. I shall explain it to you."

Hearing this, the Bodhisattva Foremost in Virtue and Goodness was filled with joy and listened silently along with the assembly.

"Virtuous man, this sutra is expounded by hundreds of thousands of millions of Buddhas as innumerable as the grains of sand of the Ganges. It is esteemed by all Tathagatas in the past, present, and future. It is the refuge of all bodhisattvas in all ten directions. It is the pure eye of the twelve divisions of the Buddhist scriptures.

"This sutra is called the Dharani of Complete Enlightenment of the Mahavaipulya Teaching. It is also called the Sutra of the Ultimate Truth, the Mysterious King Samadhi, the Definitive Realm of the Tathagata, and the Distinctions within the Intrinsic Nature of the Tathagatagarbha. You should respectfully receive and observe it.

"Virtuous man, this sutra reveals only the realm of the Tathagatas and can only be fully expounded by the Buddha, the Tathagata. If bodhisattvas and sentient beings in the Dharma Ending Age rely on it in their practice, they will gradually progress and reach Buddhahood.

"Virtuous man, this sutra belongs to the sudden teaching of the Mahayana. From it sentient beings of sudden [enlightenment] capacity will attain awakening. This sutra also embraces practitioners of all other capacities who engage in gradual cultivation; it is like a vast ocean which allows small streams to merge into it. All who drink this water, from gadflies and mosquitoes to *asuras*, will find fulfillment.

"Virtuous man, if there were a man who, with the purest intentions, gathered enough of the seven treasures[57] to fill a great chiliocosm and gave them all as alms, he could not be compared to another man who hears the name of this sutra and understands the meaning of a single passage. Virtuous man, if someone teaches hundreds of sentient beings as innumerable as the grains of sand of the Ganges such that they attain arhatship, his merit cannot be compared to that of an expounder of half a gatha of this sutra.

"Virtuous man, if a man hears the name of this sutra and has faith in it without any doubt, you should know that he has sown the seeds of merit and wisdom not with just one or two Buddhas; indeed he has cultivated roots of goodness and heard the teaching of this sutra from Buddhas as innumerable as the grains of sand of the Ganges. Virtuous man, you should protect all practitioners of this sutra in the Dharma Ending Age so that evil demons and heretical practitioners will not disturb their bodies and minds and cause them to regress."

At that time in the assembly, the Fire Head Vajra, the Wrecking Vajra, the Nila[58] Vajra, and other vajra [guardians] numbering eighty thousand, together with their retinues, rose from their seats, prostrated themselves at the feet of the Buddha, circled him three times clockwise, and said in unison: "World Honored One! If in the Dharma Ending Age there are sentient beings who practice this definitive Mahayana teaching, we will guard and protect them as we would our own eyes. We will lead our retinues to their place of practice to guard and protect them day and night so that they will not regress. We will see to it that their families will forever be free from all calamities and hindrances, that they will never have any plagues and illnesses, that their wealth and treasures will be ample, and that they will not be in need."

Then Mahabrahma-devaraja,[59] the king of the twenty-eight heavens,[60] the king of Mount Sumeru, and the [four] Lokapalas rose from their seats, prostrated themselves at the feet of the Buddha, circled him three times clockwise and said in unison: "World Honored One! We too will guard and protect those who observe this sutra so that they can live in security and peace without regression."

Then the powerful king of demons, Kumbhanda, and one hundred thousand other demon kings rose from their seats, prostrated themselves at the feet of the Buddha, circled him three times clockwise and said: "World Honored One! We also will guard and protect those who observe this sutra from morning to night so that they will not fall back in their practice. If ghosts and spirits approach within one *yojana*[61] of their dwelling, we shall pulverize them."

When the Buddha had preached this scripture, all who were in the assembly, including bodhisattvas, devas, nagas, and others of the eight groups[62] with their retinues, as well as the deva kings and Brahma kings, having heard the teaching of the Buddha, were filled with great joy. With faith, they respectfully received and practiced this teaching.

¹ Great Illuminating Storehouse of Spiritual Penetration, *shen tong da guang ming zang* 神通大光明藏. Spiritual, *shen* 神 signifies inconceivability; penetration, *tong* 通 refers to nonobstructedness; great illuminating, *da guang ming* 大光明 signifies the manifestation of the Buddha's merit and wisdom; storehouse, *zang* 藏 refers to the repository or essence from which all dharmas arise and manifest. One can understand the Spiritual Penetration and Great Illumination as the function, *yong* 用, whereas the Storehouse is the essence, *ti* 體.

² Quiescent-extinction is a rendering for *ji mie* 寂滅, which is a Chinese rendering for the Sanskrit word nirvana. Quiescent, *ji* 寂 signifies the stillness of the nature of emptiness; extinction, *mie* 滅 signifies the purity of nirvana, free from defilements.

³ "equal and identical" is one of the many shades of meaning of *ping deng* 平等. *Ping* 平 can be translated literally as level or equal but also connotes impartiality. In this context, *deng* 等 may be rendered as identical, same, or indistinguishable. Within the context of time (past, present, and future), the translator has chosen to render *ping deng* as equal and identical. Elsewhere, the term has been rendered impartial equality.

⁴ Literally, this should be translated as "joined his palms together with the tips of the fingers crossed," *cha shou* 叉手. This is one of the ancient Indian gestures for respect. It symbolizes the non-duality of the realm of the Buddhas (the left hand) and the realm of ordinary sentient beings (right hand).

⁵ Causal ground, *yin di* 因地 can also be understood as the mind-ground, *xin di* 心地. It refers to both the circumstance when the Buddha first initiated the bodhi-mind, *chu fa pu ti xin* 初發菩提心 and to the intrinsic nature of mind, *xin xing* 心性 or Buddha-nature, *fo xing* 佛性. Original arising, *ben qi* 本起 simply means the fundamental starting point of Dharma practice, *fa xing* 法行, which refers to the practice that accords with the nature of all dharmas, *fa xing* 法性, that is, emptiness, *kong xing* 空性.

⁶ Dharani, *zong chi* 總持 means universal control. See glossary for further information.

⁷ Complete Enlightenment, *yuan jue* 圓覺 in this sutra does not refer to thorough enlightenment where practice is no longer necessary, as the sutra will reveal in later chapters. Rather, it designates the perfection and completeness of Buddha-nature intrinsic to all beings, *yuan man xian cheng zhi fo xing* 圓滿現成之佛性.

[8] Ignorance, *wu ming* 無明 is *avidya* in Sanskrit. See glossary for further information.

[9] The four great elements, *si da* 四大 are: earth, water, fire, and wind. Together, they constitute the physical body of a living human being.

[10] Impressions, *ying* 影 may also be translated as reflections or shadows.

[11] Tathagatagarbha, *ru lai zang* 如來藏 is synonymous with Buddha-nature, *fo xing* 佛性. See glossary for further information.

[12] The four conditions, *si yuan* 四緣 of vision, hearing, perception, and awareness, *jian, wen, jue, zhi* 見聞覺知 refer to the ability to experience external phenomena. These four qualities occur because of the illusory six sense faculties. When the internal six sense faculties and the external four elements of earth, water, fire, and wind combine, they create an "energy" *qi* 氣 which comes into existence due to these different conditions. In this case, "energy" refers to the conditioned impressions, *yuan yin* 緣影 or mental images of the perceived external sense objects. Because of attachments, this energy or impression does not disperse, and thereafter gives rise to the six corresponding consciousnesses or awareness of these impressions. In this process, there seems to be a separate existing mind which is cognizant of the illusory external world.

[13] See glossary for further information about these technical terms.

[14] Here, nature, *xing* 性, should be understood as *te xing* 特性, or characteristics and activities.

[15] Resolute faith *jue ding xin* 決定信 is a stage where one's faith no longer backslides *xin xin cheng jiu* 信心成就. This is a stage where a bodhisattva has reached at least the first level of the Ten Faiths. This level in the doctrinal system is referred to as the Path of Seeing. See glossary for further information on Bodhisattva positions.

[16] ". . . in motion" refers to ". . . samsaric."

[17] Illness or *yi* 翳 refers to ignorance.

[18] Flower signifies birth and death and nirvana.

[19] These four terms — affection, love, craving, and desire, *en, ai, tan, yu* 恩愛貪欲 — are subtle distinctions of attachment and desire, which, despite their role in the secular world, are all causes for the continuance of cyclic existence. Here love, *ai* 愛 should be understood as attached love, *zhi ai* 執愛 or self-centered love. The translator has simply translated this term as attached love or grasping in some later passages. The same word is sometimes translated into like, as in the case of like and dislike, in later paragraphs and chapters.

[20] "The different types of births in the world . . . are created by sexual desire" points to the fact that all samsaric beings still have within them the roots and potential of sexual desire, *yin yu xing* 淫欲性, *yin yu xi qi* 淫欲習氣, which perpetuates cyclic existence. This sentence does not mean that all births literally come into being through sexual activity, because births through humidity and transformation are not results of sexual activity. Births through humidity and transformation are either caused by the combination of various conditions in the natural environment such as moisture, sunlight, and air or by the power of a deity or spirit. Bodhisattvas can also manifest transformation bodies for the purpose of liberating sentient beings.

[21] Activity is a rendering of *xing* 性, which is usually translated as nature, as in 'the nature of Complete Enlightenment.' However in this context, *xing* refers to *te xing* 特性, which means characteristic, quality, function, or activity.

[22] Obstruction of principle, *li zhang* 理障 is an obstruction one may have in understanding or accepting the ultimate truth or view of Reality.

[23] Obstruction of phenomena, *shi zhang* 事障 refers to all the vexations and afflictions one may have that bind one to samsara.

[24] Here, nature, *xing* 性 should be understood as capacities or dispositions.

[25] The Two Vehicles, *er cheng* 二乘 are the sravaka, *sheng wen* 聲聞 and pratyekabuddha, *bi zhi fo* 辟支佛, *du jue* 獨覺 vehicles.

[26] This sentence is difficult to understand because in each case the word *xing* 性 — sometimes translated as nature — refers to different things. One interpretation is: even though there are five distinct natures or capacities as mentioned previously, each nature or capacity is endowed with the intrinsic nature of Complete Enlightenment. What the sutra is saying is that the five distinct natures make the nature of Complete Enlightenment possible. For example,

one perceives existence because of nonexistence; one perceives nonexistence only through existence. Therefore, the five natures are not apart from the nature of Complete Enlightenment.

[27] "Those who extinguish vexations" refers to sravakas and pratyekabuddhas; "those who do not" refers to bodhisattvas.

[28] "The succession of arising and perishing thoughts" refers to the sixth consciousness, *di liu shi* 第六識. The mind or self is just the continuous stream of deluded thoughts, *wang nian* 妄念. "That which grasps on to the self" refers to the seventh consciousness, *di qi shi* 第七識. Because of attachment, this continuous flux of thoughts creates karmic seeds, *ye zhong* 業種 which are planted in the eighth consciousness, *di ba shi* 第八識, the *alaya*, *a lai ye shi* 阿賴耶識. Although the *alaya* cannot grasp itself — it is just a storehouse of karmic seeds — the seventh consciousness attaches to the *alaya* as the self. See glossary for an explanation of the eight consciousnesses.

[29] There are two sets of five desires, *wu yu* 五欲. The most obvious or coarse desires are for wealth, sex, food and drink, fame, and sleep. The subtle desires refer to the five sense objects. In themselves the sense objects are not defilements, but they are potential objects of desire.

[30] This stage is equivalent to an ordinary person's realization of emptiness. In the Ch'an tradition, it is referred to as seeing one's self-nature, *jian xing* 見性. In the doctrinal system, this is referred to as the Path of Seeing, *jian dao wei* 見道位 within the stages of Ten Faiths, *shi xin* 十信. After perceiving emptiness, usually one's realization is not deep enough to eradicate all vexations. Therefore, one is still an ordinary person and still needs to continue one's practice. However, after reaching the position of Ten Faiths, one's faith will never regress , *xin bu tui* 信不退. Beyond the position of Ten Faiths are the Ten Abodes, *shi zhu* 十住, Ten Practices, *shi xing* 十行, and Ten Transferences, *shi hui xiang* 十迴向, which elevate one to the level of sagehood, *xian wei* 賢位. After one fulfills all the practices and realizations in the position of Ten Faiths, one enters the position of Ten Abodes, which is the beginning of Path of Practice, *xiu dao wei* 修道位. When one fulfills the three stages of Ten Abodes, Ten Practices, and Ten Transferences, one enters the position of Ten Grounds, *shi di* 十地 or *bhumis* and moves to the position of sainthood, *sheng wei* 聖位. This is referred to as the Path of Ultimate Attainment, *jiu jing wei* 究竟位. The above are gradual levels of realization and practice. However, depending on the depth of one's realization of emptiness, it is possible for a practitioner to ascend to the highest position, bypassing, *dun chao* 頓超 the lower stages.

31 This is the attainment of one of the three positions, *san xian wei* 三賢位, of Ten Abodes, Ten Practices, and Ten Transferences, depending on one's realization. These three positions are all subsumed under the Path of Practice, *xiu dao wei* 修道位.

32 Illumination is a literal translation of *zhao* 照. In this context, *zhao* refers to understanding, as in understanding *jie* 解 of Dharma. Realization is a rendering for *jue* 覺, which can mean awareness of, awakening or realization. In this case, *jue* refers to realization or perception, *jian* 見.

33 This section refers to the attainment of at least the first stage of the Ten Grounds. At this stage, one's 'practice' will never regress, *xing bu tui* 行不退. If one attains the eighth ground or *bhumi*, one's 'position' will never regress again, *wei bu tui* 位不退.

34 These are what are known as the Three Higher Studies, *san zeng shang xue* 三增上學, which subdue the three poisons of greed, anger, and delusion.

35 Wisdom of All Aspects, *yi qie zhong zhi* 一切種智 is one of three wisdoms of a Buddha. Wisdom of All Things, *yi qie zhi* 一切智, *sarvajnata* in Sanskrit, is the omniscient wisdom which realizes the emptiness of all things. Wisdom of the Path, *dao zong zhi* 道種智, *margajnata* in Sanskrit, refers to the wisdom of knowing all there is to know about the conventional realm, especially with regard to saving sentient beings. Wisdom of All Aspects, or Universal Wisdom, *sarvakarajnata* in Sanskrit, refers to the perfect knowledge of Reality as it is.

36 "Body and mind" refers to the six sense faculties, *liu gen* 六根 and consciousnesses, *liu shi* 六識. "Guests and dusts," *ke cheng* 客塵 refers to the six sense objects, *liu cheng* 六塵.

37 At this stage one is free from the bondage of the five skandhas and the eighteen realms of existence.

38 There are different degrees of "lightness and ease," *qing an* 輕安. Sometime it means an experience of physical and mental pliancy. On a deeper level, it is an experience of enlightenment, where one is free from the burden of body and mind. In this case it refers to an enlightened state since it is experienced in the state of quiescence and stillness, *ji jing* 寂靜.

39 In this paragraph, "quiescence" signifies the state of dhyana, while the wisdom derived from "stillness" signifies the previous practice of *samatha*.

Therefore, even though the bodhisattva in this section solely practices *samapatti*, since the bodhisattva is holding dharani — which means the essence of all methods — he is actually upholding all three Dharma doors of dhyana, *samapatti*, and *samatha*.

[40] The nature of enlightenment is quiescent and extinct, free from all dualities. Therefore, this state refers to dhyana.

[41] The essence of all dharma natures is stillness. Therefore, this state refers to *samatha*.

[42] Phenomena are illusory projections. Therefore, this state refers to *samapatti*.

[43] "Practices of purity" refers to, on the one hand, severing sexual desires; on the other hand, the bodhisattva practice of overcoming afflictions and benefiting sentient beings.

[44] Sign, *xiang* 相, includes many shades of meaning such as form, mark, trace, appearance, feature, characteristic, aspect and phenomenon. These words differ slightly in meaning. The translator will choose one of these words to bring out the meaning of the text.

[45] Principle refers to enlightenment.

[46] Realized, *liao* 了, in this and next paragraph actually means to be done with or to end.

[47] "Practicing with attachments" is a rendering of *you wei* 有爲, *samskrta* in Sanskrit. See glossary for further information.

[48] Storehouse consciousness, *a lai ye shi* 阿賴耶識 is also known as the eighth consciousness, *di ba shi* 第八識, *alayavijnana* in Sanskrit.

[49] Attachment to the dharma of nirvana, *fa ai* 法愛 refers to the arhats who, have realized the emptiness of the self, *ren wu wo* 人無我, and have not yet realized the emptiness of dharmas, *fa wu wo* 法無我.

[50] In this context, the Bodhisattva of Universal Enlightenment is referring back to the answer that the Buddha gave to the previous bodhisattva about the teaching as a guiding vision for future practice. Therefore, the translator has taken the liberty to add this line in the text.

⁵¹ Perfect enlightenment refers to *anuttara-samyak-sambodhi*.

⁵² Walking, standing, sitting, and lying down.

⁵³ Wisdom of Equality, *ping deng xing zhi* 平等性智, *samatajnana* in Sanskrit, is the enlightened realization that self and others are equal and identical.

⁵⁴ "The three kinds of periods of retreat" refers to 120 days, 100 days, or 80 days.

⁵⁵ Counting is a literal translation of *shu* 數. This approach actually includes methods such as counting and following the breath, Five Contemplations of Stilling the Mind, *wu ting xin guan* 五停心觀, Four Foundations of Mindfulness, *si nian chu* 四念處, Sixteen Special Practices, *shi liu te sheng* 十六特勝 associated with the Four Noble Truths, *si shen ti* 四聖諦, and Contemplation of the Four Immeasurable Minds, *si wu liao xin* 四無量心.

⁵⁶ The mind of Complete Enlightenment.

⁵⁷ The seven treasures are: gold, silver, lapis lazuli, crystal, mother-of-pearl, red pearl, and carnelian.

⁵⁸ Thunderbolt.

⁵⁹ Mahabrahma-devaraja, *ta fan wong* 大梵王 is the king or controller of the world of samsara.

⁶⁰ Twenty-eight heavens are the three realms in samsara. There are six heavens in the realm of desire, eighteen heavens within the realm of form, and four heavens within the formless realm.

⁶¹ *Yojana, you xun* 由旬 is a measurement in India. One *yojana* is approximately forty miles.

⁶² The eight groups are: 1. devas, 2. nagas, 3. *yaksas*, 4. *gandharvas*, 5. *asuras*, 6. *garudhas*, 7. *kinnaras*, 8. *mahoragas*.

Complete Enlightenment

Commentary on the sutra
by
Master Sheng-yen

Prologue

Thus have I heard. At one time the Bhagavan entered the Samadhi of the Great Illuminating Storehouse of Spiritual Penetration. This is the samadhi in which all Tathagatas brightly and majestically abide. It is the ground of the pure enlightenment of all sentient beings.

[The Bhagavan's] body and mind were in the state of quiescent-extinction, where past, present, and future are intrinsically equal and identical, and his completeness filled all ten directions, and was in accord with everything without duality. From within this condition of non-duality, he caused various Pure Lands to appear.

[The Bhagavan] was accompanied by one hundred thousand great bodhisattvas and mahasattvas. Chief among them were Bodhisattva Manjusri, Bodhisattva Samantabhadra, Bodhisattva of Universal Vision, Bodhisattva Vajragarbha, Bodhisattva Maitreya, Bodhisattva of Pure Wisdom, Bodhisattva at Ease in Majestic Virtue, Bodhisattva of Sound Discernment, Bodhisattva Cleansed of All Karmic Obstructions, Bodhisattva of Universal Enlightenment, Bodhisattva of Complete Enlightenment, and Bodhisattva Foremost in Virtue and Goodness. Together with their retinues, they all entered samadhi, abiding in the Tathagata's Dharma assembly of impartial equality.

The passage above introduces the main body of the sutra. Sutras attributed to the Buddha follow a set format and can be divided into three parts. First is the introduction; second is the main body of the sutra, which contains the Buddha's actual discourse; and third is a section that explains how to protect and transmit the teachings of the sutra.

The introduction usually includes six parts: the recorder of the sutra, the time the sutra was spoken, the location of the assembly, the person or being who delivered the sutra (who is almost always the Buddha himself), the speaker's state of mind or level of awareness, and the audience who listened to the teachings.

"Thus have I heard" marks the beginning of this and all other formal discourses given by the Buddha. It is an affirmation that the words and teachings are authentic, that they were indeed spoken by Sakyamuni Buddha. The "I" refers to Ananda, cousin to the Buddha and a close disciple. After the Buddha entered nirvana, efforts were made to record and preserve the Buddha's teachings by the arhat disciples. Ananda remembered all of the Buddha's formal discourses in detail and recited them so that the Dharma would survive.

Ananda then marks the time at which the Buddha spoke. There are two ways to mark time. One refers to local or specific time, such as Eastern Standard Time or Greenwich Mean Time. The other refers to universal time, or the standard time for all worlds. The Buddha is not limited by time or space; he encompasses the entire universe. Ananda could not give a specific time or date, so instead he says, "Once" or "At that time."

Before the Buddha spoke he entered into a deep samadhi described as the Great Illuminating Storehouse. This reveals the location of the assembly and in which form the Buddha spoke this sutra. Since this sutra was revealed to bodhisattvas in samadhi, we can deduce that it was spoken by the Sambhogakaya of Sakyamuni Buddha in the Pure Land of True Reward. Sambhogakaya is one of the three bodies — the other two being the Dharmakaya and the Nirmanakaya — possessed by a Buddha according to the Mahayana view. The Sambhogakaya, or Body of Beatitude, is the body the Buddha enjoys in a Pure Land as a result of his previous actions and virtues; the Dharmakaya is the true nature of the Buddha; and the Nirmanakaya is the earthly body in which a Buddha appears to sentient beings in order to fulfill his vows.

In this "Samadhi of Great Illuminating Storehouse of Spiritual Penetration," the Buddha's mind was tranquil and non-discriminating. His mind was in a state of "correct receptivity" free from all defilements.

There are shades of meaning and symbolism behind these lines of "entered the Samadhi of the Great Illuminating Storehouse of Spiritual Penetration." "Spiritual Penetration" refers to Buddha's ability to fully understand the karmic capacity of each and every sentient being and thereby able to skillfully deliver him or her from all kinds of suffering. "Great Illumination" signifies the Buddha's wisdom, virtue, and compassion. The Chinese rendering of the word "Storehouse" or *garbha* means concealment and repository. It also connotes something inexhaustible and boundlessness. Here, it means the inexhaustible jewel-repository — the Buddha-nature — the essential nature of all the Buddhas. It is the Absolute Reality in all of us.

In this intrinsic samadhi, the Buddha's mind was the same as that of all Tathagatas. Such awareness is not gained; rather, it is uncovered. Though this enlightened mind is within us, it is veiled by our endless need to possess and repell.

The luminous aspect of the enlightened mind of the Buddha is not like the light of the sun or moon. The inner light of pure wisdom is limitlessly profound. It is also inexplicable, for any description would limit it. Calling the light of wisdom beautiful would taint it with emotional connotations.

A Chinese character often used to describe the light of wisdom may be translated as "majestic," but this word does not convey its true meaning either. The same character has other shades of meaning — stately, serious, soft — and is used to describe the Buddha's compassion. In this context, "majesty" refers to the compassion that spontaneously arises with wisdom. With wisdom, the Buddha observes and contemplates. With compassion, the Buddha helps sentient beings. Where there is wisdom, there is no attachment or vexation. Where there is compassion, there is the impetus to help all sentient beings.

The sutra states that this samadhi is actually the "ground of the pure enlightenment of all sentient beings." The ground of pure enlightenment is what all the Buddhas are awakened to, abide in and manifest. It is also what all of us have never separated from. The "ground" refers to "storehouse" previously mentioned. It conceals all the virtue and wisdom of the Buddha. "Enlightenment" here refers to the intrinsic enlightenment; an idea highly esteemed in the Mahayana Buddhism, especially Ch'an Buddhism. Actually, intrinsic enlightenment is spoken of in response to unenlightenment. It is on the one hand, the potential for full Buddhahood in all living beings and on the other, the nature of emptiness. It is because of unenlightenment, that the Buddha spoke of intrinsic enlightenment. We should not think that all of us are enlightened already but we just don't know it. Rather, we have always been deluded by our emotional afflictions and deceived by our poisoned minds. However, because intrinsic enlightenment is also the nature of emptiness, through practice, all of our problems and vexations can also be realized as emptiness.

The sutra states that the bodies and minds of the Buddha and liberated bodhisattvas are in the state of quiescent-extinction. Quiescent-extinction is another rendering for nirvana. It is quiescent because its nature is ever still. It is extinction because it is free from all poisons of the mind. Only in such stillness and purity can the illumination of wisdom and its accompanying compassion manifest. It is sentient beings who are controlled by desires. Bodhisattvas simply respond to the movements of sentient beings. Wherever sentient beings are, there bodhisattvas will manifest. Hence, bodhisattvas can manifest in innumerable places. Yet, in the mind of the bodhisattva, there are neither beings to be saved nor an "I" who saves. Ordinary sentient beings, on the other hand, are well aware that they act when they help others.

A bodhisattva's mind and body are stable under all conditions. The Chinese character used to describe this universal stillness can be translated as "original," "highest," or "reality," and it refers to the genuine basis of all things, that which is intrinsically there. As in the case of wisdom and compassion, there are no words that can adequately describe a great bodhisattva's enlightenment. If there were, the enlightenment would not be genuine.

The stillness of a bodhisattva's enlightenment permeates the entire universe, and within this completeness there is no discrimination — neither subject nor object, neither perceiver nor perceived. All is Buddha-nature and it is as still as the unmoving surface of a lake.

The volitional activity of sentient beings causes things to manifest, just as wind creates ripples on a lake. All things experienced by sentient beings are the result of this karma, created by their volition, their egocentric desires and erroneous views. These innumerable manifestations of ripples, however, are of the same nature. Clay pots may vary in form, but their substance is the same. The Buddha, too, can manifest in innumerable worlds and Pure Lands in order to help sentient beings in infinite ways. Fundamentally, however, all is Buddha-nature.

The Pure Lands mentioned in the sutra include the world we inhabit now. Buddhas and bodhisattvas view this world as a Pure Land. Ordinary sentient beings are unable to see it as such because they cannot overcome their addictions to negative patterns of self-attachment and discover this intrinsic samadhi. On the other hand, practitioners who enter the door of Ch'an would not view the world as impure, miserable, or chaotic. To them it would be a beautiful place. People who reach this level in their practice recognize beauty in everything.

Actually, it is not necessary to enter samadhi to experience such feelings. If you can put aside, for a moment, all anxieties and concerns in your mind, and just gaze upon something without discrimination, you may experience the world as a lovely place — a world that is fresh and alive. But if you have a mind that is plagued with attachment and aversion, then you will always be filled with turbulent and disturbing thoughts; nothing will appear beautiful and serene. Your mind will project an image or atmosphere of agitation which eclipses, engulfs, and keeps you from perceiving the serenity all around you.

Once, in the middle of a retreat in Taiwan, a young woman noticed one of the monks dozing during the work period when everyone was sweeping and cleaning. He was not handsome by any means, but because the woman had had a good meditation experience earlier in the day, she looked at him and saw a beautiful being. Never in her life had she seen such beauty. She was so taken by his appearance that she wanted to hug him, but she refrained because he was a monk.

An hour later, she saw him again, but the effects of her experience had worn off, and he looked like an ordinary person again. Later she said to me, "How could I have thought that he was so good looking a little while ago?" Without the power of samadhi, such experiences are fleeting.

The sutra then describes the assembly that listened to the Buddha's discourse. When the Buddha entered deep samadhi, one hundred thousand bodhisattvas appeared at his side. Of course the sutra does not list every name, but it does mention the most important figures — the twelve bodhisattvas who asked specific questions related to the practice that leads to Complete Enlightenment.

All of the bodhisattvas, as well as their retinues, were able to enter the same samadhi in which the Buddha resided, through the power and grace of the Buddha. They were absorbed, so to speak, in the Buddha's light of wisdom and compassion. The Buddha helped them enter this samadhi so that he could transmit the Dharma to them.

But this does not mean that the bodhisattvas and their retinues were equal to the Buddha in terms of enlightenment. They were able to see what the Buddha saw, but they could not maintain that level as long as the Buddha. Furthermore, their sphere of perception was not limitless like the Buddha's.

The light of the sun is often used as an analogy for enlightenment. Although sunlight shines without discrimination, not everyone sees it in the same way. People in houses with the shades drawn may only see a narrow shaft of light. Those outside see more, but the sun may still be blocked by clouds; and even on the clearest day, the sun will eventually set. Just as it is impossible for us, on earth, to see the sun continuously, so too the bodhisattvas were unable to perceive all that the Buddha perceived.

Each of the bodhisattvas mentioned in the sutra has a different quality of enlightenment and each one follows a different method of practice. Their differences are reflected in their names and in the order and content of their questions. Thus, the sutra follows a proper sequence.

Their names are, in order of their appearance: Bodhisattva Manjusri, Bodhisattva Samantabhadra, Bodhisattva of Universal

Vision, Bodhisattva Vajragarbha, Bodhisattva Maitreya, Bodhisattva of Pure Wisdom, Bodhisattva at Ease in Majestic Virtue, Bodhisattva of Sound Discernment, Bodhisattva Cleansed of All Karmic Obstructions, Bodhisattva of Universal Enlightenment, Bodhisattva of Complete Enlightenment, and Bodhisattva Foremost in Virtue and Goodness.

The names of the bodhisattvas correspond to their particular character, merit, and ability, which differs from the custom of most people, whose names are given because of tradition, religion, or the sound of the word. Whereas a name generally bears little resemblance to one's personality or character, the names of Buddhas and bodhisattvas almost always reveal the natures of their characters and merits.

Bodhisattva
Manjusri

Now I will discuss the actual discourse of Sakyamuni Buddha. The first chapter of *The Sutra of Complete Enlightenment* begins with the questions asked by Manjusri Bodhisattva:

> *Thereupon Bodhisattva Manjusri rose from his seat in the midst of the assembly, prostrated himself at the feet of the Buddha, circled the Buddha three times clockwise, knelt down, joined his palms, and said: "O World Honored One of great compassion! Please expound to the multitude who have come to this assembly the Tathagata's Dharma practice of the original-arising purity of the causal ground. Please also expound to us how bodhisattvas may initiate this state of pure mind within the Mahayana and leave all illness. [Pray teach us] so that sentient beings in the future Dharma Ending Age who aspire to the Mahayana will not fall into erroneous views." Having said these words, he prostrated himself on the ground. He made the same request three times, each time repeating the same procedure.*

The Buddha's disciples followed a special ritual when they wanted him to speak on a certain subject. The Buddha rarely spoke about the Dharma without being asked. For the sake of listeners and sentient beings in the present and future, bodhisattvas posed questions in a formal manner. It is comparable to modern day press conferences in which well known politicians publicly answer

questions. It would be impossible for politicians to accommodate
every reporter in the audience, so they choose particular senior
reporters. These reporters ask questions they feel are relevant to the
entire audience. Similarly, bodhisattvas represented the entire
assembly and, in a larger sense, all sentient beings.

In a sutra, a bodhisattva poses a question which the Buddha
answers. In most sutras, the Buddha rarely speaks unless asked a
question — the *Heart Sutra* and *Amitabha Sutra* are exceptions to
this usual format. This question and answer ritual was a traditional
practice in ancient India and China. In the *Analects of Confucius*, for
example, students asked questions and Confucius responded. It is
also a familiar practice in the Ch'an sect, where students ask and the
master responds.

The special ritual described in this and other sutras is unique
to ancient India. Manjusri rose from his seat and prostrated with his
head at the feet of the Buddha. The head is considered the most
esteemed part of the body, the feet the least. Prostrating in this
manner, a person displays profound respect for the other. Manjusri
then circled the Buddha "three times clockwise." In doing so,
Manjusri kept the Buddha to his right. Such circling is another
means of showing respect; it also expresses admiration. The
Buddha's appearance and presence is so noble and awe-inspiring
that other beings cannot turn their eyes from him.

Why did Manjusri circle to the right instead of to the left?
According to Indian tradition, circling to the right demonstrates
greater propriety and respect. Circling someone to the left indicates
an attitude of contempt and disrespect. The origin of this custom is
unclear, but it persists to this day. "Left" is considered derogatory,
and there is a Chinese phrase which describes those who are not on
the correct path as followers of the "left path." This ritual is also
symbolic of purifying the body, speech, and mind. Rising from the
seat and prostrating is purifying the body. Circling the Buddha
three times clockwise expresses sincerity and reverence of mind.
Joining the palms and beseeching the Buddha to expound the
Dharma is purifying the speech.

Manjusri asked the Buddha to expound for the assembly the
"Tathagata's Dharma practice of the original-arising purity of the

causal ground." In simpler terms, Manjusri was asking the Buddha about his practice based on Buddha-nature before his attainment of Buddhahood. When the Buddha was still immersed in vexation, he practiced the Dharma of the Tathagatas of his own accord and initiative. The practice was the basis for his enlightenment, for his attainment of Buddhahood.

The Dharma practice of the Tathagatas which Manjusri speaks of involves the immaculate Buddha-nature — that which is free from vexations, that which is wisdom. The purpose of practice is to discover for ourselves the essence of our very being — the Buddha-nature. It is very meaningful and worthwhile for us to practice until this intrinsic nature — our wisdom — is uncovered.

One often reads in sutras and commentaries phrases such as "original nature" or "original wisdom." It can be misleading. To say that we were originally pure and that vexations arose later is only a manner of speaking. In reality, there was no time when we were originally pure. Nor was there a time when we became buried in vexation. It is not a matter of historical progression; nor is it a falling from grace. To say that we were originally pure means only that we all have Buddha-nature as our basis, and that we all have the rare potential to realize it. We are Buddha-nature. It is our true condition. For this reason I prefer the phrase "intrinsic nature."

Manjusri asked the Buddha how a bodhisattva can develop the "pure mind within the Mahayana." The phrase 'bodhisattva' refers to a being who has the ability to attain Buddhahood but has postponed its final attainment in order to remain in the world to help sentient beings. Even though Sakyamuni Buddha reached supreme enlightenment, it is possible for him to continue helping and saving sentient beings. When the Buddha helps, it can be said that he is adopting the role of a bodhisattva. The bodhisattvas who pose questions in this sutra, as well as Bodhisattva Avalokitesvara, are great bodhisattvas.

Emphasis on the role of the bodhisattva has made Buddhism especially tolerant of and receptive to other religions and practices. Buddhism sometimes views great religious leaders, saints, and philosophers of other traditions as "transformation bodies," or incarnations, of bodhisattvas. When Buddhism was transmitted to

Japan, the ancient deities of the Japanese were regarded as bodhi-sattvas. The same is true for certain prophets of Islam and Christianity. In China, such philosophers and sages as Confucius and Lao-tzu are sometimes considered incarnations of enlightened beings.

How can practitioners on the Bodhisattva Path develop the pure Mahayana mind? How can people and bodhisattvas be free of vexations? There are two major obstructions a bodhisattva can encounter. A bodhisattva may develop a feeling of aversion toward the world and want nothing to do with it. Such a being is not, in fact, a true bodhisattva as he or she has no real intention of helping sentient beings. At the other extreme, a bodhisattva may develop strong desires and attachments to the world. Such a being cannot be considered a true bodhisattva either. A genuine follower of the Mahayana Bodhisattva Path is neither attached to the world nor attached to liberation from it, neither filled with desire nor filled with aversion. He or she will not cling to or run away from anything.

Ordinary sentient beings possess both of these mentalities. When their careers and families are causing them problems, people may want to escape and be free from suffering. But if everything is going well, people cling tightly to their possessions and, in fact, desire more. A person with one sexual partner may want two or more. A person with a hundred thousand dollars may want a million, and a person with a million may desire ten million.

Such mentalities are not aspects of the Mahayana mind. Desire and aversion are flip sides of the same coin. Whether people get attached to things or try to give them up does not matter. They are still trying to satisfy their own selfish interests. It is for the sake of sentient beings who demonstrate such behavior that Manjusri asks his questions. He himself does not experience such feelings. However, he asks the Buddha for the correct practice so that sentient beings will have the proper guidance.

Once when I was lecturing in Taiwan, I became annoyed at a man in the audience who asked stupid questions after every comment I made. Finally I asked, "Why are you acting this way?" He answered, "I'm not asking for myself. I know this already, but

many of the people in the audience are too embarrassed to ask such
stupid questions, so I ask for them. If I didn't ask, they wouldn't
understand the lecture. I'd be the only one who knew what you
were talking about." I said, "Thank you. You must be a great
bodhisattva." Fortunately, most people don't do this. If they did,
I'd never be able to finish a lecture. Some people ask questions to
flaunt their intelligence while others ask questions to get attention.
Some people raise opposing views because they enjoy debates. Such
intentions are different from those of the bodhisattva. A bodhisattva does not ask questions for his own sake or self-interest. He
has no desire, so there is no need to show off. He asks solely for the
benefit of sentient beings.

> *At that time the World Honored One said to Bodhisattva*
> *Manjusri: "Excellent, excellent! Virtuous man, for the benefit of*
> *the multitude of bodhisattvas you have asked about the*
> *Tathagata's Dharma practice of the causal ground. For the benefit*
> *of all sentient beings in the Dharma Ending Age who aspire to*
> *Mahayana, you asked how they can attain correct abiding and not*
> *fall into erroneous views. Listen attentively now. I shall explain it*
> *to you."*
>
> *Hearing this, Bodhisattva Manjusri was filled with joy and*
> *listened silently along with the assembly.*

This paragraph is straightforward, and its format is repeated by the
Buddha throughout the sutra before he answers questions posed by
bodhisattvas. The Buddha praises Manjusri's compassion for sentient beings in the Dharma Ending Age and says that he will answer
the question.

The phrase, "Dharma Ending Age," which appears throughout
this and many other sutras, has two meanings. In one definition, as
time goes on, fewer and fewer people will hear the Dharma, and of
those who do, fewer still will accept it and walk the Buddha Path.
Today, there are scholars who study the history of Buddhism and
debate in an intellectual manner its influence on culture, philosophy, and religion. However, most of them are not interested in
practicing Buddhism and some regard it as superstition. In a second

definition, the "Dharma Ending Age" refers to the existence of
people who are geographically cut off from Buddhadharma. It is
difficult for people in certain regions of the world to hear Buddhadharma, and if they do encounter the Dharma, it is likely that their
contact will not be strong or genuine. They may learn false or
distorted Dharma.

> *"Virtuous man, the Supreme Dharma King possesses the method of
> the great dharani called Complete Enlightenment, out of which
> emanates pure true suchness, bodhi and nirvana, as well as the
> paramitas to teach bodhisattvas. The original-arising [purity] of
> the causal ground of all Tathagatas relies on the complete illumi-
> nation of [intrinsic] enlightenment, which is pure [in essence] and
> permanently free from ignorance. Only then do the [Tathagatas]
> accomplish the Buddha Path."*

The Supreme Dharma King is one who has been liberated from all
dharmas, or phenomena. What is "liberation from dharmas"?
Consider a kingdom in which the ruler has absolute power. He is
completely free to do what he wants with anyone and anything. He
is above rules and laws. Likewise, a person who has attained
Buddhahood is completely free from dharmas or phenomena. He
feels neither attachment to nor aversion from thoughts, ideas, or
external situations. In this sense he is a "King of dharmas." Most
sentient beings cannot be called kings or queens of dharmas. We do
not have control over our emotions and environment. We are
controlled by situations. As we respond to events we may become
happy, sad, or angry. Those who are kings and queens of dharmas
are not bothered by phenomena or circumstances.

Once in Taiwan a young monk and I were on a bus when an
older woman with her children came on board. The monk offered
his seat to her and she accepted. Two stops later the woman got off,
but first she gave her seat to one of her children, forgetting that the
monk had been sitting there originally.

The monk later complained to me about the situation. I asked,
"Isn't it true that you want to help all sentient beings? If, because of
this experience, you never offer your seat to another person, then

instead of helping sentient beings, you have allowed others to influence you negatively."

Most people do not have a firm grasp of Buddhadharma. Instead of being masters of their environment and emotions, they are enslaved by them. We are free of dharmas if we don't view painful things as being painful and if we don't crave more happiness after experiencing a joyful event. This is a difficult level to attain. After all, pain is pain and happiness is happiness. Avoiding pain and craving happiness is the natural inclination of sentient beings.

Buddhas and bodhisattvas are detached from suffering, yet they immerse themselves in the suffering of sentient beings in order to help them. They are like parents who aren't healthy or skilled, who, for the sake of their children, perform arduous tasks. They may be aware of their painful situation, yet they persist because they only desire the best for their children. The suffering taken on by the bodhisattvas is essentially different from the retributional suffering of sentient beings. We have vexations when we are suffering. Bodhisattvas take on necessary suffering as the result of their vows to deliver and benefit sentient beings. For them, there is no suffering.

I ask people if they remember a period in their lives when they didn't suffer much. Some answer that childhood is trouble-free and happy, but that the responsibilities of adulthood bring suffering. Is this the case? The first thing a newborn baby does is cry, and it cries often through its infancy, sometimes for no apparent reason. The same is true for adults; sometimes we become angry or sad and we do not know the cause. All of us, at any time in our lives, are subject to pain and suffering. There are many people in other countries who wish to move to the United States. They believe it is the best, freest, and happiest country. It may be better than some other countries, but it is not free of problems. The world is intricately intertwined. Problems in one area lead to problems elsewhere. A cold winter or poor harvest in one region is apt to affect the entire world, either directly or indirectly. There is no way to escape our problems. They are our own creations and follow us wherever we go.

Thus it can be seen that the world is enmeshed in suffering. Even happiness is a form of suffering, because eventually it disappears. As long as we have psychological or physical problems, as long as we are controlled by the environment and emotion, we will find insecurity and pain in our lives. Life as we know it is an ocean of suffering, and we are all lost in it; in its vastness there is no definite sense of direction nor is there an ascertainable shore of safety. The teachings of the Buddha exist to help sentient beings pull themselves out of this "ocean of suffering." Through the methods of practice expounded by the Buddha we can transcend the pain of our bodies and minds. We can choose to break the seemingly endless cycle of birth and death and the vexations that are inherent in it, because these vexations are of our own making.

The sutra says, "The Supreme Dharma King possesses the method of the great dharani called Complete Enlightenment." Dharani may be interpreted here as the thread that holds something together. For instance, if you hold the main line of a fishing net, you control the entire net. Similarly, the collar of a jacket is small, but it gives the entire piece shape, and if you grab it you possess the entire jacket. The method of practice — great dharani — is like this main line or collar. Actually, even if you hold a small string of the fishing net or just a thread of the jacket, you are connected to the whole thing. I can control a person's movements just by pulling a few strands of his or her hair. Any one part of a whole offers access to the entire entity. In terms of Buddhism it means that everything within the Dharma is connected — any method of practice in accordance with Buddhadharma is an entrance to Complete Enlightenment.

Practice is necessary in order to attain Complete Enlightenment. Ordinary sentient beings are unenlightened because they do not realize the basis of their own existence — Buddha-nature. Even practitioners at higher levels may not have complete realization. Hinayana arhats have one-sided enlightenment because they emphasize only the "emptiness" aspect of the Dharma. Many Mahayana bodhisattvas are similarly only partially enlightened. Although they understand that the world is illusory and impermanent, and although they have the compassion to help sentient beings, they have not yet fully realized the Dharma; there is still need for practice. Practitioners may have reached enlightenment, but their stock of merit and virtue have not yet reached completion and fulfilment. Only Buddhas have fulfilled all wisdom, merit and virtue.

Pure true suchness, bodhi, nirvana and the paramitas emanate out of the practice of the dharani called Complete Enlightenment. Fundamentally, each one of us possesses pure true suchness. True suchness is the intrinsic wisdom-nature of Complete Enlightenment, revealing all things as they are, free from the relative conditions of distinction and change. We are unaware of it because it is obscured by our vexations of attraction, repulsion, and indifference. The situation is quite different for people who are fully enlightened. They are free from the birth and death of the physical body and from the arising and perishing of emotional afflictions. It is because of the arising and perishing of afflictions that sentient beings experience physical birth and death. They will continue this unending cycle and remain prisoners of this self-inflicted world of samsara until they fully realize their true suchness. If we did not possess true suchness, then practice would be futile. It is because of this intrinsic nature that practice is possible. When vexations are gone, true suchness is revealed.

Bodhi is an enlightened state. Bodhi is also wisdom. There are different kinds of bodhi, depending on the level of enlightenment. The bodhi of Sakyamuni Buddha is unexcelled supreme enlightenment. The bodhi of great bodhisattvas and the bodhi of arhats are profound, yet they do not match that of the Buddha. Ordinary sentient beings are completely ignorant of bodhi. In order to realize it fully, they must make sincere vows to reach enlightenment not only for themselves, but for the benefit of all. This necessites diligent practice.

Practice means developing the bodhi mind and cultivating it in all circumstances. When someone accomplishes this goal and completes his or her bodhi mind, the cycle of the birth and death of the physical body and its every possible affliction is severed. Such a state is called nirvana. The methods used to reveal bodhi and attain Buddhahood are called "paramitas" or perfections. There are numerous paramitas described in the Buddhist sutras, and each one signifies the perfection of a particular aspect of the practice. There are six basic paramitas: charity, moral discipline, patience, diligence, meditation, and wisdom. Actually, any method that helps to alleviate vexation in our minds and bodies can be called a paramita.

People who study with Dharma teachers know that practice is extremely useful. Once they practice and begin to see results, however, it doesn't mean that their problems, suffering, and vexations will disappear. Genuine practitioners are aware of this. Only people who haven't made the initial effort to practice, or who haven't gotten results, may fantasize about enlightenment. "Once enlightened, always enlightened" is such a fantasy. Practice should not end after you achieve initial results. If anything, you must practice even harder! It is only after you first get a taste of enlightenment that true practice begins. Eventually, the experience of enlightenment will become deeper and deeper, until finally, enlightenment is complete and Buddhahood is reached. Only then are vexations and delusions permanently eradicated.

A young man has been visiting me on and off for three years. He is interested in experiencing enlightenment, but he doesn't want to practice. He won't come to classes. I tell him to meditate, but he refuses. He says he cannot because he has too many mental problems. He believes that there is a magical method that will automatically enlighten him and end his psychological and neurotic problems. I cannot help him.

In order to remove habitual patterns of vexation permanently, you must practice for a long time. In this manner, vexations will be cast off — gradually and thoroughly. Our minds are like muddy water. It takes time for the silt and impurities to settle. The water must remain still, otherwise the silt will whirl up into the water again. It is best to wait until the impurities solidify and sink to the bottom, too large and heavy to ever rise again. Only then will the water be pure and clear. It is the same with our practice, our minds, and our vexations. Only when our vexations solidify and sink will our minds be clear and pure. Until that time, the slightest movement will give rise to vexations again.

Some people experience pleasant sensations when they practice. When they are happy, they may think that their problems are gone forever. This happy feeling is itself a problem. While people experience this feeling, they may have no discernible vexations — no hate or love. But once they re-enter daily life and encounter people and the environment, problems will return. One of my students told me that she frequently experiences a variety of emotional afflictions in her life. I asked her, "What do you feel when they arise?" She replied that she often feels strong emotions of either affection or enmity. "When you feel neither of them," I asked her, "do these vexations still appear?"

For most people, vexations exist even in a state of apparent calm. The vexations may be less conspicuous, but they are there. Only when you completely still your mind and become calm and clear can wisdom and compassion develop.

We should practice until all the dust-like particles of vexation have solidified. Only then can we fulfill our original vows to attain Complete Enlightenment. This is Buddhahood. All those striving for Buddhahood ultimately must rely upon great bodhi — great enlightenment — so that vexations can be eradicated. This is what the Buddha encourages us to work toward through the various paramitas. It is not an easy endeavor. Nonetheless, regardless of the difficulty or the length of time it may take, we must proceed, putting forth our best effort in our spiritual evolution.

> "*What is ignorance? Virtuous man, since beginningless time, all sentient beings have had all sorts of delusions, like a disoriented person who has lost his sense of direction. They mistake the four great elements as the attributes of their bodies, and the conditioned impressions of the six sense objects as the attributes of their minds. They are like a man with an illness of the eyes who sees an [illusory] flower in the sky, or a second moon.*
>
> "*Virtuous man, there is in reality no flower in the sky, yet the sick man mistakenly clings to it. Because of his mistaken clinging, he is not only deluded about the intrinsic nature of the empty space, but also confused about the arising of the flower. Because of this false existence [to which he clings], he remains in the turning wheel of birth and death. Hence this is called ignorance.*

> "Virtuous man, this ignorance has no real substance. It is like a person in a dream. Though the person exists in the dream, when [the dreamer] awakens, there is nothing that can be grasped. Like an [illusory] flower in the sky that vanishes into empty space, one cannot say that there is a fixed place from which it vanishes. Why? Because there is no place from which it arises! Amidst the unarisen, all sentient beings deludedly perceive birth and extinction. Hence this is called the turning wheel of birth and death.

> "Virtuous man, one who practices Complete Enlightenment of the causal ground of the Tathagata realizes that [birth and extinction] are like an illusory flower in the sky. Thus there is no continuance of birth and death and no body or mind that is subject to birth and death. This nonexistence of [birth and death and body and mind] is so not as a consequence of contrived effort. It is so by its intrinsic nature.

> "The awareness [of their nonexistence] is like empty space. That which is aware of the empty space is like the appearance of the illusory flower. However, one cannot say that the nature of this awareness is nonexistent. Eliminating both existence and nonexistence is in accordance with pure enlightenment.

> "Why is it so? Because the nature of empty space is ever unmoving. Likewise, there is neither arising nor perishing within the Tathagatagarbha. It is free from conceptual knowledge and views. Like the nature of dharmadhatu, which is ultimate, wholly complete, and pervades all ten directions, such is the Dharma practice [of the Tathagata] of the causal ground.

> "Because of this [intrinsic completeness], bodhisattvas within the Mahayana may give rise to pure bodhi-mind. If sentient beings in the Dharma Ending Age practice accordingly, they will not fall into erroneous views."

The preceding paragraphs are the heart of the Buddha's answer to Manjusri and should be considered as a whole. "Since beginningless time" is a phrase often used in Buddhist sutras. According to Buddhadharma, we cannot speak of a beginning. There is a practical reason for this. If we speculate on the origin of the universe or humankind, we will succeed only in raising unanswerable questions, such as, "When does this beginning start?" or "What was here before the beginning?" If we say that God created the universe, it only leads to other questions, such as, "Where does God come from?" or "Why did God pick a particular time to create the universe?" or "People create so many problems. Why would God create so much trouble?" These questions cannot be resolved. Buddhadharma is not concerned with speculation. By stating "since beginningless time," such questions are rendered unnecessary.

Since beginningless time, sentient beings have had all sorts of delusions. In fact, the nature of their "sentience" and their reactions to it is their very problem. Hence they are sentient beings. What are delusions? It is like losing one's orientation and confusing east for west and north for south. The directions haven't changed. It is the person who is confused. Mistaking east for west is a delusion; likewise, mistaking this body to be ours is also delusory. The body is only a combination of elements. It was not our body in the past and it will not be our body in the future. It will certainly not be our body after we die. Even at this moment, this body does not really belong to us. It is constantly changing, with new parts being manufactured from different things. Yet, a person can attach the idea of "self" to the body and consider it a permanent entity. This is an illusion. This is delusion.

Of course, some may agree with me, but they are using the intellect, acknowledging an idea through the power of reason. What about the mind or the spirit? Surely, they must be the self, you say. The mind interacts with the environment through the senses: the eye sees shape and color, the ear hears sounds, the body senses temperature and other forms of contact, and so on. However, if you were to carefully analyze the interaction of the senses with the environment, you would realize that there is no continuous, unchanging self within the mind. Even in dreams there is no continuous self. A dream is merely the mind's calling up and interaction with memories of past experiences; it is the continuation of the generation of the moving "pictures" of the subconscious mind.

The mind is but an impression, a reflection of the body coming into contact with the environment. If you shine a light on an object, a shadow will appear, but the shadow has no substance. Just so with the mind. The mind is only the reflection formed when the body interacts with objects in the environment. Both the body and the environment have no separate self.

People believe that the self is the body and mind, and that this self is real. They are mistaken. We are attached to the interconnection of body, mind, and environment. We remember the past, think about the future, enjoy things that are good, avoid things that are unpleasant. We feel pride when we succeed and disappointment when we fail. We grasp and cling to the thoughts, feelings, and sensations that form in our minds.

Those who take the body and mind to be the self are like one who sees and believes that flowers grow in the sky. Most of us know that there are no flowers in the sky, but it is hard to convince someone who feels that he clearly sees them otherwise. If you try to explain that it is an illusion, that person will think that you are crazy. According to Buddhadarma, the mind and spirit are also illusions. When we speak of the spirit, the soul, and the self, we are clinging to our fantasies of permanence and existence.

On the other hand, we cannot say that nothing exists. That is nihilism, which is also delusion. If this view were true, it would be pointless to practice and strive for enlightenment. In saying that things do not exist, people can loosen their attachment to forms and ideas and be relieved of the burden of anxieties and afflictions that arise from these attachments. In saying that things are not non-existent, people will not become lax in their efforts to practice diligently in accordance with the Buddhadharma and will work toward revealing their Buddha-nature. Buddha-nature is neither existence nor non-existence.

The line of the sutra "the nature of empty space is ever unmoving" refers to Budddha-nature. Buddha-nature is not material. It is empty; therefore it cannot be said to exist. But "empty" does not mean that it is nonexistent. Buddha-nature is free from the relentless cycles of arising and perishing. It is unmoving and unchanging. If Buddha-nature were also a process of arising and perishing, it would be something conditioned. Hence, it is beyond the grasp of the ceaseless motion of discrimination. We may think that external phenomena move, but it is not the case. Everything, from the smallest speck to the largest universe, is unmoving and unchanging. It is the mind, acts, and thoughts of sentient beings that make external phenomena appear to move and change.

The world appears to move because the mind moves. It has strayed from the present moment. If the mind comes to a halt and rests in the present moment — even if it is in the midst of commotion — all phenomena will be unmoving. If practitioners are determined in their practice, they can attain a level where the mind becomes pure and unmoving. At this point, everything else will also be unmoving. It is only when we are attached to the existence of self and external phenomena that we see the world as existent. If in our minds there is nothing, then outside of them there will also be nothing.

There is a famous story in the *Platform Sutra* that illustrates this idea. As the Sixth Patriarch, Huineng, entered the gates of a monastery, he heard two monks arguing. They were staring at a flag waving in the breeze. One monk insisted that the flag was in motion, while the other monk believed it to be the wind that was moving.

Huineng said, "Neither flag nor wind is moving. Your minds are moving."

Such a concept is not easy for us to understand. We may object to this story, maintaining that regardless of whether or not our minds are moving, the flag still moves. If we close our eyes, the flag will continue to move. By ordinary reasoning, it would seem that the Sixth Patriarch spoke nonsense.

To understand this story, we need to understand the words spoken in *The Sutra of Complete Enlightenment*. When the mind is not moving, the entire universe, from the smallest speck to the largest galaxy, is not moving. Accepting it intellectually or repeating this idea is not enough. Furthermore, it isn't enough to say that it is the moving mind that causes external phenomena to appear to move. Really, it is the "mind of vexation" that causes them to appear to move.

This unmoving reality also connotates changelessness. If one were to sip water from a glass, it would seem that some water has disappeared, but that is not the case. The amount of water remains the same, only some of it is now in that person's stomach. The water remains on the earth; there is no change in its quantity. On a larger scale, if I were to leave this planet, I would still be in the universe. I don't really "disappear." In the context of total existence, there is no arising or perishing, no creation or extinction.

Steadily reflecting on this principle is the real practice. Awakening to this unmoving state is awakening to the pure mind. In this awakening, vexations will disappear. This is the correct view. Erroneous views, on the other hand, will only increase vexations.

External phenomena arise because of the mind of vexation. Although it seems that we all share the same objective reality, actually the world I experience is quite different from the world you experience. Each one of us has different feelings and experiences which are reflected in the so-called objective reality around us. The tree I see is not the tree you see. Even those who share the same family or lifestyle may have markedly different perceptions about the world. The world varies as vexations vary. For some, the mind is in constant motion; their heads are filled with ideas, worries and preoccupations. For others, the mind is calmer. Buddha-nature, however, does not move at all. It is utterly quiescent.

Buddha-nature, which is also known as Tathagatagarbha, contains the seed of Buddhahood. It is not that a Buddha arises when someone becomes enlightened, for Buddha-nature has never been separate from that person. Tathagatagarbha never increases or decreases. It is better to say that with Buddha-nature there is the potential to realize Buddhahood. "Coming and going, arising and perishing" are viewpoints of ordinary sentient beings.

> *At that time, the World Honored One, wishing to clarify his*
> *meaning, proclaimed these gathas:*
>> *Manjusri, you should know*
>> *that all Tathagatas,*
>> *from their original-arising causal ground,*
>> *use wisdom to enlighten*
>> *and penetrate ignorance.*
>> *Realizing that ignorance is like*
>> *a flower in the sky,*

they are thus liberated from the continuance
[of birth and death].
Like a person [seen] in a dream who
cannot be found when [the dreamer] awakens,
awareness is like empty space.
It is impartial and equal, and ever unmoving.
When enlightenment pervades all ten directions,
the Buddha Path is accomplished.
There is no place where illusions vanish,
and there is no attainment
in accomplishing the Buddha Path,
for the intrinsic nature is already wholly complete.
By this, bodhisattvas
can give rise to the bodhi-mind.
Sentient beings in the Dharma Ending Age
through this practice will avoid erroneous views.

People who meditate sometimes have illusory experiences. On one retreat I observed a woman looking at the sky, and I asked her what she saw. She pointed to what she thought was Bodhisattva Avalokitesvara. I told her there was nothing in the sky. She said, "Shifu, do not deceive people. If I can see bodhisattvas, surely you must be able to."

Similarly, believing that the body and mind are the self is also an illusion. I say this knowing that most people think I am talking nonsense. Yet we are deluded, and because of our ignorance we continue through an endless cycle of birth and death.

We desperately cling to the belief that body and mind are the self, that they are indispensable, inseparable. This belief limits us, constrains us, and causes us to be controlled by wandering thoughts and external phenomena in the environment. On the other hand, if we can control our minds and think the thoughts we want to think, then we control the environment. Under the first condition, environment controls mind; under the second condition, mind controls environment.

A man obsessed by his desire for a woman may try anything to win her love. If he fails, but his desire persists, he may vow to pursue her lifetime after lifetime. The woman he desires is not controlling him. It is he who cannot liberate himself from his own desire. This is an example of a reaction to an environment which controls the person. How much more do we desire and cling to our own bodies and minds?

Recently, I read a story that may or may not be true. It occurred in Stalinist Russia and concerned a man with psychic powers. One day he walked into Stalin's private office and startled the Soviet leader, who was not expecting visitors. Stalin asked the man how he had evaded his guards and the man answered, "I thought of myself as the head of the KGB, and so no one bothered me. In fact, your men saluted me as I walked by." Stalin was naturally skeptical, and he asked for a demonstration. In a flash, Stalin thought he was looking at his KGB man. After a while, the man "returned" and said, "Really, I am just myself, not the man you think you see." Stalin was impressed by the man's power and used him in foreign intelligence. Whether or not the story is true, it illustrates the possibilities of mind control. The psychic manipulated the environment and the minds of others.

Although this man's power of mind seems impressive, it is not liberation. He still had attachments and vexations because he was still immersed in the reflections formed from the body and its environment. He simply had stronger mental powers than most people.

Many people have asked me, "Shifu, am I dreaming this moment? I know I dream at night, but even my daily life seems like a dream." I answer, "Yes, you are dreaming now. At night you are dreaming within your dream." Which is the true self? Which self is more real? Such questions are irrelevant because whether asleep or awake, you are still dreaming. To fully realize this, you must wake up from all your dreams.

Other people say to me, "Sometimes I go somewhere I've never been, and I get the feeling that I know the place. What is the significance of this?" I tell them, "Probably in your dreams you have been to a place that looked similar to the place you actually visited, but most likely it is not the same place."

Dreams are usually foggy and confused. You may readily admit this, but you'll probably insist that you are clear in your waking life.

It isn't true. Even now your mind is not clear. Are you aware of every detail of what you've done and seen and come in contact with today? Most people pass the day as if in a blur. In fact, even at the moment when you experience things you are not clear. If you were, it would be like the negative of a photo, where every detail becomes indelibly stamped.

The so called mind that arises from our identification with the body and reactions to objects in the environment is not real. It is empty and unreliable. With practice, we can liberate ourselves from this false self; at that moment we will see the true self, which does not move or change, which is pure. This true self is Buddha-nature. To realize Buddhahood, we must practice hard in order to truly understand that body, mind, and the so-called objective world are unreal. If successful we will be liberated from the vexations that arise from attachment. We will be liberated from the cycle of birth and death.

Birth and death have no self-nature. If they did, they would be permanent, and it would be impossible to be liberated from them. Perhaps you think that there is a Complete Enlightenment to be attained. No. Complete Enlightenment is empty. It cannot be possessed or owned. If Complete Enlightenment had a permanent self-nature, it would be impossible for the unenlightened to become enlightened. There was a hard-practicing monk during the Ming dynasty (1368-1644) who read two lines of verse:

> *After liberation there are more vexations.*
> *After one has experienced True Reality*
> *   one will enter samsara.*

The monk was puzzled because it seemed to contradict what he had been told. If one has vexations after liberation, what is the use of liberation? If after enlightenment one continues the cycle of birth and death, why practice? He realized there must be a deeper meaning underlying the words, so he made a vow not to eat or sleep until he understood the verses. Eventually he attained enlightenment and realized that if a person were attached to liberation, it would only be more vexation. If he thought he had attained true suchness, it would just be one more attachment, and he would sink deeper into the cycle of birth and death.

Our sense of personal identity, the self that arises from the body and mind, is false. On the other hand, a "true self" waiting to be discovered is also false. We have to let go of all concepts of existence and emptiness in order to be in accordance with Complete Enlightenment. If you say you are devoid of attachment and yet persist in saying that there is enlightenment and a Buddha Path to follow, then you are still moved by vexation. The Path *is* the ultimate totality of all things. There is nothing separate from it. If you say, "I have attained the Path," then there is still a separation of subject and object, something to be gained and something to be left behind. There are no relative conceptions in Complete Enlightenment — no Buddhahood to be reached, no enlightenment to be attained.

Bodhisattvas following this teaching will reach Buddhahood. Sentient beings who are in accordance with this teaching will not become trapped in erroneous views, even in the Dharma Ending Age. There are two main inverted erroneous views. People are either attached to their concepts of existence, which leads to a life filled with struggle and frustration, or they are attached to a concept of non-existence, which leads to apathy and escapism. Buddhadharma embraces neither view. There is a story about a wolf who couldn't find food. He searched without luck until he went insane. One day he thought he found something. It was his left leg, but he didn't realize it, and so he ate it. It was delicious. Afterwards, his stomach was satisfied, but he realized he'd lost something else. If in reaching the Buddha Path we feel we've attained something wonderful, then we are no different from the wolf. We must practice until we reach the stage of no gain or loss. We are all like the wolf in that we feel happy if we attain or are given something. We don't realize that it is only our own left leg. The universe is whole and complete. Nothing has ever been separate from us. It is ourselves that create the feeling of separation.

"Realizing that ignorance is like a flower in the sky" aptly describes our awakening from delusion. There is no such thing as a flower growing in the sky. If people see one, something is wrong with their eyes! Likewise, it is only because our minds are agitated that we sense opposition in the environment. As there is no flower in the sky, the nature of reality has no duality. Dualistic perception is the result of a mind of vexation. If we understand this directly, we are free from vexation, suffering, birth, and death. In a dream one may experience anger, happiness, and sadness, but when one awaken one realize it was all unreal.

Do you realize what you are doing this very moment? Are you dreaming or awake? We may be awake relative to those who are sleeping, but in comparison to those with true wisdom, we are sound asleep. We are dreaming the dream of vexation. We are lost in the dream of birth and death. All sentient beings are dreaming. Only in reaching Buddhahood will we completely awaken. In our "dream of existence" we experience many things: family, career, fame, failure, happiness, shame, sickness, death. When one is thoroughly enlightened, one sees that none of these things has any more substance than a mirage.

Enlightenment is like a clear sky, whereas the mind of vexation is like a sky filled with moving clouds and rain. For those who have awakened, the vexations that clouded the mind and created the illusion of movement no longer exist. There is nothing to obscure the mind's intrinsic brightness and purity. Such a mind is genuinely non-discriminating, all-pervasive, and unchanging. It is Complete Enlightenment.

Bodhisattva
Samantabhadra

*Then Bodhisattva Samantabhadra rose from his seat in the midst
of the assembly, prostrated himself at the feet of the Buddha,
circled the Buddha three times clockwise, knelt down, joined his
palms, and said: "O World Honored One of great compassion! For
the multitude of bodhisattvas in the assembly, as well as for all
sentient beings who cultivate Mahayana in the Dharma Ending
Age, please explain how they should practice having heard about
this pure realm of Complete Enlightenment.*

*"World Honored One, if these sentient beings come to
understand illusion, then body and mind are also illusory. How
can they then use illusion to remedy illusion? If all illusory
characteristics were exhausted and extinguished, then there would
be no mind. Who is it that practices? Why, then, do you say that
practice is illusory?*

*"If sentient beings originally had no need to practice, then
they would remain confined to illusory projections amidst birth
and death and never discern the state [in which all is seen to be]
like an illusion. How could they be liberated from illusory
conceptualization? For the sake of all sentient beings in the
Dharma Ending Age, please explain the expedient method of
gradual cultivation of practice in order that sentient beings may
permanently leave the state of illusion." Having said these words,
he prostrated himself on the ground. He made the same request
three times, each time repeating the same procedure.*

> At that time the World Honored One said to Bodhisattva
> Samantabhadra: "Excellent, excellent! Virtuous man, for the
> benefit of the multitude of bodhisattvas and sentient beings in the
> Dharma Ending Age, you have asked about the expedient, gradual
> stages of the bodhisattva's practice of the samadhi in which all is
> seen to be like an illusion, and which frees sentient beings from
> illusion. Listen attentively now. I shall explain it to you."
>
> Hearing this, Bodhisattva Samantabhadra was filled with
> joy and listened silently along with the assembly.
>
> "Virtuous man, all illusory projections of sentient beings
> arise from the wondrous mind of the Tathagata's Complete
> Enlightenment, just like flowers in the sky which come into
> existence from out of the sky. When the illusory flower vanishes,
> the nature of the sky is not marred. Likewise, the illusory mind of
> sentient beings relies on illusory [cultivation] for its extinction.
> When all illusions are extinguished, the enlightened mind remains
> unmoved. Speaking of enlightenment in contrast to illusion is
> itself an illusion. To say that enlightenment exists is to not have
> left illusion yet. [However], to say that enlightenment does not
> exist is also no different. Therefore, the extinction of illusion is
> called the unmoving [mind of enlightenment]."

Bodhisattva Samantabhadra asks the Buddha to explain how it is
possible for sentient beings to practice if the world and their
existences are illusory. The life of a sentient being is a long dream.
Existence only appears to be real. When one finally awakens, or
attains Buddhahood, existence is seen for what it is — a sequence of
illusions. Until that time, people will remain obsessed by the body,
mind, and external phenomena, not realizing that they are illusory.
You will live in a dream, thinking that it is reality. However, in
order to understand the illusory nature of mind and body, it is
necessary to practice. To do so, we must use our illusory minds and
bodies. There is no other way.

Relying on illusion to realize that we are an illusion might
seem foolish, an impossible task to accomplish. If something is
unreal or illusory, then it follows that it is empty — nothing is
there. If our minds are unreal, then it is empty. If this is true, then

there is no mind with which to practice. Who is practicing? Our bodies are also unreal. If I am unreal, then who is talking? If you are unreal, who is listening?

Bodhisattva Samantabhadra is concerned that people who hear these words will consider practice an illusion and not bother with it. If, as the Buddha says, practice doesn't exist, then it shouldn't matter if we practice or not. Do you agree? If you have such an attitude, then you will remain in samsara, never realizing that you live in a dream.

Generally, unless a sleeping person is having a nightmare, he or she will not want to wake up. The dreamer prefers to remain in the dream. In the same way, if your daily life is relatively pleasant, you probably won't care to practice in order to realize that your life is illusory. No one likes to be wakened from nice dreams. Sentient beings mistakenly view their moment-to-moment illusory existence as a continuous, connected lifetime. Because they are unaware that their life is unreal, they do not attempt to wake up. For this reason, Bodhisattva Samantabhadra asks the Buddha for an expedient method that will encourage sentient beings to practice Buddhadharma so that they may eventually awaken from the dream of existence.

The Buddha says that illusions do not exist. When illusions disappear, all that remains is wondrous emptiness. Realizing this is enlightenment — liberation from the suffering of illusory existence. To say "I am enlightened" is wrong. To what are you enlightened? One would just be creating comparisons between enlightenment and existence, between enlightenment and worldly phenomena. Existence and worldly phenomena are all illusory. Only illusions can be compared to illusions. If a person say that he is enlightened, then he is attached to the belief that there is something called "enlightenment" that can be attained. He would still be living in a dream.

On the other hand, if a person say that there is no such thing as enlightenment, he is also wrong. He is attached to yet another concept and are still deluded. The correct approach is to say nothing. Only through the eradication of labeling and attachment is one in accordance with the unmoving nature of enlightenment. Realizing the unmoving, the realm of illusions and dreams is transcended.

There is a story about an old monk who sat on a train reciting the Buddha's name. A young man remarked loudly, "Monk, how come you don't do anything? The rest of us have jobs. We contribute to society. What do you do?"

The monk answered, "Within a watch there are many gears, constantly turning, but in the center there is an axle that never moves. If it were to move, the gears would foul up and the watch would stop working. Which is more important, the gears that move or the axle that doesn't move?" The young man acknowledged the wisdom of the story, but he was not ready to equate the monk with the unmoving axle, and he was not convinced that the monk did anything worthwhile. What do you think?

A certain political theory maintains that a ruler should be relaxed and not ponder too many problems. Instead, his ministers should do most of the work. The theory maintains that a country under such leadership will benefit. However, if the ruler works too much and the ministers have too much leisure time, the country will eventually fall apart.

The same principle applies to our health. If we use our minds all day and don't exercise our bodies, chances are we won't live a long, healthy life. On the other hand, if we remain calm and tranquil while diligently working our bodies, we'll be healthier and happier. In your practice, it is important that you still your mind. Once the mind moves, it enters the realm of illusions. It is as if someone struck you on the forehead causing spots to dance in front of your eyes. The spots do not exist, but you see them anyway. Likewise, in our lives we see and experience things as ours or mine, beautiful or ugly, pleasant or painful. All of these ideas and feelings exist because of attachments. Because we cannot break the bonds of attachment to our minds, bodies, and external phenomena, problems inevitably arise.

Everyone has problems, but it would be wrong to say that everyone is mentally ill or insane. In a sense, however, all people, sane and insane, have something in common. We are all dreaming. The mind that moves is like turbulent water; it swirls so fast we cannot even distinguish the impurities within it. Only when the mind settles and stops moving are we able to see the tenuous connection between thoughts. Only then will wisdom arise.

You will realize that this "mind" has no existence. If the mind is unreal, then the thoughts within it are also unreal, and the vexations that arise from our thoughts and feelings are also unreal. If vexations were real, it would be impossible to get rid of them. Because they are illusory, we can liberate ourselves from them. Practice, for this reason, is only for ordinary sentient beings. Buddhas do not need to practice. When the turbulent waters calm and impurities settle and sink, then purity is complete. No further calming is required. In our practice we use the unreal mind to transcend the unreal mind. We use an illusory thought to watch for the arising of other illusory thoughts. Unless we concentrate on one thought, an endless sequence of thoughts will follow, sweeping us along in their never-ending cycle. If we can truly fix on one thought, the mind will stop, and it won't be necessary to use that thought anymore. There is no need to keep a watchdog in a house if there are no thieves.

When all illusory conceptualizations in the mind disappear, wisdom spontaneously arises. Wisdom is the absence of illusion; wisdom is emptiness, and emptiness is unmoving. It is inconceivable and ungraspable. One can't carry a bit of emptiness or wisdom around. Things that are graspable, whether thoughts or forms, are unreal. Emptiness is the only true reality. To understand this is enlightenment.

If a person still carry ideas of self, of good and bad, of man and woman, and of right and wrong, he is dreaming. We will enter emptiness only when we stop discriminating. A genuinely enlightened person realizes that everything is an illusion, yet chooses to remain in the world for the benefit of others. In a truly awakened state, awareness is undefiled.

"Enlightenment" is a term that is contrasted with illusion. It is only a word which describes a concept. As such, it is also an illusion. Words and concepts cannot describe enlightenment; we only use them for the sake of expedience. If enlightenment were relative to illusion, then it too would be an illusion. For instance, students are relative to teachers. Teachers exist only because there are students to teach. If everyone were qualified to teach, what need would there be for teachers? Only those who are still in samsara need to have an idea of enlightenment. Thoroughly enlightened beings have no need for the name or concept. A sage sees no difference between himself or herself and ordinary sentient beings. On the other hand, it would be incorrect for a sentient being to view a sage as being the same as an ordinary person. Comparisons — enlightenment and illusion, masters and disciples — still exist for sentient beings.

Sakyamuni Buddha said: "I am not unique. I'm just another member of the Sangha." This is true. The Buddha was a member of the Sangha who attained Buddhahood. But if his disciples thought they were no different from the Buddha, they never would have learned from him. For one who is not enlightened, it is necessary to set goals, follow a teacher's guidance, and practice.

> *Virtuous man, all bodhisattvas and sentient beings in the Dharma Ending Age should separate [themselves] from all illusory projections and deluded realms. [However], when one clings firmly to the mind that separates [from all illusory projections and deluded realms], this mind [should also be taken as] an illusion, and one should separate oneself from it. Because this separation is an illusion, it should also be separated. One should then be free from even this 'separating from the illusion of separation!' When there remains nothing to be separated from, all illusions are eliminated. It is like rubbing two pieces of wood together to obtain fire. When the fire ignites and the wood completely burns, the ashes fly away and the smoke vanishes. Using illusion to remedy illusion is just like this. Yet even though illusions are exhausted, one does not enter annihilation.*
>
> *"Virtuous man, to know illusion is to depart from it; there is no [need to] contrive expedient means! To depart from illusion is to be enlightened; there are no gradual steps! All bodhisattvas and sentient beings in the Dharma Ending Age who practice accordingly will permanently leave illusions behind."*
>
> *At that time, the World Honored One, wishing to clarify his meaning, proclaimed these gathas:*
> *Samantabhadra, you should know*

that the beginningless illusory ignorance
of all sentient beings
is grounded on the Tathagata's
mind of Complete Enlightenment.
Like a flower in empty space,
its appearance relies on the sky.
When the illusory flower vanishes,
the empty space remains in its original unmoving state.
Illusion depends on enlightenment for its arising.
With the extinction of illusion,
enlightenment is wholly perfect,
for the enlightened mind is ever unmoving.
All bodhisattvas and sentient beings
in the Dharma Ending Age
should forever leave illusions far behind
until all illusions are extinguished.
It is like producing fire with wood,
when the wood is burned out,
the fire is also extinguished.
Enlightenment has no gradual steps;
the same applies to expedient means.

We all have attachments, or to use a contemporary term, addictions. They may be material or mental; they may be worldly, philosophical, or physical. Attachments may be superficial and transient or deeply ingrained and stubbornly fixed. Attachments have one thing in common, however: they all create aggravation, turmoil in our lives.

Through practice, it is possible to separate yourself from attachments. Gradually, step by step, you can drop attachments, until all vexations are eliminated. The sutra speaks of four levels of attachment to transcend. Some teachers speak of the process as "separation," but this is misleading because it implies that one is escaping or running away from attachment. This is not the case; rather, recognizing attachment is *itself* separating from attachment.

Recognizing attachment usually proceeds sequentially. First, we detach ourselves from the illusions of worldly phenomena.

Second, we regard our own minds as illusory, and in so doing, detach ourselves from it. Third, we realize that the thought of being free from the mind is also an attachment, and in so doing cease clinging to that concept as well. Fourth, we detach ourselves from separation itself.

It is extremely difficult to progress through these four levels of separation, and detach oneself from innumerable attachments. Achieving the first level of separation, that of detaching oneself from worldly phenomena, is the easiest task of the four. However, it is still an enormous undertaking. One must detach oneself from the material world: money, possessions, career, family, and physical body. It doesn't mean that you have to give up all these things. You still lead a normal life, but you remain detached from them, less dependent on them. In other words, one do not become elated over having possessions and experiencing pleasurable events, and one do not despair over loss and misfortune. In detaching oneself from worldly phenomena, one realize that all experiences — good, bad, or neutral — are the result of causes and conditions that come together and then disperse.

Once a student who was upset told me that he wanted to leave his family. I asked him where he would live. He said he wanted to leave his body too. So I asked him what he would do after he left his body. He replied, "At that point I imagine I would be free." Unfortunately, this is not the case. He is caught up in yet another attachment. If he left his family and body through a natural process, without pain or regret or happiness, that would be all right. But this student did not understand freedom. He desired to be free from the confines of his family and body because he was annoyed by them. He wanted to escape. This is not the kind of separation that the sutras advocate.

Most of us cling to things we like and avoid things we dislike. However, if we aspire to follow the Buddha Path, then we must learn to detach ourselves from worldly phenomena. It is difficult to reach the first level of separation. Yet mastering the next three levels is even more difficult. In mastering the first level of separation one separates himself from the body and the situations around him, but as long as one reflects upon what is seen and experienced, he is still attached to a mind that perceives and discriminates. This mind still exists.

When a person detaches himself from the mind of discrimination, he has reached the second level. However, although there is no longer attachment to the mind or its functions, there is still clinging to the idea of a self that avoids attachment. In order to reach and pass the third level of separation, one must drop his attachment to a self that avoids, subtle though this may seem. Achieving the third level, a person will no longer have any problems with attachment or non-attachment.

Progressing to the fourth and last level is a positive step. At this level, one is free from all levels of separations and are completely enlightened. If he stopped at the third level, he would exhibit an attitude called "stubborn emptiness." It is a view that negates the existence of everything. Although it is free from attachment to materialism, it is still a form of attachment because it adheres to the idea of annihilation. At the fourth level, the final obstacle is transcended. You are completely free. If there remains something to separate from, or if the idea of separation persists, then practice must continue.

In the sutra, the Buddha uses the analogy of fire being produced by the rubbing together of two pieces of wood. When the wood is consumed and turns to ashes, the fire goes out. The wood represents attachment, and the fire represents separating oneself from all attachment. When there are no more attachments, there is no more need for separation, just as fire disappears when there is no more fuel. Once the wood and fire disappear completely, there will be no possibility of another fire starting again. A practitioner who reaches the fourth level will not have any problems with attachment, non-attachment, or separation.

People who are striving to reach the first level and those who have reached the fourth level are completely different. However, in outward appearances, the difference may not be noticeable. People at the fourth level behave in many ways like ordinary people, but there is a big difference between ordinary sentient beings and completely enlightened sentient beings. People who have not yet mastered the first level are attached to mind, body, and worldly phenomena. They discriminate between themselves and other things. They desire good things and avoid bad things. People at the fourth level may say, "This is good, this is bad," but their thoughts, words, and actions do not stem from discriminations and attachments. They are genuinely free from attachment. Their thoughts, words, and actions are a product of wisdom.

A Buddha or bodhisattva would not say, "Since I am fully enlightened and have no more attachments, I can do whatever I want. I can kill and steal and lie." Enlightened beings adhere to morality and worldly conventions and conduct themselves accordingly. They do so because of wisdom, not attachment.

The sutra says that when we recognize illusions, we should detach ourselves from them without the use of expedient means. How can we perceive illusions as illusions? What methods can practitioners use to progress through these four levels?

First, we must settle our minds. This method is known as "stilling the mind." In order to see illusion as illusion, we must be mentally calm. Once this is achieved, we can effectively use the second method of practice: contemplating the self and worldly phenomena, or worldly dharmas. It is extremely difficult to detach oneself from the body, mind, and worldly phenomena without practicing these two methods.

You can read books on Buddhism or attend lectures and classes, but if you are unable to directly realize and penetrate Buddhadharma, you will continue to experience vexations. Contemplating ideas is not forceful or enduring enough to help you overcome the fundamental problems of life and vexations. Once you personally experience the world and self as illusory, however, all attachments will naturally disappear. Wisdom will rise instantly, automatically.

We designate four different levels in order to differentiate among the four major obstructions an individual faces during the course of practice. Enlightenment, however, is instantaneous and immediate. Enlightenment does not begin to appear at the first level and gradually grow until it becomes complete at the fourth level. Only when one is completely unattached will one experience enlightenment. When one has a genuine enlightenment experience, it is of exactly the same nature as the Buddha's enlightenment. However, since a normal person's practice is not as strong as the Buddha's, the experience does not last. He will not remain enlightened. A flash of enlightenment may come but it will fade. For this reason, we must persist in our practice. Experiencing and then losing enlightenment should not dishearten us. For that brief moment of enlightenment we perceive what the Buddhas perceive. It will increase our faith in ourselves and Buddhadharma, and we will be more determined in our practice.

Bodhisattva of
Universal Vision

Then the Bodhisattva of Universal Vision rose from his seat in the midst of the assembly, prostrated himself at the feet of the Buddha, circled the Buddha three times clockwise, knelt down, joined his palms, and said: "O World Honored One of great compassion! For the sake of the multitude of bodhisattvas in this assembly and all sentient beings in the Dharma Ending Age, please expound on the gradual stages of the bodhisattva's practice. How should one contemplate? What should one abide in and uphold? What expedient methods should one devise to guide unenlightened sentient beings, to universally enable them to reach enlightenment?

"World Honored One, if these sentient beings do not have the correct expedient methods and contemplation, they will be confused when they hear you expound this samadhi [in which all is seen to be an illusion] and will be unable to awaken to Complete Enlightenment. Would you be compassionate enough to expound the provisional expedient methods for our benefit and for sentient beings in the Dharma Ending Age?" Having said these words, he prostrated himself on the ground. He made the same request three times, each time repeating the same procedure.

At that time the World Honored One said to the Bodhisattva of Universal Vision: "Excellent, excellent! Virtuous man, for the benefit of the multitude of bodhisattvas and sentient beings in the Dharma Ending Age, you have asked the Tathagata about the gradual stages of cultivation, what contemplation one should abide in and uphold, as well as the various expedient methods one should use. Listen attentively now. I shall explain them to you."

Hearing this, the Bodhisattva of Universal Vision was filled with joy and listened silently along with the assembly.

"Virtuous man, newly initiated bodhisattvas and sentient beings in the Dharma Ending Age seeking the Tathagata's pure mind of Complete Enlightenment should hold the right thought of separating from myriad illusions. First, they should rely on the samatha practice of the Tathagatas and strictly observe the precepts. They should reside peacefully among an assembly of practitioners and sit in meditation in a quiet room.

"They should always be mindful that the body is a union of the four elements. Things such as hair, nails, teeth, skin, flesh, tendons, bones, marrow, and brain all belong to the element of earth. Spittle, mucus, pus, blood, saliva, sweat, phlegm, tears, semen, urine, and excrement all belong to the element of water. Warmth belongs to the element of fire. Motion belongs to the element of wind. When the four elements are separated from one another, where is this illusory body? Thus one knows that the physical body ultimately has no substance and owes its appearance to the union [of the four elements]. In reality it is not different from an illusory projection.

"Due to the provisional union of the four conditions [of vision, hearing, perception, and awareness], the illusory six sense faculties come to exist. The inward and outward combination of the six sense faculties and the four elements [of earth, water, fire, and wind] gives rise to the illusory existence of conditioned energy. [In this process], there 'seems to be' something which is cognizant. This is provisionally called 'mind.'"

The Bodhisattva of Universal Vision asks the Buddha three questions. First, what methods of practice should people on the Bodhisattva Path adopt? Second, what understanding should people have of their methods as they progress on the Path? Third, how should people actually approach and work on a particular method?

Bodhisattva of Universal Vision asks these questions for the benefit of those who have not yet been enlightened. He is asking the Buddha to expound expedient methods so that sentient beings who do not know how to contemplate and practice correctly will not be confused when they hear Buddhadharma.

According to the sutras, there are fifty-two levels of Bodhisattvahood. Reaching the fifty-second level is the same as reaching Buddhahood. Bodhisattvas on the first through fortieth levels are still considered ordinary sentient beings. Therefore, when the Buddha speaks of newly initiated bodhisattvas, he is talking about any sentient being who has accepted Mahayana Buddhadharma, has generated the bodhisattva aspirations, or vows, and has begun to practice.

Here, an explanation of the Buddha's term "expedient methods" is necessary. We speak of expedient methods because, in regard to Buddhadharma, there really is nothing to talk about. Teachings are expounded to help those who have no other way of understanding. Therefore, teachings and methods of practice are expedient methods for the unenlightened. They are unnecessary for the already enlightened. To cross an ocean you need a boat. Once you reach the other shore, the boat has served its purpose and is no longer necessary. It is an expedient device, and so are methods of practice.

When the other shore is reached, however, the boat is not burned. It is saved so that others can use it. Similarly, those who have become enlightened do not abandon their methods and practice. Instead, their practice serves as a model for others, and they teach so that others will be able to cross the ocean of ignorance. This is the bodhisattva way. Buddhas and bodhisattvas continue to speak of and use methods of practice for the benefit of sentient beings.

In order to practice correctly, you must first have the right thought. The true definition of "right thought" is "no thought." You should not hold onto thoughts of wisdom or vexation because all thoughts, even thoughts of enlightenment, are illusory. "No thought" is not a blank mind. Someone at the level of "no thought" is clearly, fully conscious, completely aware, and free of illusions.

In order to reach the level of "no thought" you must adhere to the precepts. The precepts that the sutra refers to are three in number: (1) to avoid anything that is harmful to you and others; (2) to carry out all activities that are beneficial to both yourself and others; (3) to carry out all activities that are beneficial to others even if they are not beneficial to you. These are precepts for bodhisattvas and are difficult to put into practice. Do not be deterred by them. They are guidelines to follow, standards to aspire to. If you are willing to adopt these precepts even though you know you may fail, that is already good.

After accepting the precepts, you must then use a method of practice. In this section of the sutra, the Buddha speaks of two methods: "contemplation on impurity" and "contemplation on divisions of the constituents." These methods are especially useful for people who are extremely attached to desire. To seek or desire things is normal, but desires of a powerful and persistent nature create problems and cause suffering. The attachment and desire between the sexes has always created enormous vexations for humans.

It is true that we have basic needs that must be satisfied. We need clothes and shelter to keep us warm and safe, we need food for energy and health, and most people need to satisfy their sexual urges. These needs and urges are normal, but if we are overly attached to any of them, they will create problems and vexations. For instance, people who are narcissistic are usually hurt by criticism.

The methods described by the Buddha can help to alleviate and eventually eliminate strong attachments. If you practice the methods sincerely and diligently, you will be less affected by external phenomena, other beings, and your own body. Of course you will still need food, clothing, and perhaps sex, and you will continue to interact with others and the environment, but you will experience less suffering. It is better to view the interaction between body and environment as the natural order of things and not allow yourself to become too attached to them. With attachment comes suffering. Furthermore, practitioners should regard their bodies as "the union of the four elements." In so doing, they can use the method of contemplating impurities, asking themselves, "What is this illusory body of mine?"

Our bodies, as well as the external environment, are an aggregate of the four elements: earth, water, fire, and wind. The four elements come together, interact, and then disperse. What permanent body can be found in the midst of all this?

One of my students suggested that we modernize the sutra, replacing the four elements with atoms and molecules, since chemistry and physics have deepened our intellectual understanding of the world and universe. Sakyamuni Buddha was not aware of this modern method of categorization and in fact was drawing from an even older system used in India. But the four elements are tangible and accessible to most people, whereas the world of sub-atomic physics is abstract and understandable to only a few. It is simpler to stay with the older system, even if it isn't entirely correct.

In carefully examining ourselves, we usually say that there are two facets to our existence: the material and the mental (or spiritual). The material body can be extended to include the so-called objective world, or what I often refer to as the environment, external phenomena, or worldly phenomena. We consider the physical body to be the personal self and the environment to be that with which we interact. We think that our bodies belong to us and that they are enduring, but we are mistaken. Though our bodies were originally created in our mothers' wombs, they have completely changed since birth. The body changes with each passing moment. We ingest food, convert it into energy and bodily materials, and excrete wastes. The water we drink eventually leaves our bodies in the form of sweat or urine. We breathe in air, use oxygen, and exhale carbon dioxide. Metabolism requires the continual intake, transformation, and elimination of materials. The body is the interaction of the four elements, and it is always changing.

When the interaction of the four elements combines with the mind, a sense of self emerges. The mind, however, is not a fixed entity, for if we separate each thought from the continual flow of thoughts, we realize there is no mind or spirit apart from them. The existence of the mind is dependent upon the continuation of our thoughts. It is the coming together of the four elements that gives rise to our sense of body, and it is the unending chain of thoughts that gives rise to our sense of mind. The combination of mind and body creates what is called "self."

I once asked a student of mine, "Can you describe your girlfriend?" He said that she was a unique configuration of the four elements with a mind and heart. I told him that he could speak of the four elements with accuracy, but he could not know or describe her mind. In fact, even the girl does not know what her mind is. She might say, "I love you," but she probably isn't clear as to what love is. It is the same with the existence of mind. The mind is an abstract idea. If you try to talk about it in a concrete manner, inevitably you must conclude that it is a continual sequence of thoughts. There is really no such thing as mind.

Our lives are transient, and whatever we seemingly acquire is even more so. You should treasure the present moment and make good use of it. If you can do this, you will not be too perturbed when things come and go in your life. Furthermore, you should understand that your body is not separate from external phenomena. If the elements are constantly interchanging between the body and its environment, then there is no clear cut distinction between self and other, or self and world. Your body is part of my body. Our bodies are part of the environment. Anything that is part of me may eventually become part of you. Over the long process of constant change in the universe, who can say where the elements that make up your body have been?

Right now in this room we are sharing the air. I am inhaling what you are exhaling, and vice versa. This is not simply limited to the air we breathe. Our bodies are excreting things into the atmosphere every second. It may sound unclean, but are you willing to claim that it isn't happening? Do you think that you've never taken anything from another individual or that you've never given any part of yourself to others?

In order to practice well, you must detach yourself from worldly phenomena. Whatever you gain you may lose. You should also consider any thing or any being in the world as a part of yourself. This method is a good one. It can help to alleviate vexations. Through contemplation meditation you will realize that your existence is temporary. You will also realize that you cannot deny your existence. Therefore, you should take good care of your body and your surrounding environment, and make use of them for the benefit of others as well as yourself.

> *"Virtuous man, this illusory mind cannot exist without the six sense objects [of sight, sound, smell, taste, touch, thought]. When the four elements disperse, the six sense objects cannot be found. Once the elements and the sense objects disperse and are extinguished, ultimately there is no cognizant mind to be seen.*
>
> *"Virtuous man, when the illusory bodies of sentient beings become extinguished, the illusory minds also become extinguished. When the illusory minds become extinguished, the illusory sense objects also become extinguished. When the illusory sense objects become extinguished, the illusory extinguishing also becomes extinguished. When the illusory extinguishing becomes extinguished, that which is not illusory is not extinguished. It is like polishing a mirror. When the defilements are wiped off, brightness appears."*

The Buddha elaborates further on the transient nature of the body and mind. The body is an collection of the four elements and the six sense faculties (eyes, ears, nose, tongue, body, and mind); and the mind is created by the interaction of the six sense faculties with the six dusts, or sense objects (what is seen, heard, smelled, tasted, felt, and thought). Everything is in a continual state of change. Thoughts unceasingly come and go; the body and its environment unceasingly interact. Arising, perishing, birth, death — everything changes.

However, we all believe in existence: we exist, the world exists, the Buddha exists. But who is it that senses this existence? It is your self, separate and untouched by the feelings and thoughts of others. Only you have the unique idea of existence that is yours. Who is this self? This self is the mind, and the mind is merely an unending succession of thoughts. Between these separate thoughts there is nothing. Therefore, I ask, "What is the mind?"

The mind is an illusion. There is no such entity called mind.

This is the correct view. But if this is true, then who is reading these words? Who is thinking these thoughts and claiming that there is no-mind, no-self? If I ask you to tell me if your mind is true or false, you will be in a quandary. You might say that the mind is true, or real, or enduring, but if your mind is following these words, then it is moving. If your mind is moving and changing, then it is not real, and if the mind is not moving, how can you read these words and think about what I am saying? On the other hand, if you say the mind is false, that it does not exist, then who is reading these words? How can you think or read at all? The best thing to do would be to avoid the question.

It is important that we read and trust the Buddha's words in the sutra, trust that the Dharma is spoken from a level of Complete Enlightenment and that the Buddha would not mislead us. The mind is false, transient. To know this through direct, personal experience is to be enlightened. When the false mind disappears, so too does the unreality of the false mind. This is enlightenment.

The false mind arises from the external environment. More specifically, it arises from the external sense objects' interaction with the sense faculties of the body. It is in the interaction of sensation, body, and worldly phenomena that the idea of mind arises. Objectively speaking, I am a mass with shape, contour, and color. I also produce sounds. But because human beings have a memory of experience that makes the shape familiar, and because the stream of sounds that comes from my mouth is understandable to you, you call me a person. Other things have shape and color and make sounds, but only humans do so in a way that is recognizable and understandable to humans.

At this point you should be clear about one thing: there is nothing that exists outside of yourself — no body, no mind, no environment. Even the spirit is something that you produce, something that your mind experiences. Without a mind, you are nothing more than a mass of flesh. Without a mind, you cannot react to my words or to worldly phenomena. Nothing external exists independent of the mind. It is our feelings and sensations that mediate the world, but even they do so within the context of mind.

Common sense leads you to say, "I exist." You believe that

you have a mind and that there is an external world. In this external world the world exists, other sentient beings exist, God exists. However, without your mind, there is no existence: no world, no people, no God. If you know that your own mind is false (merely a succession of uninterrupted thoughts), then all external objects are also false. To directly experience this emptiness is enlightenment. Simultaneously, you realize that the mind and the objects perceived by the mind do not exist. From this description, enlightenment sounds like a frightening proposition. Are you willing to go to a place where nothing exists? If I invited you into a house, telling you that when you entered everything would disappear, including your body, your mind, and the entire world, would you accept the invitation? Sakyamuni does not speak of such a place. To say that body, mind, and environment will disappear when you are enlightened is a figure of speech. It does not mean that there will be nothing left. In fact, this "disappearance" refers only to its illusory dimensions and qualities.

Mind, body, and environment have an illusory existence, therefore they have an illusory cessation. The cessation of all false things is itself false. Then what is real? You must realize that everything is transitory. This is the only reality, the only truth. Enlightenment is realizing this truth.

After enlightenment, we do not deny the existence of things. A rock is still a rock; it does not vanish. But there is nothing that exists continually. Everything is in constant flux. We cannot say that things continue to exist from moment to moment. The false mind is a mind that constantly changes. The false world is a world continuously undergoing transformations. We cannot say that after enlightenment there is a false mind but not a false body, because then the body would be real. If the mind did not exist but the body did, then the body would just be a corpse. In that case, reaching enlightenment would be easy — just wait until you die. After death, everyone would be enlightened.

In the sutra, the mind is compared to a mirror. When the mirror is dirty and dusty, it does not reflect well. Objects that pass in front of the mirror are not clearly reflected. But if the dust is swept away, the mirror accurately reflects once again. Just like a clean mirror, the mind of an enlightened person sees clearly because it is swept clean of vexations.

Vexations are the self. If you have a self, then you have a view. There is "I and you," "I and others." With separation and discrimination come opposition, avoidance, yearning, craving. As long as you hold onto an idea of self, then you will also perceive an external world, and you will want to possess and avoid things. The self creates vexation, and vexation, in turn, reinforces the sense of self. When a self exists, nothing you see is true. Everything is subjective, seen from your particular viewpoint. You cannot view anything without placing a value on it, judging it, or comparing it to something else. This is the illusory mind. When there is no self, however, we cannot say that the mind ceases to function. When there is no vexation, and therefore no self, the mind of discrimination is replaced by the mind of wisdom.

In ancient times, mirrors were made of bronze instead of glass. The bronze was polished until it could reflect images. In the same way, when the mind is cleansed of vexations and thoughts of self and others, it becomes bright, clear, and luminous, able to reflect everything exactly as it is. For an enlightened being, there is no such thing as a real mind. If a person says he has an enlightened mind, then he also possesses a sense of self. If he has a self, then he has vexation, and if he has vexation, he is not enlightened. For ordinary people, there is such a thing as an enlightened mind, but for those who have already attained enlightenment, mind in the ordinary sense no longer exists. This does not, however, mean the person is dead or a zombie.

> "Virtuous man, you should know that both body and mind are illusory defilements. When these appearances of defilement are permanently extinguished, purity will pervade all ten directions.
> "Virtuous man, for instance, the pure mani jewel reflects the five colors as they appear before it, yet the ignorant see the mani as actually possessing the five colors. Virtuous man, although the pure nature of Complete Enlightenment likewise manifests as body and mind, [people] respond in accordance with their capacities, yet the ignorant speak of the pure Complete Enlightenment as

having intrinsic characteristics of body and mind. For this reason, they are unable to depart from illusion. Therefore, I say that body and mind are illusory defilements. It is in terms of separating from illusory defilements that bodhisattvas are defined. When defilements are thoroughly removed, their corresponding [cognition] is [completely] eliminated. Since there is nothing corresponding to defilement, there is also no 'one' there to designate."

Ordinary people do not understand that the mind and body are illusory. Just as forms and colors reflected in a mani jewel may be taken to be real colors and forms, so too the body, mind and worldly phenomena are perceived to be real by people.

Originally, your mind is identical with the Buddha-mind. It is complete and pure. But with the perception of having a body and mind comes the false idea that the body and mind are outside and separate from Buddha mind. At that moment, perfect enlightenment is gone, and it will return only with cultivation and practice. Upon realizing that body and mind are transitory and unreal, Complete Enlightenment returns. Enlightenment can come in an instant. People would like to contrast perfect enlightenment with the illusory nature of body and mind, but this itself is the essence of the problem. Eliminating comparisons is enlightenment. You cannot attain enlightenment by leaving illusion. If enlightenment were separate from illusion, it would be impossible to attain.

"Illusion" and "enlightenment" are names and nothing else. It does not matter whether we talk about any of this. In fact, talking about enlightenment and illusion is a waste of time; but because there are people who need to hear it, the sutras exist.

If there is a wooden peg in a table, you can try to remove it by hammering it out with another peg. Of course, you have only filled the hole with another peg. You could repeat this nonsensical process over and over; in so doing, at least you will get a clearer idea of the emptiness of the hole. Once you can say, "Yes, now I know the hole is empty," then there is no further need to replace one wooden peg with another. This is an analogy for the teachings and for our practice. Each person must realize the illusory nature of his or her own mind.

> *"Virtuous man, if bodhisattvas as well as sentient beings in the Dharma Ending Age realize the awakening of the extinction of illusory appearances, at that time, unlimited purity and infinite emptiness will be revealed and manifested in their enlightenment. Because the enlightenment is complete and illuminating, it reveals the mind in its purity. Because the mind is pure, objects of vision are pure. Because vision is pure, the eye faculty is pure. Because that faculty is pure, the visual consciousness is pure. Because the consciousness is pure, hearing is pure. Because hearing is pure, the faculty of hearing is pure. Because that faculty is pure, the consciousness is pure. Because the consciousness is pure, perception is pure. The same holds true for the nose, tongue, body, and mind."*

Only with practice is it possible to realize that sense faculties, sense objects, and sense perceptions are illusory and impermanent. Practice is a process. At first you are entangled in illusion. With practice you can reach the next level, wherein you perceive that body, mind and environment are illusory and empty of real substance. Still, this is not the end of practice. Ultimately, you realize that this emptiness is also illusory. First you are immersed in the phenomenal world. Next you are in utter emptiness. In the final step, however, you re-enter the phenomenal world once again.

It might seem as if practice is a journey that leads you in circles, but the person who has reached the third step is no longer an ordinary sentient being. Such a person is completely enlightened and has taken an active step in returning to the world to help those who are still entangled in illusions. The second stage can be described as a passive state where nothing exists, neither ignorance nor wisdom, neither samsara nor nirvana. There is no self nor any sentient beings. In the third stage, that of complete and thorough enlightenment, there is no place that is not pure and undefiled. In other words, ignorance is wisdom and samsara is nirvana.

There is a sect of Buddhism in which people aspire to reach the Pure Land. Perceptions of the Pure Land are divided into different levels depending on the experience of practitioners. If the practitioner's mind is filled with vexation and discrimination, the world is perceived as being imperfect and unclean and the Pure

Land is seen as a perfectly pure place or a place to emulate. If the mind is pure and clean, then the world is perceived as being pure and clean; then, any place can be the Pure Land. In this sense, the Pure Land is identical to Ch'an. Outside of the mind there is no Pure Land. Similarly, it is not necessary to seek the Pure Land. When the mind is pure, the Pure Land is manifest. But answer me this: if the mind is pure and clean, who is it that has a mind? Is there a mind at all? Only people who have deep experience from the practice can truly answer this question.

On a retreat in Taiwan, one of the participants had a shallow experience. When he went outside everything he saw seemed beautiful and likable. He approached a dog, feeling a strong attraction to it. The dog licked him, and he in turn licked the dog. He felt happy, so he wanted the dog to feel happy as well. He also saw people sweeping in front of their homes, and he thought it strange, because to him the world seemed immaculately pure.

Is this enlightenment? No. Such an experience is still part of the first level of practice. The person still discriminates; he still sees his surrounding environment apart from himself. Although shallow, the experience is nonetheless worthwhile.

If we look at the world only with our eyes and do not think about what we are seeing, is the world pure and clean? Once, during class, I asked my students if they looked at their excrement in the toilet after moving their bowels. One student said that he did. I asked him if it was dirty. He replied that he did not know, since all he did was look at it. "In that case," I asked, "would you be willing to pick it up to take a closer look?" He changed his mind after that.

Once I watched a mother removing a diaper from her child. I said, "Oh boy, it looks really dirty in there!" The woman replied, "Not at all. This is great." She smelled the diaper, smiled and said, "It smells great." She was happy because the child had a healthy bowel movement. There are workers in some hospitals who look at stool samples for a living. They analyze them in order to diagnose patients.

Clean, pure, dirty, these are all subjective terms. The meaning changes with each individual's experience. Clean and dirty are concepts that exist only in the mind. When your mind is pure, then external objects will also be pure.

I knew a person who had diabetes. His foot started to decay. Throughout this process he was very protective of his foot and did everything he could to make it better. Eventually it was amputated. Afterwards, the doctor asked if he would like to see his dismembered foot. He replied with disgust, "I don't want to see that dirty rotten thing."

Once the foot left his body, he no longer viewed it as his, but while it was attached to his leg, the foot was precious. Both views are subjective. At the first level of experience, concepts of clean, pure, and dirty are strictly subjective. Once your mind reaches the level of purity, everything you see is also pure — external objects as well as the body.

The following is a famous kung-an (Jp: koan): A student asks his master, "What is the Buddha?" The master replies, "A piece of dry dog shit."

Are the Buddha and dog shit the same thing? If the Buddha is pure, is dog shit pure? If your mind is pure and clean, it's easy to say that the Buddha is also clean, but are you willing to say the same about dog shit? If mind and body are pure, why bother to brush your teeth or wash your face? Why not put shit on the table while you eat? Why bathe?

These questions are absurd, but I ask them for a reason. Do not misunderstand the idea of purity. The purity that the sutra speaks of is purity of the mind. Although external objects are pure and clean, we must still discriminate. After all, shit is shit and food is food. We must still discriminate in a conventional sense. We must still bathe and brush our teeth. It's wise to avoid strange or harmful behavior. In the practice we pass through levels. The first level is the level of illusion, but we do not know it as such. At the second level, everything is seen as being illusory, unreal. It is a negation of self-centeredness and the world. We return to the ordinary, common world at the third level. Although enlightened, we lead a normal life, knowing which things are conventionally clean and unclean.

After attaining thorough enlightenment, Sakyamuni Buddha said that all men are his father, all women his mother. Yet, when his father died, he went to the funeral and helped carry the coffin. Although the Buddha saw all things as being equal, he still recognized his father as his father and acted accordingly.

> *"Virtuous man, because the sense faculties are pure, the objects of sight are pure. Because the objects of sight are pure, the objects of sound are pure. The same holds in the cases of smell, taste, touch, and thought.*
>
> *"Virtuous man, because the six sense objects are pure, the earth element is pure. Because the earth element is pure, the water element is pure. The same holds for the elements of fire and wind."*

The sutra divides the interaction of the self and external world into three categories: sense faculties, sense dusts, or objects, and sense perception. Actually, if the mind is pure and clean, then all three categories are pure and clean. It does not matter which category you start with. These categories are expedient teachings, invented to help explain the Dharma better. If one of the categories is pure, it follows that they must all be pure. All things, however, start with the mind.

> *"Virtuous man, because the four elements are pure, the twelve entrances, the eighteen realms, and the twenty-five existences are pure. Because these are pure, the ten powers, the four kinds of fearlessness, the four unhindered wisdoms, the eighteen exclusive attributes of the Buddha, and the thirty-seven aids to enlightenment are all pure. The same holds for the purity of everything all the way up to the eighty-four thousand dharani doors."*

Once one is enlightened, there is no realm — from that of ordinary beings to that of the Buddha — which is not pure. The terminology in this paragraph of the sutra is extensive and complex, yet the meaning is clear: when the mind is free of vexation, everything is pure.

The four elements of air, fire, water, and earth describe the physical form of human beings as well as the so-called objective world. The "twelve entrances" refer to the six sense faculties and six sense objects. The twelve entrances together with the six mental activities associated with them are the "eighteen realms." The "twenty-five existences" refer to the different types of sentient beings that inhabit the three realms of samsara, the realms of desire, form and formlessness. The "ten powers," the "four kinds of fearlessness," the "four unobstructed wisdoms," and the "eighteen exclusive attributes of the Buddha" are all functions of the Buddha's wisdom.

The "thirty-seven aids to enlightenment" are methods and guidlines for practice. We need not go into these methods in detail. The important point is that if we can maintain a mindful, concentrated mind and diligently avoid non-virtuous thoughts, speech, and action, then all thirty-seven methods are encompassed.

The "eighty-four thousand dharani doors" refer to the infinite, uncountable ways one can enter the door of enlightenment. Dharani literally translates as "complete control." What it means is that all methods are interdependent and mutually penetrate each other. To master one method is to master all methods. You need not master every dharani door. If a house has fifty doors, you only need to walk through one to enter the house. If you can penetrate one method or fully understand one sutra, then you have mastered all methods and all sutras. In prostrating to one Buddha you acknowledge and pay homage to all Buddhas. If you attain perfection, your merit, virtue, and wisdom encompass all merit, virtue, and wisdom.

It is important to remember this in your practice. One method is as good as another. If you constantly change methods while meditating, then you are fooling yourself. A method does not change; it is you who changes. Changing methods is like trying to enter a house with fifty doors and barely turning the knob of one door before trying another. In time you'll try every door, but you'll still be outside. You must be persistent with your method and with your practice.

Students who have been on several retreats sometimes ask me for new methods. They feel that not using a new method on each retreat is a sign of stagnancy or failure. This is common. I tell them that the method may be the same, but how they approach and apply the method changes. Furthermore, the energy they put into practice changes, and they themselves change as time and experiences come and go. In the beginning, most students have neither seen the door nor know where to look for it. Later, when they are at the door, they may not believe it or recognize it as such. After they discover that it is a door, they may not know the technique for opening it; later still, they may know the technique but may be unsuccessful in their attempts to open this "door" and cross the threshold. These are different stages of practice, and my guidance must change accordingly. Methods may remain the same, but everything else changes.

Just as it is unnecessary to explain all the dharani doors, so it is unnecessary to explain the other terms in this paragraph of the sutra. What is purity, after all? If there is water in a cup, we can say that the water is pure, but is the cup? Many people enter this center. They may all be neat and clean, but when they leave, the center is dirty, and the air stale. As long as there is existence there will be impurity. This holds for all categories, from the four elements to the eighty-four thousand dharani doors. In order to realize that all things are pure and free of conceptual contamination, all terms, concepts and thoughts must be erased. Only then will purity reveal itself.

Using the mind to understand such terms — analyzing and categorizing — only creates more vexation. Do you really want to know the eighty-four thousand dharani doors? In complete, perfect enlightenment, there is nothing that can be attached to. There are no sentient beings, no gradual steps to Buddhahood, no Buddha.

Philosophy, religion, and science have different ways of explaining the workings of the body, mind, and worldly phenomena. Buddhism explains the mind as a series of uninterrupted thoughts. If the thoughts are separated, there is no mind to be found. The mind that seems to exist only does so because of the body's interaction with its surrounding. Eyes receive light, ears receive sound, and so on, and the mind perceives them through a continuum that we call space and time.

The experience and knowledge that we have accumulated from the past and our expectations and imaginings about the future cannot be separated from the external environment. There is no such thing as the mind outside of the external environment and the body that makes contact with it.

For an enlightened person, there is no mind, no sentient beings, no external environment, no Buddha, no vexation, no wisdom. But only people who are enlightened have the right to make this statement. For ordinary people, the four elements and the eighty-four thousand dharani doors still exist.

> *"Virtuous man, because the nature of Absolute Reality is pure, one's body is pure. Because one's body is pure, a multitude of bodies are pure. Because a multitude of bodies are pure, likewise sentient beings in all ten directions are completely enlightened and pure."*

We must remember that the words spoken above come from a completely enlightened being, not an ordinary person. However, if you see into your self-nature, then you perceive what the Buddha perceived and absolute reality is manifest. You perceive that everything in the universe has been, is, and always will be pure and clean. When this is understood directly, it is called enlightenment.

An enlightened person sees everything as Buddha-nature. Of course, it is extremely difficult to attain this level. Only with sincere and diligent practice can the mind become and remain undisturbed by vexations.

Sakyamuni Buddha does not refer to "purity" in the relative or comparative sense. He speaks of absolute purity. Light is a relative phenomenon. If I turn off the lights, the room becomes dark, but not completely so, because light still filters through the windows. If I turn the lights back on again, one by one, the room gets brighter and brighter. These are all relative comparisons. The light that manifests when one enters deep levels of samadhi, however, comes from within and cannot be compared to light from a lamp, the sun, or anything else. The light of samadhi is absolute. Likewise, the purity of enlightenment is absolute.

If we discriminate between pure and impure, clean and dirty, good and bad, less and more, we are using our minds of vexation.

We always compare, categorize, judge. We are repelled by the smell of sweaty socks, yet entranced by the aroma of incense and perfume. Odors are a natural phenomenon that exist and nothing more. It is we who have preferences among them. Sentient beings have always had the tendency to discriminate, but to one who has reached the level of non-discrimination, everything is absolutely pure. If you perceive that your nature is pure and clean, then you see that your body, the environment, and the entire universe are also pure and clean. To an enlightened person, all sentient beings are Buddhas and all places are Buddha lands. Flowers, mountains, garbage, shit: none is different from the Buddha.

Does this mean that an enlightened person loses the ability to make worldly judgments? No. An enlightened person would not eat his own excrement or purposely ingest poison. Enlightened beings are not fools. They know good from bad. Pure and clean refer to the mind, not to external phenomena.

Under special circumstances, an enlightened being might use supernormal abilities to do something out of the ordinary, but it would be for a specific purpose. It would not be common practice. An enlightened person's physical body is subject to the same ills as anyone else's body. The Ch'an sect does not emphasize supernormal abilities in its teachings. It emphasizes removing vexations and seeing directly into one's intrinsic nature. Ch'an masters rarely exhibit supernormal abilities; rather, they stress practice in daily activities. Through practice, the mind gradually becomes purified as more and more vexations disappear. Upon attaining Complete Enlightenment, nothing is left, including the mind. If anything — even a single self-created thought — is in the mind, attachment remains.

> "Virtuous man, because one world is pure, a multitude of worlds are pure. Because a multitude of worlds are pure, all things completely exhausting empty space in the past, present, and future are impartially equal, pure, and unmoving."

The Buddha progresses from speaking about the purity of a single being to the equal and unchanging nature of the universe. It is a sweeping statement, yet it is true. The unchanging nature of the universe can only be perceived and understood by those who have purified their minds. Normally, our minds are like a cluttered house. Through practice we reorder the house, making it easier to move around, but this is only a partially correct analogy, a relative purity. If the mind were a blackboard and vexation were chalk marks, one might think that the goal of practice would be to erase the scribbles from the board; and in the case of the mind, to gradually remove all thoughts and vexations until it becomes pure and bright. However, when all marks are erased and the board is clean and empty, practice is not over. An empty, clear, and bright mind is still a mind. If a mind exists, then so does attachment, and complete liberation has not yet been attained.

When Complete Enlightenment is attained, nothing remains, yet all is encompassed. Buddhist teachings divide the universe into two material realms and one mental realm. The body and the so-called objective world make up the two material realms and the interaction of the body with worldly phenomena makes up the mental realm. Through the interaction of body and worldly phenomena, sentient beings experience pain, pleasure, past, future, time, and space. When one is completely enlightened, the three realms no longer exist and there is no further need for cultivation. If there is no longer a body, an objective world, or their interactions, how can there be a need for practice?

At this point, there are no more attachments. Space and time are boundless. There are no limiting notions of future or past, great or small. There are no distinctions. Buddha-nature pervades everything. At this point, a grain of sand is as vast as limitless space, and a single moment encompasses all of time.

Space and time are only attachments. If you are not limited by a self, then you transcend the bounds of space and time. Small and large are equal. Past and future are equal. Mental and material are equal. When all things are equal, all is encompassed. This is complete liberation.

> "*Virtuous man, since empty space is equal, identical, and unmoving as such, you should know that the nature of enlightenment is*

also equal, identical, and unmoving. Since the four elements are
unmoving, you should know that the nature of enlightenment is
also equal, identical, and unmoving. Since [everything] up to the
eighty-four thousand dharani doors are equal, identical, and
unmoving, you should know that the nature of enlightenment is
also equal, identical, and unmoving."

Space is everywhere impartially equal and unchanging. It has been
so since time without beginning and will be so for innumerable
eons to come. Space is formless, therefore it can assume any shape.
Is the space in the United States different from the space in the
Orient? Sometimes I think it must be because everyone wants to
move here. The Chinese often say that the moon is fuller and
rounder in the States, but of course it is the environment that
differs. Space is the same no matter where you are. Buddha-nature
is like this. Although we all have our own forms and thoughts, our
Buddha-nature is the same.

When Huineng, the future Sixth Patriarch, met Hungren, the
Fifth Patriarch, Hungren asked, "Where do you come from?"
Huineng replied that he came from the extreme southern region of
China. The people in Hungren's province considered southerners
to be barbarians. Hungren said, "You're a barbarian. How can a
barbarian expect to be a Buddha?" Huineng answered, "Although
there are northerners and southerners, north and south make no
difference to their Buddha-nature." Immediately Hungren realized
that Huineng was no ordinary man.

Most people make distinctions based on what they see, hear,
and experience. Even today, some Chinese people consider people
of the West to be barbarians or "foreign devils" for as silly a reason
as having body hair. Westerners, too, look down upon other races
and nationalities. Even animals discriminate. A small dog in his
own home will bark furiously at any strange dog walking past, even
if that dog is twice its size. Humans and animals are able to distinguish among places and forms. When we seize upon these differences and cling to them, vexations appear.

Buddha-nature is "impartially equal." It is the same with space
and time. "Impartially equal" means that space is everywhere

without distinction; there is no difference between this space and that space. There is no difference between one time and another.

If everything has the same fundamental nature, then there should be no attachment to any one thing. If you can let go of all attachments and distinctions, you will uncover your Buddha-nature.

Since we all have Buddha-nature, would you be willing to share yours with someone else? Would you be willing to part with some of your Buddha-nature? Such ideas are nonsense. Buddha-nature pervades all things. My Buddha-nature is your Buddha-nature is everyone else's Buddha-nature. However, it does not mean that if we all uncover our Buddha-nature we will all be one Buddha.

True, Buddha-nature is impartially equal, and space, time, and form do not exist, but Buddhas still have their own power and vows; and they still help others. Sentient beings perceive Buddhas to be active individuals, but Buddhas do not perceive themselves in the same way. They perceive all space, time, and forms as being equal, so they do not feel that they are moving, changing, helping. Where, then, is the Buddha? All things, small or large, sentient or non-sentient, are Buddha. Even the most infinitesimal thing is the complete Buddha. Buddha has no fixed spatial location; thus any particle contains the totality of all Buddhas.

When I sit in this chair, I'm taking up space. Nobody else can sit here. No one can occupy another person's position. However, if we imagine that our bodies do not exist, then one room could easily accommodate all the people of the world. We could run a marathon on a grain of sand. A grain of sand would encompass the entire universe.

It is impossible for most of us to accept that the universe is within a grain of sand. As long as we make distinctions between this and that and experience the world from our self-centered points of view, a grain of sand will always be a tiny speck. As long as we hold onto a concept of who we are, what kind of situation we are in, and what we like and dislike, then our self-created worlds will be quite small. We will see everything through the narrow vision of our personal lives. Our world is created by our attachments, by our self-centeredness. If we put down our conceptions of ourselves, others, and worldly phenomena, the world becomes limitlessly large.

I knew of a famous person in Taiwan who was married to an attractive young woman. Once she ran off to Hong Kong with an American. Some urged him to take action against her, but he said, "No, there is no need. If she really loves this American, then she should be with him. If she eventually decides that I'm not a bad person and comes back, then it means that she still cares for me and she should be with me. If the American really cares for her, then she must be a loving person. In that case I was not wrong in believing she was so." Some time later his wife came back, and he hosted a huge dinner to celebrate her return. He said to his friends, "This marriage is like a diamond. It's unbreakable and will never go bad."

If we could maintain an attitude similar to the one this man demonstrated, then we would not suffer as much when we encounter unsatisfactory situations. Even this, however, is not the ultimate stage — the stage where everything is equal and unchanging.

The last few lines of the sutra paragraph cited above deal with the essentially unchanging nature of our own bodies. Of course we are growing older and cannot say that our physical form remains the same; yet the constituents of our bodies — the four elements — are indeed unchanging. They cannot be made to disappear from the universe. They are not created or destroyed. If, for example, we wash our faces, the water will flow down the drain, run into a river, sea or lake, eventually become rain and then moisture for a plant, an animal, another human being. Water is transformed in this way. Moment by moment our bodies change. The components and configuration constantly evolve, appear and perish, but the elements do not disappear.

This does not mean that everything is the same. If it did, then I suppose I could cut off my leg and cook it for supper. This is not the meaning of the sutra. We cannot ignore the differences between things just because we have an idea that they are all the same; rather, we should understand that in an enlightened state there simply is no attachment to any particular form.

I tell people that the goal of practice is to enter the door of Ch'an, but there is no door. If a door existed, then it would be separate from us. For this reason, Ch'an states that no door is the door. After you enter the door through your practice, you realize that there never was a door to enter. Ch'an is not a place or destination. It's an awakening.

Some time ago I lectured at Columbia University. The lecture took place in a basement. After I had finished speaking, we exited through the wrong door and wandered deeper into the building, opening door after door. We were like mice running through a maze. Finally we came out onto what seemed to be a roof-top tennis court with taller buildings around us. We thought we would have to climb one of the fire escape ladders to a higher roof and call for help, but there was a door across the court. We entered that door and climbed another flight of stairs, only to find that we were at street level again. We hadn't been on a roof as we had assumed.

The door of Ch'an is like this. If you put all of your effort into your practice, you will eventually get to the final point and discover that there never was a door at all.

> *"Virtuous man, as the nature of enlightenment is pervasive and full, pure, and unmoving, being perfect and boundless, you should know that the six sense faculties also fully pervade the dharmadhatu. Because the sense faculties are pervasive and full, you should know that the six sense objects also fully pervade the dharmadhatu. Because the sense objects are pervasive and full, you should know that the four elements also fully pervade the dharmadhatu. So it is with everything up to all the dharani doors, which also fully pervade the dharmadhatu."*

This and the previous paragraphs have to do with the nature of enlightenment. They also talk about the six sense faculties and six dusts, or sense objects. They refer to them as being universal and complete. If something is universal, it does not discriminate between this and that. If something is unchanging, then it must be complete; and if any one thing is universal and complete, then all things must be. In the midst of completeness and universality there cannot be something that is not so.

Before enlightenment, the six consciousnesses are muddled and impure; they are forever being moved and influenced by external phenomena. On attaining enlightenment, one realizes that the six consciousnesses have no true existence. Yet they continue to operate, in a much improved and purer manner.

Most of the time our consciousness is focused on whatever we are sensing at that time. Our consciousness is fixed where our senses are fixed. We are inexorably tied to the ever-changing phenomenal world. When things move, we move with them. We are in a continual state of compelled transition. It is impossible to be the master of one's consciousness under such conditions. Of course we may think that we are our own masters, but this is a fantasy. We are fooling ourselves. In reality we are constantly influenced by and reacting to outside events.

Before enlightenment, the activity of the six consciousnesses is extremely limited. Because we identify with our senses, we remain within the bounds of that which can be perceived by the sense faculties. This is what causes vexations in our lives. Who among us can say that he or she is not moved, influenced, or controlled by his or her senses? We are not liberated. Therefore we all experience some form of suffering, and this stems from our attachment to our senses and perceptions. On attaining Complete Enlightenment the six consciousnesses no longer exist in name. They still function, but boundlessly, extending throughout all of space and time. They are not limited by self-attachment. In the enlightened condition, the consciousnesses have been transformed into wisdom. Perfect wisdom exists everywhere — in America, in China, all over the world, throughout the universe. Yet those who have not seen it are countless in number.

The Bible says that the grace of God exists everywhere; it is only a matter of whether one is able to perceive it. It is the same with the air we breathe. We cannot breathe if we plug up our noses and mouths, but that doesn't mean that the air is gone. It's still all around us. It is also the same as trying to describe a sunset to someone who was born blind. No matter how well you describe what you see, the blind person will probably never have a clear impression of it; and yet the sun continues to shine and set.

The six consciousnesses, the six objects of consciousness, and the six sense faculties are the most important part of our lives; but do we really know what they are, where they are, or if we really possess them? One might say that if we did not have senses, we wouldn't be able to tell the difference between ourselves and anyone or anything else. If we ask where these sense consciousnesses reside, one might reply that they are a part of the mind, the soul, or the spirit; but where is the soul, the spirit, the mind?

Consciousness is always where the senses are. When you are hungry, your consciousness is in your belly. When you have a headache, your consciousness is in your head. If someone catches your eye, your consciousness is on that person. I ask you then, is consciousness inside or outside your mind? If someone yells at you, is your consciousness in your ear? in that person's mouth? in the sound coming from the person?

Sakyamuni Buddha posed similar questions to his disciple, Ananda. He asked, "Where is your mind?" Ananda thought, "Is it inside of me, outside of me, or somewhere in between?" He couldn't answer with certainty. The Buddha told him, "There is no mind. There is nothing that can be called mind."

The sutra states that the six consciousnesses "fully pervade the Dharmadhatu." If this is so, then they cannot emanate solely from the mind, and they cannot solely be a part of the mind. The unlimited cannot be derived from the limited. A finite, fixed entity cannot extend throughout all of space and time. The six consciousnesses are universal. If they are universal, then they must be unmoving and unchanging. Conversely, anything that changes or has a particular function is limited. For example, air is always moving, so it is limited. The space that it flows through, however, does not move. Space is unlimited. If you travel to a distant place, you can say that you have moved, but space has not. Furthermore, it is impossible to see space. Likewise, we cannot see the six consciousnesses; and, like space, the six consciousnesses are universal and unlimited. This should be of great encouragement to you. If they were finite and measurable, then it would be impossible to transform them into the nature of enlightenment — wisdom.

As the six consciousnesses are universal and complete, so too are the six sense faculties and the objects that they perceive. They are all pure and unmoving. This may pose a problem. If the sense faculties are universal, does that mean your eyes, ears and nose are infinitely large? If your eyes are everywhere, then as I stomp my foot on the floor I am also stomping on your eyes. The world would be a very painful place if this were the case. Obviously, this is not what the sutra means.

The Buddha is talking about the experience of someone who has already attained Complete Enlightenment. This person no longer has any attachments. He would not say, "These are my eyes, this is my nose." He sees no difference between one body and another. Of course the question can then be raised: "If you are enlightened, why don't you hand over your eyes, ears, and nose?" To answer this we must make a distinction between the Buddha's Nirmanakaya, or Transformation Body and Dharmakaya, or Dharma Body. The Dharmakaya is universal, with no separation from anything else. It is the Dharmakaya that the Buddha speaks of.

The Nirmanakaya — the Transformation Body, that manifested as a prince in India 2500 years ago and attained Buddhahood — exists for the sake of sentient beings. Its function is to adapt to whatever area, world, or place the Buddha enters. Therefore it is not something that he can frivolously give up. It has a use. From the Buddha's standpoint, the body is not important, except that it is used for the benefit of sentient beings. Thus the body ceases to belong to the person who becomes enlightened. The body of an enlightened being exists for others.

After enlightenment the six consciousnesses become pure, unlimited, and unmoving. They are still. The mind does not run off in every direction after what it likes or away from what it dislikes. Naturally, when this happens all other things become pure, unlimited, and unmoving as well. It doesn't mean that your nose will grow to an unlimited size. Rather, because you have given up your attachment to your nose and its function, it becomes limitless in its ability. The sutra says that everything up to all the dharani doors fully pervades the dharmadhatu. As the six consciousnesses, the sense faculties, and the objects of perception become pure and unbounded, all of the dharani doors — the methods leading to enlightenment —

are also transformed in the same way. They too become universal and unlimited.

When one has attained Complete Enlightenment, there is no longer a need for the many methods of practice for themselves. A Ch'an master once said to someone reading the sutras, "All of these books are nothing but used toilet paper." For someone who is already enlightened, the dharani doors are like used toilet paper. They have fulfilled their function in helping the practitioner to awaken, and so they are no longer of any use to him or her. For such an individual, the dharani doors do not exist. In this sense they are pure. Of course, for those who have not yet discovered their Buddha-nature, the sutras should still be treated with respect and the dharani doors should still be followed. For the innumerable unenlightened sentient beings, there are still innumerable methods of practice.

> *"Virtuous man, because the nature of wondrous enlightenment pervades everything fully, the nature of the sense faculties and the sense objects is indestructible and clear. Because the sense faculties and the sense objects are indestructible, [everything] up to all the dharani doors is indestructible and clear. It is like hundreds of thousands of lamps illuminating a room: their illumination pervades fully and is indestructible and clear."*

A person who has attained complete, perfect enlightenment no longer discriminates between this and that. To an enlightened being, everything is unlimited. This limitlessness is beyond existence and non-existence.

If we say that enlightenment exists, then we are making it relative to non-existence. We are giving it a specific form and placing it within boundaries; as such it is fixed and cannot be complete, unlimited, and universal. If we say that it does not exist, then we risk regarding it as if it has disappeared altogether. If enlightenment did not exist, then it would be impossible to attain. Thus, it would logically follow that if anyone could somehow become enlightened, then that person too would disappear and cease to exist. If there is no such thing as Buddhahood, then there is no need for us to respect the Buddha, study the sutras, or struggle with practice. For these reasons, we can neither say that enlightenment exists nor does not exist.

In any religion there are certain questions that cannot be answered. The questioner is inevitably left with a great paradox. According to Buddhadharma, non-existence is existence and existence is non-existence. This sounds nonsensical, but actually it is the most logical and profound teaching.

Discussing existence and non-existence in terms of enlightenment is difficult to grasp for most people, so let's talk about something closer to home: our bodies. If asked, most of us would reply that our bodies exist; but, if our bodies are not eternal, then they cannot really exist. A body that grows from childhood to adulthood does not have any permanent form. As people get older, their bones begin to shrink and become brittle, their hair whitens, and their skin loses its elasticity. Since the body changes so much throughout one's life, how can one say that it truly exists as the same thing?

Actually, we exist amidst non-existence. If all through your life you ate and drank but never had a bowel movement, you would be enormous. If this were true for everyone, there would be nothing in the world but people. Of course, this is not the case. Whatever we obtain is ultimately lost or discarded. We cannot hold onto anything. Existence must exist with non-existence.

We should understand that our desires and our vexations — our search for fame, power, wealth, and physical pleasure — stem from our inability to realize and accept the changing nature of all that is. Everything in the world is transitory. When Mao Zedong was alive, all he had to do was cough and all of China trembled. Now that he is dead, where is he? Where are the things that he obtained? Mao Zedong exists within non-existence. He is not a permanent entity. After ordinary people have satisfied themselves with clothing, food, and a place to live, they begin to seek other things. Some may look for fame. When they acquire that, they may seek power so that they can control other people. Perhaps they hope that their names and reputations will live on after they die. Such people have unquenchable ambition, and because of it they create problems for themselves and society. Envious outsiders might consider them to be fortunate, but in fact they live with the constant fear that others will do them harm in one way or another. In trusting no one and guarding their every thought, word, and action, these people suffer a great deal.

Obviously we do exist in some way. Our existence is not static; we are always changing. We have lived countless lives before this life, and after we die we will live many more. We are born, we get old, we die, we are born again. Therefore we still have to pay great attention to our lives. Whatever we do will affect us.

The non-existence Buddhadharma speaks of is not nihilistic. Rather, it is an absolute proclamation: the nature of enlightenment is complete, universal, and perfect. Within all sentient beings, everything right here and right now is total liberation.

Are you questioning your existence? If you are, then pinch your cheek. If it hurts, then you exist. Thus you cannot say that Buddhism is nihilistic, that it expounds emptiness in the sense of there being nothing at all. The sutra says that everything always has and always will exist. Perhaps this seems confusing in light of what I said earlier.

I recently received a letter from a woman in Taiwan which said, "I've had my teeth for twenty-five years and now the dentist has pulled them all out. They aren't mine anymore."

I wrote her back, saying, "Don't worry about it. Eventually, none of your body will be yours." This is equitable. If you take sustenance to create and maintain your body, it's only fair that you give your body back and allow it to become something else.

An earthworm eats soil and eliminates soil, so why does it bother to eat at all? In the same way our bodies are destined to decompose and return to the earth. We may ask, "Why trouble ourselves to live?" When all is said and done, we are not much different from earthworms. We should understand, however, that it is because of our karma that we are born. For that reason we should continue with our human lives.

There is a story about a man who, after he died, was reborn as a snake. He retained his intelligence and memory, so he knew that he had become a snake due to the retribution of previous karma.

He grew fast as a snake and needed to eat all the time; but he was not a good hunter. He always felt pangs of hunger. He thought to himself, "The life of a snake is not good. I know I'm a snake because of bad things I did in the past, but I did some good things too. After this lifetime things will probably change for the better."

He looked for a way to die. One morning before dawn he crawled to the gate of a city and waited for the day to arrive. A man saw the snake and called to others, "There's a huge snake outside the gate!" People picked up bricks and grabbed clubs and beat the snake to death. As life left him, the snake was happy. He thought, "Now the retribution for all my evil past actions is finished. In the future I'll have a happier life."

Do you think the snake got what he desired? If the snake did accomplish his goal, then you might as well commit suicide when you run into difficulties. This way, nobody would ever have any problems for very long. Obviously something is wrong with this logic. The snake's death was not an accident. In intentionally seeking death, the snake only succeeded in creating more karma. I'm sure you have already guessed that he was reborn as another snake. When he realized that he was in the same miserable condition, he thought to himself, "This is unfair! Who is doing this to me?"

At this point someone said to him, "The reason that you are again a snake is because you haven't yet paid back your karmic debt. You tried to escape your situation. Not only do you have to take care of the principal of your loan, but you must pay back interest as well."

The snake thought carefully about this and decided, "I'll finish my life as a snake. I'll live no matter how much suffering I have to endure." As soon as he made up his mind, he died and was reborn as a man. He remembered his previous two existences as a snake and told his story.

Our lives are analogous to the story of the snake. If we face dangers and difficulties as they arise, accepting them and dealing with them, then they will no longer be perceived as dangers and difficulties. People who live their lives in this way are happiest. Those whose personalities are bright and tranquil will likely see their way through difficulties more easily than others and will live, if not longer lives, then at least fuller lives. Those with an inordinate fear of death will likely die sooner than those who do not have this fear. It is said that soldiers who have a great fear of death die in more sizable numbers on a battlefield than those who do not.

The snake could not escape his karma. He could only accept it and live his life as best he could. With this attitude he was able to work with his attachments and vexations. It is the same with our desire to become enlightened. If we give up our mistaken ideas, we will likely replace them with correct ideas; but even correct ideas aren't the end of it all. In going from the incorrect to the correct we are still making distinctions. We still have a concept of self and others. We have to transcend ideas of correct and incorrect and self and other in order to attain complete liberation.

The nature of enlightenment is universal. We cannot attain it as long as we attach to any particular thing. Instead, if we accept our bodies and everything in our environment as being no different from eternal, unchanging nature, then we are one with enlightenment.

In fact, we are not separate from Complete Enlightenment. We just do not realize it. There is nothing to gain or find. If enlightenment were something outside of us, then the Buddha would have been very selfish not to have given us some of his own. Sakyamuni Buddha could have at least broken off a little piece of it to give to us.

The truth is, the Buddha has nothing to give. From the perspective of Buddhas, sentient beings are intrinsically Buddhas because the Buddha-nature which exists in all sentient beings has never been destroyed or reduced in any way. It is like hundreds of thousands of lamps that light a room, the whole of which is filled with light that is indestructible and unadulterated. Some of the lamps may shine more brightly than others, but this does not diminish the light that shines from them. There is no obstruction or conflict among them.

Our nature and that of the Buddha are the same. Although we are ordinary, common people, our essence is perfect, complete, and universal. It is simply because we have not given up our attachments and still have vexations that we are not able to realize this truth. If we can affirm this original perfection and have faith that we can attain it, then there is hope for us in practice. Eventually we will discover our Buddha-nature. If we cannot do this, however, there is no possibility of our reaching our goal.

In order to attain Complete Enlightenment, we must open our minds to our own potential. Setting aside ideas of existence, non-existence, perfection, imperfection, ordinary people, and Buddhas, we are free to embrace everyone and everything within our minds. This is the working of our universal Buddha-nature.

> *"Virtuous man, since his enlightenment is fully accomplished, you should know that a bodhisattva neither is bound by dharmas nor seeks to be free from dharmas. He neither detests birth and death nor clings to nirvana; neither reveres those who uphold the precepts nor condemns those who violate them; neither esteems experienced practitioners nor slights beginners. Why? Because all [sentient beings] are enlightened. It is like clear vision that is completely aware of what is in front: when this clarity is perfect, it has no likes or dislikes. Why? Because the essence of this clarity is non-dual and itself has no likes or dislikes."*

This paragraph describes a being who has perfected his or her realization of enlightenment: a great bodhisattva. Bodhisattvas neither revere nor condemn, neither esteem nor slight, feel neither limited nor liberated. These examples represent polarized attitudes. If you experience such feelings, then you are an ordinary sentient being, because such feelings arise from attachment. Bodhisattvas who have perfected their enlightenment are not attached to personal feelings and ideas. These bodhisattvas have realized that which is non-differentiating, unchanging, universal, complete, indestructible, and unadulterated. Such lofty goals might dissuade practitioners, but we must remember that the Buddha speaks of ultimate principles. We are where we are, and we must take one step at a time. We should continue to practice and study the Dharma.

Sakyamuni Buddha says that great bodhisattvas neither tie themselves to nor try to free themselves from dharmas. Here, "dharmas" refer to all forms and phenomena, whether they be physical or mental, whether they be "with outflows" or "without outflows." They include the four elements, the six sense faculties, and six sense data — every object and thought.

Ordinary sentient beings are attached to dharmas with outflows — activities related to a self. Sentient beings cling to the belief that these dharmas truly exist. Arhats are attached to dharmas without outflows — dharmas that are free from the self (phenomena of liberation). As such, they are fettered by dharmas without outflows. Being tied neither to dharmas with outflows nor to dharmas without outflows — is the attitude of a true bodhisattva.

Bodhisattvas are not attached to phenomena, yet they do not try to deliberately free themselves from phenomena. Bodhisattvas exist in the midst of dharmas. They are not separate from dharmas, but they are not bound by them either. For example, Hanshan (Cold Mountain), who lived in the mountains, possessed nothing and desired nothing, yet he did not shun anything either. As a result, the whole world was his household. The mountains were his bed and pillow, the clouds his blanket, the sea his bathtub. He felt comfortable in any environment, and everything, in essence, was his.

In the next phrase, Sakyamuni Buddha says that bodhisattvas neither detest birth and death (in this case, samsara) nor cling to nirvana. Ordinary sentient beings cling to samsara. Arhats cling to nirvana. Bodhisattvas do not cling to samsara or nirvana. Ordinary sentient beings do not know about nirvana and cannot escape the cycle of birth and death. They are in the midst of vexation and often are not even aware of it. Vexations run deep. To hold onto life is vexation; to fear death is vexation. Samsara is not limited to the birth and death of the physical body. Within a lifetime there are innumerable momentary births and deaths. Samsara includes the arising and perishing of every thought and every phenomenon. Attachment to thoughts and phenomena is also vexation.

Ordinary sentient beings strive to leave samsara and enter nirvana, but is nirvana genuine? From the perspective of Buddhas and bodhisattvas, if nirvana is separate from samsara, then it too is temporary and finite. Hence bodhisattvas neither detest samsara nor cling to nirvana. The bodhisattva attitude is true liberation.

Sakyamuni Buddha says that bodhisattvas neither revere those who keep the precepts nor condemn those who break them. By ordinary standards, it would seem that bodhisattvas are amoral. Most people revere precept holders and condemn precept breakers, but precepts are relative ideals; they are not ultimate principles. Although bodhisattvas follow precepts, they do not discriminate between people who hold precepts and people who do not. Likewise, bodhisattvas neither esteem experienced practitioners nor slight beginners. Ordinary people tend to respect experienced practitioners.

What people admire in others can be amusing. If my actions were out of the ordinary — if I only ate one banana a day, if I didn't sleep at night, if I spent the entire day meditating and prostrating — some people would surmise that I was a great practitioner and would respect me more. Or if I were an old monk, people would think I was a wise man with a lot of experience under my belt. Years ago in Taiwan there was a gathering of many Buddhists. One monk there was obviously very old. Even though his head was shaved, people could see that his hair was white. When he arrived, people crowded around him and prostrated to him. I was young at the time, and though I had been at the gathering for a while, no one paid respect to me. I had been a monk for over twenty years, but I was young and my hair was still black. I knew that the old monk had left home only a couple of years earlier, but people assumed he was a wise sage. Age does not necessarily make one a good practitioner or a strict adherent of the precepts.

Great bodhisattvas, on the other hand, have realized the essence of non-differentiation and would not discriminate or cling to extreme views. Such ideas and actions would be vexation. Bodhisattvas rely on genuine wisdom. The wisdom of bodhisattvas can be compared to the non-discriminating quality of light. Light does not choose to shine on one thing and not another. If we see one thing and not another, it is entirely our own affair. The light is not making distinctions between this and that. It does not choose to illuminate beautiful things and neglect ugly things. The non-differentiating mentality of enlightened beings is like this light.

At this point I must offer a word of caution. We are still

ordinary sentient beings, so we should act in a manner befitting ordinary sentient beings. For us, birth and death are still birth and death; suffering still exists; nirvana is still nirvana. Breaking precepts should be avoided. Experienced practitioners and people who hold precepts should still be respected and emulated. Beginners need not be discouraged, but they should understand that they are beginners. If we did not make such distinctions, no one would practice and no one would act morally. We cannot pretend that we are bodhisattvas and act in ways that we believe bodhisattvas would act. The fact is, we discriminate whether we want to or not. Therefore, for us, there is still Dharma to study, precepts to follow, and methods to practice.

> "*Virtuous man, these bodhisattvas and sentient beings in the Dharma Ending Age who have gained accomplishments through cultivating the mind have neither cultivated nor accomplished anything. Complete Enlightenment is universally illuminating in quiescent-extinction without duality. Hundreds of thousands of millions of asamkyas of Buddha worlds, as innumerable as the grains of sand of the Ganges, are like flowers in the sky, randomly arising and perishing. They are neither identical to nor separate [from the nature of Complete Enlightenment]. Since there is no bondage or liberation, one begins to realize that sentient beings have intrinsically accomplished Buddhahood, and that birth and death and nirvana are like yesterday's dream.*"

The last sentence speaks of yesterday's dream. My question is, in looking back on yesterday's dream, does it mean that we are awake now? Most people are not aware that they are dreaming while they dream. It is only after they wake up that they are aware that they had been dreaming, yet it does not mean that they will not dream again. They may in fact have the same dream a few nights later, and during the dream they will again not know they are dreaming.

There are three levels to dream awareness. In the first level, one dreams and is not aware of it, and then awakens. In the second level, one awakens from the dream, but later has a similar dream, and is again unaware that it is a dream. In the third level, one dreams and, on waking, wishes that the dream were real and could eventually be realized. These are three levels of people's delusory dreams, with the third level being most delusory.

We are all on the third level. We are ordinary sentient beings who live in dreams, yet cannot accept that we do so. We have enormous expectations. We want to see, do, and attain this and that. We all have grand ideas to actualize and goals to accomplish. Most things we seek fall into the categories of fortune, fame, position, or power.

There are those who say that we are dreaming when things are going well and we are in a position of fortune, fame, or power. But when things go badly and we lose our positions, then we are awake. The truth is, we are dreaming either way.

A long time ago I read a novel called Three Dreams. The protagonist was a man who kept falling in love with different women. Every time he lost a woman he loved, he would say that he had finally woken up from his dream, but sure enough, he would fall in love again and go through the same process. This happened with three different women. I believe that the novelist could have continued the novel indefinitely. Why stop after three dreams?

During a recent retreat here at the Center, someone received an emergency phone call from his brother, who told the retreatant that he had lost a lot of money, perhaps through his business or the stock market. Since the man was on a retreat, however, he felt that he had not lost or gained much, so he continued to meditate. The last day I asked him how he felt, and he still believed that he had not lost anything; but when I asked him what he was going to do, he answered that he would work hard to make his money back. Here we find someone waking from one dream only to dive right back into another.

Psychologists generally agree that if we did not dream at night and have daydreams during our waking lives, we would be unhealthy and unhappy. Our lives and our future would seem hopeless without dreams. If there is no hope for the future, then why continue living? I have said that true Buddhist saints do not dream. Some people hear this and tell me that if this were true, they would prefer not to be saints. They feel that a life without dreams would be empty and hopeless. Remember, though, that we are not saints. Our nature is to dream, and we do so on the third and most delusory level. It is natural. As long as we remain in delusion, it is impossible not to dream.

Hard-working practitioners have already reached the second level of dreaming. While they practice, they know that nothing is permanent. They realize that they come into the world alone and leave alone. During practice they are clear about this, but afterward they cannot maintain the power and clarity of their meditation. Life and its ever-changing situations again draws them. They are seduced by the environment and fall into another dream.

A practitioner on a previous retreat was kneeling and crying heart-brokenly because he was afraid to be alone. I said, "Don't you realize that everyone comes into the world and leaves it alone?" He replied that indeed he knew that, but all the same he was afraid. I asked if he were afraid right then and there during the retreat. He replied that he wasn't, but once he returned to his daily life he knew that the fear and insecurity of being alone would return. He knew he would crave to have someone he could turn to and rely on. Knowing that he would feel this way made him all the more sad. This is a man who has woken from a dream and is afraid because he knows he will fall into the same dream again and again.

In Taiwan there is a young woman who wants to leave home and become a nun. Her mother visited and told me she would not let her daughter do it. She wanted her daughter to marry. I asked why. She said that now it would be fine for her daughter to become a nun because her daughter would have Shih-fu to rely on. But she said I was old and she wondered who the girl would rely on once I died. I asked the mother whom she depended on, and she said she depended on herself. Her husband, she said, was quite useless and unreliable. So I asked, "If you do not rely on your husband, why do you insist that your daughter have a husband?" She said that at least there was a chance her daughter would find a worthy husband, but if she became a nun, she wouldn't have anyone. Here is a woman who has already woken up from one dream, yet she is ready to fabricate the same dream for her daughter. If the mother were a practitioner, perhaps she would feel differently, but in her present state of mind she is willing to pass on the dream to the next generation.

From their experience of practice and their understanding of Buddhadharma, practitioners may already know that every aspect of their lives is a dream; yet they are not liberated from their attachment to their bodies, minds, and the environment. Though they know their lives are dreams, they cannot refuse them, and so they continue to be immersed in them.

We have all experienced the feeling that we are not always in control of ourselves, that our bodies and minds seem to be on their own, doing whatever they want, pulling us along. There may be things we do not want to do, yet we cannot restrain our bodies from doing them. There may be thoughts we do not want to entertain, yet we cannot stop ourselves from thinking them. It is so because we are ordinary sentient beings, not sages or saints. We have been unable to free ourselves from our dreams.

The first level of dreams is that which is described in the sutra. When we know with our entire being that everything we have experienced is part of yesterday's dream, then we are free from the disturbances and vexations of those dreams. When such a person wakes up, he sees that everything he thought and did up to that point was one long dream, and that the dreams he had at night were but dreams within a dream. Such a person has truly woken up. His experience is the beginning of liberation.

I remember an old uncle whose mind was clear but who was in constant pain. He could hardly move, so he needed to be cared for. He was afraid of the night because he was left alone, and his sleep was filled with nightmares. He would sleep only a few minutes at a stretch, and during those times he would have nightmares. When he woke up the nightmares seemed like an eternity. Daytime was all right, but he spent most of it dreading the evening. Days passed quickly, but nights, slowly. Eventually he began to fear the day as well, because he saw it as being only a short respite between one night and the next. This was his life.

Such is the life of ordinary sentient beings. Before liberation, our lives are analogous to my uncle's. There will be brief interludes when we wake up, and then we will fall back again into long periods of dreaming; and for many of us, there are more nightmares than good dreams. Those who do not practice rarely, if ever, wake up. Their nights and days are filled with one dream after another. Yes, there are pleasurable dreams as well as nightmares, but people tend to remember pain and suffering more than they do pleasure and happiness. Even short, pleasurable dreams end up causing suffering because they do not last long and people cling to them desperately, not wanting them to go.

It is extremely difficult to reach the level where we finally wake up for good. This is the moment of Complete Enlightenment. Those who object to a life without dreams are not enlightened. It is impossible for ordinary people to conceive of a life without dreams, and that is quite all right. It is okay to continue to dream because in our present condition we have no choice.

Bodhisattvas who have reached the stage of universal illumination and Complete Enlightenment realize that all that is done by the innumerable Buddhas for the sake of sentient beings is nothing more than flowers in the sky, arising and perishing in endless numbers. These flowers are not real. They merely seem to appear and disappear.

Before one reaches Complete Enlightenment, there is samsara and nirvana. Unenlightened people practice in order to leave samsara and enter nirvana. That is their goal. But, for thoroughly enlightened ones, samsara and nirvana are not separate. Before one awakens, one can only see different dreams: dreams of samsara, dreams of nirvana, different time periods, and different space locations. After awakening, thoroughly enlightened ones see the ultimate reality as well as the conventional reality perceived by ordinary unenlightened ones. To thoroughly enlightened ones, conventional time and space and the ultimate reality are completely merged.

When I leave Taiwan to go to the United States, it seems as if I have changed locations. People in the Orient seem to be different from people in the West. Things change in each place during the time that I am away. However, if we were to view the Earth from the Moon, we would see that all the commotion is confined to a small planet. If we were to view the Earth from another solar system, it would appear to be a stationary point of light. When viewed from a great distance, everything becomes insignificant, even time. Earthlings may scamper about struggling for things that they feel are important, but for beings in the heavens looking downward, it all appears rather foolish and ignorant.

It is a rough analogy, but people who wake up from the dream of life are like those beings who might be viewing the Earth from far away. In a dream it may seem that a lot of time has passed, that you have done many things and have traveled to many places, but upon waking you realize that no time has passed, that you haven't gone anywhere, and that you haven't done anything.

> *"Virtuous man, because birth and death and nirvana are like yesterday's dream, you should know that they neither arise nor perish, neither come nor go. That which is actualized is neither gained nor lost, neither grasped nor discarded. One who truly actualizes [enlightenment] does not contrive, stop, allow things to be as they are, nor annihilate [vexations]. In the midst of the actualization, there is neither a subject nor an object. Ultimately there is neither actualization nor one who actualizes! The nature of all dharmas is equal and indestructible."*

After the attainment of thorough enlightenment, one is free from the world of discrimination, but for the unenlightened there are different levels of discrimination depending on the number and kinds of distinctions that are made. On the first level are ordinary sentient beings; on the second level philosophers, religious teachers, and some political leaders, and on the third level are advanced practitioners. On the fourth level are beings with no self-centered discrimination whatsoever. This is full revelation of the Buddha-nature. Those beings who reach the fourth level have all the capabilities of people of the previous three levels. However, they are completely enlightened.

Discriminations that ordinary people make are based on whether things are advantageous or disadvantageous to themselves or whether they are related or unrelated to themselves. Using such criteria, people seek after or fight for that which they feel is personally advantageous, attempting to reject or leave behind that which they feel is personally disadvantageous or harmful. They also discriminate between that to which they feel they are closely related, distantly related, or not related at all. They may be enthusiastic and involved with events in their own lives, but probably care little, if at all, about what is happening in other people's lives. This attitude is common for ordinary people. It is neither bad nor good.

On the other hand, there are people who are genuinely concerned about the world and people at large. If war breaks out between two countries or famine sweeps across a continent, they feel sympathy for those who suffer. They work for peace or donate sums of money to alleviate suffering. They may or may not be people on the second level. People who are truly at the second level are those rare virtuous world leaders. Such leaders, whether they be in religion, philosophy, or politics, dedicate their lives to instituting political changes and social programs. They have a genuine concern for others. It is because of the hard work and dedication of such people that there is some semblance of order and civilization in the world.

Of course, there are people on the first level who also exhibit moral behavior and concern for others, but they are not fully driven by their own faith and experience. They are following the ideas and work of others. There is nothing wrong with this. Those on the second level, on the other hand, have great faith in their ideas, work, and vision for a better world, and they reach conclusions based on their own rational thinking. As clear and wholesome as their intentions may be, however, they are still attached to ideas of self and other, good and bad.

At the third level are advanced spiritual practitioners. Supposedly, there is an Eastern Orthodox monastery high in the mountains which accepts only those who have practiced well elsewhere. Once they enter this monastery, people are prepared to stay for the rest of their lives. Are these people doing any good for the world? After all, they are completely cut off from civilization. In China and Tibet there have been and still are many practitioners who live in seclusion. Of what use are they to ordinary people? Actually, they do help. Although direct benefits may not be perceived, through their practice they help the world. Merit is naturally transferred. Practitioners need not entertain thoughts of helping others. Their spiritual power, in fact, surpasses that which people of the second level offer to the world through their work and specific intent.

This does not mean that practitioners do not make distinctions. They may feel that there are no virtuous or evil people, that there is nothing lovable or terrifying in the world, that the world is already at peace, and that they are liberated. But if they truly made no distinctions, then it would not matter whether they lived in seclusion on some faraway mountain or in the middle of a metropolis among ordinary people. They still make distinctions between different environments — that which they find peaceful and that which they find distracting.

Of course there are those who will then ask, "If this is true, why adopt the lifestyle of a practitioner at all? Why not continue to live as ordinary people do?" When someone once asked me if I still made discriminations, I asked, "What do you think?" The person replied, "Yes, I think you do discriminate." I replied, "You're right, but why do you think so?" He answered, "If you were truly liberated, then you would go to movies, eat meat, have a drink, wear ordinary clothes. You are attached to the role of being a monk and following precepts." To this I said, "If I discard my robe and behave just like you, then I will have lost my position as a monk. Just because you can do whatever you want, go wherever you want, and eat whatever you like doesn't mean you are freer than I. It doesn't mean you make fewer distinctions. Why must you insist that I act like you? If you are attached to the idea that I am a monk, that I don't eat meat, that I don't drink alcohol, that I don't go to movies or dance, then you're making even greater distinctions than I do."

Those who reach the fourth level see no differences between monks and lay people, between being married or unmarried, between killing or saving someone. For example, drinking alcohol is considered an act of ignorance, but it is also regarded as a means of wisdom. In the Japanese Zen tradition, they call it the "soup of wisdom." Does this mean that ordinary people who drink alcohol will acquire wisdom? No, but for those who already have wisdom and do not discriminate, alcohol and wisdom are not separate, and under the right circumstances alcohol can be used as an expedient means to help others.

Ch'an practitioners who are enlightened may exhibit behavior different from ordinary monks and nuns. They might go to brothels, drink alcohol, eat dog meat. There have been such cases in Chinese Buddhist history. In artwork depicting Mahayana bodhisattvas, you will see untidy figures, some bearing long hair. They do not look like proper members of the Sangha. They represent genuinely enlightened and liberated people. Their actions are not constrained by formalities.

In the Mahayana system, the Bodhisattva Path is divided into fifty-two stages. Practitioners must reach at least the fortieth level before they attain even partial non-discrimination. For full and genuine non-discrimination, they must go beyond the forty-eighth stage. If you use the method of hua-t'ou or kung-an in your practice and generate great doubt, it is possible that you will have an experience of thorough enlightenment — genuine non-discrimination. However, the power you gain from this experience will not last. Eventually you will regress to the level of an ordinary sentient being. Hence, you need to continue to practice.

Ordinary people practice with the intention of one day entering nirvana. Once this goal is reached, they believe samsara will be something left behind in the past. This is not the case for someone who has reached the fourth level. In transcending discrimination, one also transcends samsara and nirvana. There are no discriminations made between the two realms, or between past and future. Those at the fourth level have nothing to gain and nothing to lose. In my mind, the core of the *Heart Sutra* is the phrase, "No wisdom and no attainment." This phrase precisely describes the fourth level, that of enlightenment, or genuine non-discrimination. *The Sutra of Complete Enlightenment* states that in true realization there is no Dharma realized and no subject who realizes.

There are figures in human history who attained a great deal. During Napoleon's short reign, most of Europe was his. When Mao Zedong was alive, a quarter of the human race was under his rule. But did they really acquire anything? Eventually they had to give up their own lives. In the end, nothing was really theirs. There is no attainment. Of course, practitioners must still make distinctions. Without ideas of samsara and nirvana and vexation and wisdom, there would be no reason to make any effort toward realization. When one reaches the state of non-discrimination, however, both samsara and nirvana naturally become part of yesterday's dream. Something that can be left behind or abandoned cannot be real. Something that can be attained or held onto cannot be real. Only that which can neither be lost nor gained is true reality. What this is you must discover for yourself.

> *"Virtuous man, bodhisattvas should thus practice, thus [progress through] these gradual stages, thus contemplate, thus abide in and uphold, thus use expedient methods, and thus become enlightened. In seeking this Dharma, they will not be confused and perplexed."*
>
> *At that time, the World Honored One, wishing to clarify his meaning, proclaimed these gathas:*
> *Universal Vision, you should know*
> *that the minds and bodies of*
> *all sentient beings are illusory.*
> *The body is the union of the four elements.*
> *The nature of mind is reducible*
> *to the [six] sensory objects.*
> *When the four elements are separated*
> *from one another, who is the unifier?*
> *If one practices gradual*
> *cultivation like this, all will be pure.*
> *[The nature of Complete Enlightenment]*
> *is unmoving and pervades the dharmadhatu.*
> *There is no contrivance, stopping,*
> *allowing things to be as they are,*
> *annihilation, nor is there one*
> *who actualizes [enlightenment].*
> *All Buddha worlds are like*
> *flowers in the sky.*
> *Past, present, and future are*
> *all impartially equal.*

> *Ultimately there is no coming or going.*
> *The newly initiated bodhisattvas*
> *and sentient beings in*
> *the Dharma Ending Age,*
> *in their quest to enter the Buddha Path,*
> *should thus cultivate themselves.*

This gatha, spoken by the Buddha, rephrases his answer to the Bodhisattva of Universal Vision in verse form and is meant to help people remember the teachings. Since we have already thoroughly discussed the Buddha's answer, there is no need to comment on the gatha now.

The paragraph preceding the gatha, on the other hand, is important. Contained within this seemingly straightforward paragraph are seven steps leading to Complete Enlightenment, each one representing a particular stage or level in one's practice.

At the first stage, one is engaged in "practice." Practice in this sense does not mean simply putting forth effort or repeating something over and over. Without proper methods and guidance we cannot say that we are truly practicing. Some people think that anything that puts pressure on the mind or that causes the body to exert itself or suffer is practice. This is not true. Cattle, yaks, horses, and other animals penned in or put to work are not cultivating themselves. These animals suffer and work, but they are not practicing. If this were the criterion for self-cultivation, then hardened convicts with terms of hard labor would be the best practitioners of all.

In northern China there was a man who could walk barefoot on ice and snow during the coldest part of winter. He had mastered this skill and did not appear to suffer in the least. He claimed that this was his practice. Many people had great respect and reverence for this man, regarding him as a practitioner of the highest order. A Ch'an master who heard the story brought his disciples to a frozen river. He pointed to a group of ducks waddling across the ice and said, "Look at all those great practitioners! Even the newly hatched ducklings can walk barefoot on the ice!"

Practice, therefore, does not mean causing yourself suffering.

That is not the purpose of cultivation. The actual interpretation of this term is "correcting" or "mending." In other words, problems that arise in life or practice must be resolved by the individual. We all perform non-virtuous actions, sometimes knowingly, sometimes unknowingly. In any situation, we should make an effort to realize fully what we have done and attempt to correct ourselves. Our actions can hurt ourselves as well as others.

What do we do with our minds all day? What kinds of thoughts do we get involved with? Are they useful, useless, beneficial, harmful? Most of the time I would imagine our thoughts are not that useful or beneficial to ourselves, and even less so to others. Cultivation begins here.

Buildings begin to have problems right after they are constructed. Cracks and leaks seem to appear overnight. It is the same with the physical body. Defects and problems can manifest as early as birth, or even in the womb. In the beginning of our practice we should concern ourselves with correcting these "congenital" errors, both of the body and the mind. We should try to improve ourselves, physically, mentally, and emotionally.

Many people do not pay attention to their changing mental conditions or to the way they treat their bodies; yet they may follow religious rituals. They may be vegetarians, recite sutras, and make prostrations to images of Buddhas. This, however, is not true practice. It is a kind of self-deception. Some people feel that they can go to a church or temple, ask God to forgive their sins, and assume that God has taken responsibility for their actions, leaving with lighter hearts, only to perform the same actions again. They repeat this cycle week after week, year after year. Is this practice? True repentance is admitting that you are wrong and making a sincere effort to refrain from doing that wrong action again.

The next term is translated as "gradual stages." This stage of practice is actually a series of levels related to the first stage. Someone who has been practicing for a long time will likely be at a higher position and will have cultivated more power than someone who has just started to practice. This is the principle of gradual attainment. Someone may have a sudden flash of insight into Buddha-nature, but it is the actualization and incorporation of that experience into daily life that determines how successful one's practice really is. One must pass through several levels of attainment in order to build a strong foundation of practice. After an enlightenment experience, vexations are not eliminated immediately and forever. The experience of insight is like looking at a map: one may be able to point out the destination easily enough, but that does not mean one has a clear picture of what the place looks like. One must arrive at the destination to know what the place is truly like. Hence we must be cautious and diligent in our practice, even if we have had good experiences.

On a recent retreat a practitioner was doing well. She felt tremendously confident and announced that she was willing to go to hell anytime. She had no fear whatsoever. On another retreat a different participant told me that she felt that there were no problems in the world and that there was nothing to do.

People who practice for a long time may have experiences similar to those of these two women, and the power derived from the experiences may stay with them for quite some time. However, if they have a good teacher, they will realize that they have not progressed as far as they would like to believe. They will come to realize that they are not liberated. Through their experiences, they may gain a great deal of confidence, but they must be careful that they do not become arrogant. With proper guidance, such dispositions will not linger in practitioners.

The second stage is important. Even if you are not progressing at all, or if you are regressing and encountering difficulties, it is at this second stage that you should realize the necessity of continuing to practice seriously and moving forward, step by step.

The third level of practice, translated as "contemplate," can also be understood as "right concentration." The equivalent term in Sanskrit is "dhyana." Right concentration means having the capacity to keep your mind continuously on the same object, as long as you desire, never leaving it or moving to another object. What does one keep one's mind on? There are three possibilities: something that is outside the body, something that is part of the body, or a thought. One should constantly keep the mind on the same object, and whenever one becomes aware that one's attention has slipped away, one should bring it back to the object.

Some people place their watch in front of them while they meditate, some a towel. Others choose to gaze at a spot on the floor. These are all methods of concentration using outside objects. Many people pay attention to their breathing or to a particular part of their body. These are methods of the second category. Other people watch the appearance and disappearance of their thoughts. This is a method of the third category.

On one retreat a participant could not get his girlfriend off his mind. Thoughts of her kept rising up while he practiced, so he mumbled something about her being a devil. The more he tried to push her away, the more difficult his meditation became. In an interview I gave him the solution, a simple method: "Just repeat to yourself, 'I'm thinking of my girlfriend, I'm thinking of my girlfriend'." The method worked and thoughts of his girlfriend abated.

If, on retreat, you constantly dwell on past non-virtuous actions and feel miserable because of it, it might help to switch methods and repeat, "I've done bad things, I've done bad things." In this way you can change self-indulgence into right concentration. If you cannot do this, then you will be burdened and distracted by your thoughts, and you will be unable to continue practicing.

The Chinese term for the fourth level is translated as "abide in and uphold." What you must do at this stage is retain or maintain what you have accomplished in your practice when you are not engaged in formal practice. That is, you must try to incorporate right concentration into your daily life. In fact, your life should become your practice. One of my students said, "Shih-fu, in the past I used to do sitting meditation, but I don't want to do it anymore. Every time I sit I become drowsy and fall asleep. It's come to the point where I feel that meditation is useless for me." I said, "At least you're falling asleep on the cushion and not on your bed. You'll sleep for a shorter period on the cushion and will regain your energy more quickly and efficiently. Also, sleeping while sitting is better than not sitting at all."

There are two aspects to the fourth level of practice. The first is to maintain the habit of sitting and to work hard on the method. The second is to try to maintain the level reached through prior practice. At this level, however, one should not think that it is impossible to regress. In conjuring up a lofty self-image, one only succeeds in creating more vexations. It is wise not to think too highly of one's achievements. It is also a common desire to want to reach the highest level in the shortest period of time. This is an expectation best eliminated right away. Such notions become the biggest obstructions in one's path. It is crucial to drop these ideas. Only then can one practice and make progress in a stable manner.

The fifth stage is translated as "expedient methods." It includes all methods that are helpful on the path toward perfect enlightenment. There are many kinds and levels of expedient means. The most elementary is holding the precepts and prostrating. This is the foundation of and preparation for practice. The expedient implied by the sutra is of a different nature, however. At this stage of cultivation, a practitioner works with the ten paramitas rather than the six paramitas. The six paramitas are for ordinary practitioners — those people on the Bodhisattva Path who have not yet reached the first bhumi level (the forty-first stage of the Bodhisattva Path). From the first bhumi level onward, a practitioner perfects the ten paramitas. The merit accumulated from the ten paramitas benefits all sentient beings, not just the individual. In helping sentient beings, one accumulates merit, eliminates vexation, and acquires wisdom. All can be accomplished through the practice of the ten paramitas. Ordinary practitioners can also practice the ten paramitas, but their performance will not be on a par with practitioners who have reached the first bhumi level and higher.

At this level there should be no regression. The practitioner should make steady progress, or at least maintain the current level. This is a higher stage than "right concentration," yet it is not separate from the previous levels discussed. Each successive stage incorporates the experience and attainment gained from the previous stages.

The sixth level, translated by the phrase, "and thus become enlightened," refers to Complete Enlightenment. Enlightenment can be compared to light. A match, a torch, a fluorescent lamp and the sun are all sources of light. Each of them has a different intensity. Likewise, there are different kinds or intensities of enlightenment. Some are more powerful than others. In Complete Enlightenment, all vexations disappear and the brilliance that is manifested cannot be compared with lesser experiences. The sun is incomparably brighter and more enduring than a flashlight, but even the sun has a limit to its brilliance and duration. The light of Complete Enlightenment is limitless space and time.

The first five levels are the necessary steps that lead one to Complete Enlightenment. Once Complete Enlightenment is reached, the first five levels are no longer needed. However, it is only with the attainment of Complete Enlightenment that the five previous stages are genuinely completed.

The last few words of the paragraph constitute the seventh level, which is really a summary or conclusion of the six previous stages. It is advice for the practitioner. A serious practitioner should follow the six stages on the path toward Complete Enlightenment. If one sincerely and diligently follows this path, step by step, then there will surely be steady progress with few mistakes.

Bodhisattva
Vajragarbha

Then Bodhisattva Vajragarbha rose from his seat in the midst of the assembly, prostrated himself at the feet of the Buddha, circled the Buddha three times clockwise, knelt down, joined his palms, and said: "O World Honored One of great compassion! You have wonderfully expounded to bodhisattvas the great dharani of the Tathagata's pure Complete Enlightenment, the Dharma practice of the causal ground, and the expedient methods of gradual cultivation, so that sentient beings may unveil their obstructions. Because of your compassionate teaching, all in the assembly have cleared away illusory illnesses [of the eye] and their wisdom-eyes have become pure.

"World Honored One, if sentient beings have intrinsically accomplished Buddhahood, how can there be so much ignorance? If all sentient beings originally have ignorance, why does the Tathagata say that they have intrinsically accomplished Buddhahood? If sentient beings in all ten directions intrinsically accomplished the Buddha Path and afterwards gave rise to ignorance, then when will the Tathagata give rise to vexations again? Please do not forsake your unrestricted great compassion, but disclose the secret treasury for the benefit of the multitude of bodhisattvas, so that when all the sentient beings in the Dharma Ending Age who hear of this Dharma door to the ultimate meaning of this sutra will permanently sever doubts and regrets." Having said these words, he prostrated himself on the ground. He made the same request three times, each time repeating the same procedure."

Essentially, Bodhisattva Vajragarbha asks three questions. If we are intrinsically Buddhas, why are we ignorant? If we are all ignorant, how can we be fundamentally in the state of Buddhahood? If we were intrinsically Buddhas and then gave rise to ignorance, will the Buddhas themselves give rise to vexation and become ordinary sentient beings again? Relevant questions, ones that practitioners and non-practitioners ask all the time.

When Sakyamuni says that we are all intrinsically Buddhas, he is referring to our potential. For example, anyone born in the United States and thirty-five or older has the right and privilege to run for the presidency, regardless of sex, economic, ethnic, or religious background; but how many people even run for that office, let alone actually become president? Not many have the opportunity, desire, time, or means. Barring unexpected deaths, in a forty year period there can be, at most, only ten presidents. There are many requirements and conditions that must be met, and only a few will eventually become president. Similarly, every sentient being is capable of becoming a Buddha, but not all will reach Buddhahood immediately or at the same time.

Where do sentient beings come from in the first place? Wouldn't it be much better and easier if we were all Buddhas right from the start, free from vexations? Religions and philosophies have been grappling with such questions for centuries, and there has yet to be a satisfactory answer. If you say that God created sentient beings, it only raises more questions. Why did God create suffering, too? Why is there evil in the world? Why go through all the trouble of creating a hell to punish bad people? God could have avoided all these problems.

Buddhism is not concerned with such speculative questions and chooses not to answer them. Buddhadharma addresses issues at hand; it is pragmatic and therapeutic. In relating a story about a man wounded by a poison arrow, the Buddha asked if it would be wiser for the man to immediately remove the arrow and begin treatment, or to ask a thousand questions — about the nature of the poison, the origin of the arrow, the background of the person who shot the arrow, and so on. The obvious course is to remove the arrow and treat the wound. Likewise, the main purpose of Buddhism is to cure people of ignorance, not to provide theoretical answers to philosophical questions.

Buddhism holds that there have always been sentient beings. There is no fixed time when we appeared. That we are different from the Buddha is a product of our ignorance, or *avidya*. *Avidya* refers to psychological phenomena that are localized, temporary, and changing. These three conditions must be present. They are interlocked and interdependent. A movement in space is also a movement in time, and it constitutes a change in our physical and psychological environment. One condition cannot change without the others also changing. Ignorance and vexations are transient.

Buddha-nature, however, is universal and unchanging. It is impossible for it to exist at one point and not at another. It transcends space, time, and movement. When we say that sentient beings are originally Buddhas, we are referring to their unchanging Buddha-nature, not to their local, temporary, and changing vexations.

Space is originally and fundamentally unchanging, but when it is enclosed by a container — round or square, large or small — the space seems to take on the characteristics of roundness, squareness, largeness, or smallness. The containers change and are therefore temporary in nature, but the nature of space remains unchanged. Likewise, sentient beings have different forms and behaviors. People, dogs, cats and insects are different sizes, made up of different parts, and act in different ways, yet their essential nature — Buddha-nature — is the same. When you are stimulated by your environment, you respond. Thoughts are in constant motion and vexations arise. This is *avidya*, ignorance.

Ignorance has been present and ever-changing since time without beginning. It is what leads to the creation of sentient beings. Ignorance, however, is not universal or unchanging. It is and always has been a local, temporary phenomenon in continual flux.

If we can use our methods of practice correctly and not be swayed by worldly phenomena, our minds will not move. We will not be influenced by greed, anger, and delusion, and these three poisons will disappear. That which remains is Buddha-nature.

When our minds do not move, ignorance does not exist. There is only Buddha-nature. Until we completely remove all ignorance, we will continue to discriminate and use our limited and temporary mentalities as containers to hold that which is unlimited. When ignorance and the containers are removed, only universal, unchanging Buddha-nature remains. If ignorance truly existed, it would never change.

The analogy of water and waves illustrates this point. Water is always present. Waves form when the wind blows. Waves are water, but originally they do not exist. Water can exist without waves, but the existence of waves depends on water. Water refers to Buddha-nature and waves to ignorance.

Can the Buddha again slip into a condition of ignorance? Buddha-nature is universal and eternal, but Sakyamuni the man died over 2500 years ago. The historical Buddha is not the real Buddha. The real Buddha, or Tathagata, is eternal and unchanging. The Tathagata never came and never left.

The Tathagata is ever-present. We can come into contact with the Tathagata at any time, in any place. However, we cannot ascertain this intellectually. It must come through an experience of faith or cultivation. Different people have different experiences of the Tathagata. Experiences of the Tathagata through faith are different from experiences through cultivation. This, however, does not mean that the Tathagata is different. People and their perceptions differ and change, not the Tathagata.

The Buddha that people perceive and experience is the Buddha that responds to ignorance. The Buddha must speak and act on the level of sentient beings if we are to understand his teachings. The Buddha has no ignorance, but he reflects the ignorance that is part of us. The Buddha is like a mirror. If nothing is in front of the mirror, the mirror reflects nothing. If ignorance is in front of the mirror, the mirror reflects ignorance, but the ignorance is not within the mirror. The Buddha is completely enlightened and will neither revert to a condition of ignorance nor be subject to vexations.

At that time the World Honored One said to Bodhisattva Vajragarbha: "Excellent, excellent! Virtuous man, for the benefit of

*the multitude of bodhisattvas and sentient beings in the Dharma
Ending Age, you have asked the Tathagata about the very secret
and profound ultimate expedient methods, which are the highest
teaching for bodhisattvas and the ultimate truth in the Mahayana.
These methods are capable of causing practicing and beginning
bodhisattvas in all ten directions and all sentient beings in the
Dharma Ending Age to obtain [the stage of] resolute faith and
permanently sever doubts and regrets. Listen attentively now. I
shall explain it to you."*

*Hearing this, Bodhisattva Vajragarbha was filled with joy
and listened silently along with the assembly.*

*"Virtuous man, all worlds begin and end, are born and
perish, have a before and after, exist and do not exist, coalesce and
disperse, arise and cease. Thoughts follow one another in succession, going and coming in a ceaseless circle. With all sorts of
grasping and rejecting, these [changing processes] are all cyclic
existences. If one were to discern Complete Enlightenment while
still in cyclic existence, then this nature of Complete Enlightenment would have the same [nature] as the turning flow [of cyclic
existence]! If one wished to be free from cyclic existence, then there
would be no place where [Complete Enlightenment] could exist.
For instance, when one moves one's eyes, still water appears to
have waves; when one fixes one's gaze, a circling flame appears to
be a wheel of fire. The fact that moving clouds make it seem as if
the moon were moving and a sailing boat makes one feel as if the
shore were moving also exhibits the same principle.*

*"Virtuous man, while the motion is going on, it is impos-
sible for those things to be still. How much more would this be so
if one were to discern the Complete Enlightenment of the Buddha
with the defiled mind of birth and death, which has never been
pure; how could it not [appear to] be in motion? For this reason,
you gave rise to these three doubts."*

Sakyamuni Buddha explains samsara to Bodhisattva Vajragarbha by
talking about the nature of illusion. The sutra says that one sees
waves in still water when one's sight is disturbed, and one sees a
ring of fire drawn by a circling torch when one's gaze is fixed.

Many of us have had the impression of the moon racing across the sky when in fact it was only the motion of clouds, and to people in a boat floating downstream, it may seem that the boat is still and the trees are moving. Likewise, if I rock this pen back and forth rapidly, you will see one solid object. Common sense tells us that these optical illusions are not real. Samsara, too, is illusory, but most of us are either not aware of it or don't believe it.

Many of us believe that life is long. During the years between birth and death our minds and bodies experience much, but we are aware of and remember only the most dramatic events. Even though we cannot dispute that in a few dozen years we will grow old and die, most of us believe that we are enduring entities who remain consistently the same throughout our lives.

To others, it may seem that human life is extremely brief. In relation to the vast expanse of history and time, eighty years or so is only a blink of an eye. Compared to the vastness of the Earth and the heavens, the distance we travel and the heights we reach are insignificant. This view is also illusory, although it is a step above the illusion described in the previous paragraph.

Do you ever wonder why we are born into this world? It seems quite meaningless. For no particular reason we are born, live our lives, experience all manner of changes, and then die. Do we choose to be born? If it is a conscious choice, why didn't we choose a better body, a better environment, better conditions? Why did we have to make things so difficult for ourselves? Actually, sentient beings do not experience samsara of their own free will. On the other hand, our lives are not predestined or controlled by an omniscient being or force. What we experience is determined by our karma, and thus we are compelled to remain and continue in samsara.

A man told me that he still felt the presence of his father, who had passed away some time ago. He asked, "Why do I have this feeling? He should have either entered heaven or taken another human form." Birth, life, and death are dependent on causes and conditions. One's karma must ripen for particular things to occur. In the case of this man's father, perhaps his next set of parents have not yet met; perhaps his future mother is still a girl. Until the conditions are right, he will simply have to wait.

Our karma is created by the action of our body, speech and mind, but why we think, say, and do the things we do is not always clear to us. I recently read about a famous singer who was married and having an affair with another woman. He knew it was distressing everyone involved, yet he could not stop himself. He repeatedly sought out this other woman. He was not in control, and he knew it, but it didn't matter. Such situations are not unique to famous singers. I am sure all of us have felt out of control.

Some people are not aware that they are dealing with illusion. Others are aware of it but are unable to control themselves. If I flip this pen back and forth the right way, it will appear rubbery and flexible. You know the pen is solid and straight, but you'll likely be drawn into the illusion anyway. We are pulled into the fantasy created by skillful magicians. We find appearances intriguing and alluring, and we become involved with them. This is how we continue to be pulled into samsara. We cannot ignore or rise above the illusions in our lives, so we repeatedly find ourselves caught in them.

Dharma practitioners can usually exercise greater control over their lives than non-practitioners. Those who study the Dharma may understand that their lives are illusory, yet they may be unable to control themselves. This is the first level. At the second level are practitioners who clearly recognize most illusions and act accordingly. This, however, is not foolproof, and one is still within the stream of samsara. Only at the third level, when the mind is no longer disturbed, distracted, deceived, or influenced by appearances, does one become free from samsara. This is accomplished when one is completely enlightened. This is liberation.

We are here because of our karma. It is as if we owed money to a bank and must now pay back our debt. Those on the third level will neither attempt to escape their previous karma nor create more. The rest of us are creating more karma while we make retributions for karma already created. We cannot control ourselves. Thus we sow the seeds for future lives. Liberated beings come to this world like the rest of us, but they do so through the power of their vows to help others. Buddhas appear in the world because of their vows, wisdom, and compassion, and because

sentient beings need them. Buddhas respond to the needs of sentient
beings.

How can we control our minds without leaving samsara? We
are immersed in illusion. Our very lives are illusory. It seems that
we don't have a chance. We are destined to fall again and again, our
actions establishing the appearance of future illusions. The instructions for leaving samsara are easy: stop the chain of illusion and
samsara will naturally cease to exist. Trying to escape from it,
however, will only create more karma.

To stop the cycle of samsara you must begin with yourself.
Suppose you want to see a rapidly spinning torch for what it really
is, but the more you try to stop it, the faster it goes. As you reach
for it, it recedes from your grasp. What then? Will you keep trying
to clutch at the flame, or will you address the problem at the
source? The problem is not the flame; it resides in your perception.
Similarly, in our practice, we cannot hope or wait for things
outside the mind to stop. We must go to the source. Still the mind.
When the illusory mind stops, all problems are resolved.

Someone said to me, "I have no idea what I did in my previous
lives. If I killed innumerable sentient beings, do I have to pay every
one of those debts? If I step on an ant in this life, does it mean I
have to be reborn as an ant in a future life and be killed as pay-
ment? If this is true for all my actions, when will I ever get liberated?"

The Buddha said that there is no sin. If sin existed, no one
could become a Buddha. If in your thoughts you feel you are sinful,
then sins exist. But if your mind does not move and there are no
deluded thoughts, then there is no sin either.

To leave samsara is straightforward. Simply stop the activities
of your deluded mind. Do not be pulled by the three poisons of
greed, anger and delusion. If you can do this, then you will be free
from samsara, but if your mind is constantly in motion, then you
are in samsara and will continue to discriminate, grasp, and avoid.
Such is the mind of ignorance.

Buddhism does not separate the physical element from the
mental element. The manifestation of our previous karma is physical, but it is created by the mind. A principle of physics states that

matter and energy cannot be created or destroyed, only transformed. A house is built from stone, wood, and metal, then it is
torn down, and the materials go back to the earth or are used for
something else. Crude oil is pumped from deep within the earth,
refined, and burned as gasoline. It goes through many changes, yet
its basic components remain the same. We may say the same for
our samsaric lives and the interaction between our minds and
bodies. Our minds are drawn to various illusions. How we respond
to these illusions will determine what happens to our bodies, and
this in turn will shape and influence the activity of our minds. The
process continues, seemingly without end, from life to life. This is
samsara.

> *"Virtuous man, for example, because of an illusory illness [of the
> eye], a flower is falsely seen in an empty sky. When the illusory
> illness [of the eye] is eliminated, one does not say: 'Now that this
> illness is eliminated, when will other illnesses arise?' Why? Because
> the illness and the flower are not in opposition. Likewise, when
> the flower vanishes into the empty sky, one does not say: 'When
> will flowers appear in the sky again?' Why? Because the sky
> originally has no flowers! There is no such thing as appearing and
> vanishing. Birth and death and nirvana are like the appearing
> and vanishing [flowers in the sky], while the perfect illumination
> of wondrous enlightenment is free from flowers or illnesses.*
>
> *"Virtuous man, you should know that the empty sky does
> not temporarily exist and then temporarily not exist. How much
> more so in the case of the Tathagata who is in accordance with
> Complete Enlightenment, which is comparable to the equal
> intrinsic nature of empty space.*
>
> *"Virtuous man, it is like smelting gold ore. The gold does not
> exist because of the smelting. As it has become [perfect] gold, it will
> not become ore again. Even after an inexhaustible period of time,
> the nature of the gold will not deteriorate. Therefore, one should
> not say that gold is not intrinsically perfect in itself. Likewise, the
> same holds true with the Tathagata's Complete Enlightenment.*
>
> *"Virtuous man, the wondrous and completely enlightened
> mind of all Tathagatas is originally without bodhi or nirvana; it*

*has nothing to do with accomplishing Buddhahood or not accom-
plishing Buddhahood, illusory cyclic existence or non-cyclic
existence."*

Samsara and nirvana are neither separate nor different from one
another. Two analogies in these paragraphs illustrate this point.

The sutra speaks of problems with vision. If we have defective
eyes, the world will look different to us than if we have normal
eyes. If we rub our eyes or press against our closed lids, our vision
becomes temporarily distorted. Even people with so-called perfect
vision are fooled by optical illusions. People with cataracts see the
world in a fog, and people with "floaters" disease are convinced that
objects fly past their line of vision. The sutra speaks of seeing
flowers in the sky. Most people who experience such things know
that the problem resides in the eyes, but some people actually
believe the illusions. After these people are cured of their malady,
however, they realize that the problem was with their eyes.

The second analogy refers to refining gold. Impure gold ore is
mined, smelted, and refined until nothing but pure gold remains.
The gold was always present from the first step of the process, but
some people might believe that gold ore and pure gold are two
different things. The smelter knows better, however; if there were
no gold at the start, there would be no gold at the end.

Samsara is an illusion, too, and it "exists" only as long as we
have vexations. Seeing flowers in the sky is an eye problem.
Samsara is a mind problem. When the eye problem is cured, we
realize that what we once thought to be real is in fact an illusion.
Likewise, when the mind is completely cured of its problems,
samsara and nirvana are seen for what they are — illusion. Indeed,
we realize that it never existed in the first place.

People with physical problems go to a hospital, but mental
problems are outside of a physician's realm of expertise. Psychologists may have an inkling about the workings of the mind, but
through meditation, practitioners have even deeper insight; and the
deeper one's practice, the more one understands the intricacies of
the mind and its problems. The Buddha said that if you have a
physical problem, you should go to a doctor; if you have a mental
problem, seek Buddhadharma.

I am not sure if there has ever been a person who has lived an entire lifetime without suffering illness or injury. Perhaps it is possible. On the other hand, there is not and never has been an ordinary sentient being completely free of mental problems. How many of you think you are trouble free? If you think you are completely healthy, it's a sure sign you have serious problems. A drunk rarely admits to being drunk; but if you notice that you're woozy and say that you are drunk, it indicates you're still relatively sober.

The mental problems I speak of are not limited to psychoses and neuroses. From the point of view of Buddhadharma, a sick mind is an unbalanced mind — unbalanced emotionally, intellectually, spiritually. No one's judgment is one hundred percent reliable or accurate. Our views are biased. Everyone judges and criticizes. People are ambivalent in their feelings, too. One of my American disciples says he has mixed feelings whenever I leave the United States for Taiwan. On the one hand, he is happy because he feels free. There is no authority figure to behave well in front of. On the other hand, he is sad because he will not have anyone to help him when he needs Dharma guidance. Are these serious problems? Society does not deem them so because everyone has them. We say that it is part of being human. That is true. We all have vexations. We are all in samsara. When we act from an unbalanced state of mind, we inevitably cause problems for ourselves and others.

For more obvious cases, we understand that people cannot control themselves. A drug user hates the drug he or she is addicted to, yet he or she still craves it and will do anything to get it. We do not treat criminals as harshly if it is proven that they are insane. But to a lesser degree, we are similar. If we can truly understand that people often do stupid or harmful things because they cannot help themselves, then we will not harbor as much ill will towards them. If we recognize that everyone is capable of such actions, that everyone has problems in their minds, we will be well along the path of developing compassionate minds.

Practitioners understand this. They know what they are capable of doing or saying when the mind is not balanced. They know that sometimes they will do things they are not even aware of, and at other times they will be aware but unable to control themselves. Therefore they understand the necessity of practice.

Much research exists on the study and treatment of physical diseases, but there is not as much concern for mental problems. If we were to address and work with the problems that are within all our minds, then society would be a much better place. Many of our physical problems would also disappear. Until people have this kind of vision, there will always be serious problems in the world.

It is by examining the mind — its desires, hopes, fears, judgments — that one can improve. The best way to accomplish this is through meditation. With practice, one will gradually have fewer and fewer deluded thoughts. Too many thoughts in the mind make it difficult to perceive things clearly. The fewer the thoughts, the fewer the problems. If we had no random or controlling thoughts, then all problems would disappear. We would find ourselves in harmony with others and our environment. Our judgment would be unbiased, and we would be able to accept the good and bad things that come our way without undue emotional turmoil.

When the mind is truly clear, there is no good or evil. There is no samsara or nirvana. Samsara and nirvana are concepts that we need in order to practice. Such ideas increase our faith and determination and give us a way of understanding what is and what can be, but they are only ideas. They are much like medicine. Only when you are sick do you care about the pill you need to take. Once you are healthy, the pill holds no more meaning for you. It might just as well be dust. When our minds are cleared of vexations, there is no longer a need for concepts like samsara and nirvana. We realize that samsara and nirvana are not two different things. They are not even one thing. They are illusions that a clear mind understands never even existed.

We are all like gold ore. The pure, refined gold is the pure mind in each of us. It represents our potential, our Buddha-nature. Once refined, our minds will be free of all impurities. Furthermore, according to the sutra, once gold is in its pure state, it will never become gold ore again. Likewise, once fully and completely awake, we will never again fall into the dream of samsara.

Only through practice can we refine our minds. Once our minds are free of impurities and we are enlightened, it is meaningless to ask if vexations are real. It is at this point that analogies break down. Obviously the impurities in gold ore can be gathered after the pure gold is separated, but in the case of the mind that becomes pure, vexations disappear. They do not exist for an enlightened person.

> *"Virtuous man, even the sravakas, who have perfected the state where [the karmic activities of] body, mind, and speech are entirely severed, are still unable to enter the nirvana that is personally experienced and manifested [by the Tathagata]. How can one possibly use one's conceptual mind to measure the realm of the Tathagata's Complete Enlightenment? It is comparable to using the light of a firefly to scorch Mount Sumeru; one would never be able to burn it! He who attempts to enter the Tathagata's ocean of great quiescent-extinction by using the cyclic mind and giving rise to cyclic views will never succeed. Therefore, I say that all bodhisattvas and sentient beings in the Dharma Ending Age should first sever the root of beginningless cyclic existence.*
>
> *"Virtuous man, contrived conceptualizations come from the existence of a mind, which is a conditioned [conglomeration of] the six sense objects. The conditioned impressions of deluded thoughts are not the true essence of mind; rather, they are like flowers in the sky. The discernment of the realm of Buddhahood with such conceptualization is comparable to the production of empty fruit by the empty flower. One merely revolves in this entanglement of deluded thoughts and gains no result.*
>
> *"Virtuous man, deluded groundless thinking and cunning views cannot accomplish the expedient methods of Complete Enlightenment. Discriminations such as these are not correct."*
>
> *At that time, the World Honored One, wishing to clarify his meaning, proclaimed these gathas:*
>
> *Vajragarbha, you should know*
> *that the quiescent and extinct*
> *nature of the Tathagata*
> *never had a beginning or end.*

> *To conceptualize this with the cyclic mind*
> *results in rotations in cyclic [existence].*
> *One will then remain in cyclic existence*
> *unable to enter the ocean of the Buddha.*
> *Like smelting gold ore,*
> *the gold does not exist*
> *as the result of smelting.*
> *Though it regains the original golden [quality],*
> *it is perfected only after*
> *[the process of] smelting.*
> *Once it becomes true gold,*
> *it cannot become ore again.*
> *Birth and death and nirvana,*
> *ordinary beings and all Buddhas,*
> *are but appearances of flowers in the sky.*
> *Conceptualizations are illusory projections.*
> *How much more so are such questions asked*
> *with an illusory mind?*
> *If one can put an end to this [illusory] mind,*
> *Complete Enlightenment can be sought.*

The Buddha tells Bodhisattva Vajragarbha that the wisdom of
Buddhahood cannot even be understood by sravakas — practitioners
who have been liberated from the cycle of birth and death — let
alone by ordinary sentient beings. Trying to understand Buddhahood with one's discriminating mind is comparable to using the
glow of a firefly to scorch Mount Sumeru. The unenlightened rely
on concepts, information, and memory. Their discriminating minds
enable them to understand only the material world. They are
unaware of what lies beyond.

One cannot know the Buddha's wisdom by thinking. Whatever comes out of conceptual thinking is separate from ultimate
reality. Hoping to perceive reality with the intellect is like expecting
illusory flowers to bear real fruit. Hearing the Buddha's words will
not enable us to immediately understand the wisdom of Buddhahood. Even so, in studying the sutras we can form ideas about the
nature of Buddhahood; however, they too are illusory.

We all start as ordinary sentient beings when we step onto the path of Buddhahood. Through the sutras we recognize that we are ordinary sentient beings and that there are higher levels of awareness to strive for. The concept of Buddhahood encourages us in our practice. In Indian mythology, there is a swan that is capable of separating milk from water when it drinks. Likewise, we can extract what meaning we can from the sutras to nourish our practice.

Both Eastern and Western religions agree that our lives in the temporal, physical world are filled with suffering. Most religions also say that it is possible to gain entry into another world, a heavenly realm free from suffering. In Buddhism, for example, a sravaka is a practitioner who transcends vexations and leaves samsara. Sravakas are freer and happier than the ordinary beings of this world, but they do not enter a "heavenly realm."

I once asked a friend, "What was your reason for coming to this world?" He said, "Being born was not my doing. I don't know why I came to this world. There's been a lot more suffering than happiness in my life. Coming here couldn't have been my idea. I tried to find happiness through my family, but I've been divorced three times. I tried hard each time, but each wife left and took half of my belongings and the children."

Why did you come to the world and why do you continue to live in it? Is it because you wish to have a happy marriage and a fulfilling family life? Two thousand years ago a great Chinese general named Caocao wrote a poem at the height of his successful career. He wrote that life is like dewdrops in the morning and that times of suffering outnumber times of happiness. Here was a man who had not encountered much failure in life, yet he expressed these feelings. Are your days filled with more suffering than happiness? Life is a struggle from the beginning. We struggle to be born, to talk, to walk, in our studies, and in our jobs.

Thus I told my friend, "We come into this world to pay back our karmic debts and to accumulate karmic merits. Whatever hardship we encounter occurs because of this." My friend objected, "I don't owe anybody anything. In fact, time and time again it's been my wives who have taken everything from me." I said, "You may not remember all the debts you owe. You can't remember all your dreams over the last five days. This life is a dream and your next life will be another. If you cannot remember dreams from five days ago, how can you possibly remember the dream of birth and death, the dreams of past lives? Our karmic debts may not have been incurred during this life. It is important that we make an effort to settle all our karmic debts, and, in a manner of speaking, increase our karmic credit, so that we will be in a better karmic situation the next time around."

This person said, "If life is a dream, then I don't have to do anything. It's all illusory anyway." "Yes," I said, "it is a dream, but if you don't make an effort, you'll regret it when it comes to an end." "I guess that means I'll have to work hard until I die," he said. "In that case, life is truly hard, truly suffering."

This is typical of the suffering that people experience. Sravakas, on the other hand, have transcended suffering, birth, and death. Yet, they do not fully comprehend the wisdom of the Buddha. There is a story in one of the sutras about three animals who cross a river: an elephant, a horse, and a rabbit. The elephant walks across the river and knows how deep the river is at every point; the horse crosses and knows the depth near the banks but not at the center of the river; the rabbit must swim the entire way without knowing the river's depth at any point. The rabbit represents a sravaka, the horse a bodhisattva, and the elephant a Buddha. All three have crossed the river of samsara, but their levels of attainment are different. Sravakas have no way of fathoming the wisdom of Buddhahood. Bodhisattvas have some idea, but only for a Buddha is wisdom complete. If sravakas and bodhisattvas cannot completely know the Buddha's wisdom, how can ordinary sentient beings know?

The next line of the sutra reads, "He who attempts to enter the Tathagata's ocean of great quiescent-extinction by using the cyclic mind giving rise to cyclic views will never succeed." It is possible to acquire knowledge and wisdom through study, but the highest wisdom cannot be expressed in language. Thinking requires symbols. Language is the mode of expression for reasoning. Language and symbols express the discriminations made by the mind. When the mind discriminates, it is impossible to enter the ocean of great quiescent-extinction. No doubt our technological advances have been achieved through reasoning, but reasoning cannot help us to know the Buddha's wisdom.

Samsaric mind is a mind rooted in the cycle of birth and death. It is a mind with ideas of gain and loss, a mind of vexation. Seeking happiness and avoiding suffering are also part of the samsaric mind. It is like drinking salt water to quench your thirst: the more you thirst the more you drink, and the more you drink the more you thirst.

What brings happiness? Money? Social status? Fame? A loving, stable family? Good health? These things do not bring genuine happiness. They can provide temporary satisfaction, but situations change, and the happiness cannot be sustained. The happiness we seek is like the dewdrops in General Caocao's poem — beautiful on the leaf, but soon to evaporate in the morning sun. The mind that seeks happiness is samsaric mind because it is rooted in vexation.

It is natural for people to seek happiness and avoid suffering. Without these drives and desires most of us would not want to go on living, but seeking and avoiding always end in suffering. Seeking happiness is like a dog trying to catch its own tail. Trying to avoid suffering is like trying to escape your shadow. In the end, it is these attitudes which make people weary of life.

The friend I talked about earlier asked me, "What attitude should I have toward life?" I answered, "Accept that which has already happened. If things that have not happened yet are expected to be beneficial, help them to happen. If they are not expected to be beneficial, try not to let them happen. But in all situations try to keep your mind free from thoughts of gain and loss. If you're sick, go to the doctor, but don't complain about or self-indulge in your aches. If you're not sick, pay attention to your health, but don't worry about the possibility of getting sick."

Such an attitude minimizes thoughts of gain and loss. One is not so rooted in samsaric mind at these times. Of course this is easier said than done. Bodhisattvas are not afraid of suffering, but they don't try to create it either. Unafraid of suffering, they do not anticipate it before it happens. Having no aversion to suffering, they do not attempt to escape it when it comes, nor do they see it as suffering.

In the Song dynasty, there was a respected minister who was killed when China was conquered by the Mongols. His writings showed that he did not see his execution as suffering, but as the completion of his humanity. From an ordinary point of view, his execution was death, but to him it was the fulfillment of life. Genuine practitioners understand this.

Not to have ideas of gain or loss, not to seek happiness, not to run from suffering, not to fear samsara, not to seek Buddhahood: these are marks of a mind free from samsara, free from vexation. Buddhas are free from samsara, yet they willingly return for the sake of others. The same is true for enlightened bodhisattvas. Sravakas, though they have transcended birth and death, are still afraid of it. They still have ideas of gain and loss. They are much further along than ordinary sentient beings, but they do not yet understand the Buddha's wisdom.

Mahayana Buddhism, which includes Ch'an Buddhism, teaches that the liberated mind seeks nothing, rejects nothing, is afraid of nothing. My advice is this: Accept what has happened. Do not be desirous of happiness or afraid of suffering. Do not think so much of gain or loss. If you can cultivate these attitudes, your lives will be freer and happier.

Most people use conceptual thinking in their daily lives. What does it mean to use conceptual thinking? We use the mind to analyze and investigate. We may believe that thinking is the source of all our troubles, but thinking is not necessarily wrong or bad. It is erroneous to believe that the mind stops thinking when one becomes enlightened. Buddhas and bodhisattvas can still use their thought processes. Some statues of bodhisattvas and Buddhas have their heads tilted to one side. This signifies thinking. Thought, therefore, is not something to be disparaged.

However, there is a distinction between the thinking processes of bodhisattvas and those of ordinary sentient beings. Enlightened beings think without self-motivated purpose, whereas unenlightened beings think from a position of self-centeredness. The Sanskrit terms for these two modes of thinking are *asamskrta* and *samskrta*.

Asamskrta refers to the selfless, spontaneous thought process of a bodhisattva. *Samskrta* refers to the self-centered thinking of ordinary sentient beings.

We think and act self-centeredly. Therefore our thoughts are always self-referential, goal-directed and purposeful. The thinking of a bodhisattva, however, arises from the power of samadhi. In samadhi the mind is unified. There is no self-centeredness. To have a sense of self indicates that there is a self separate from the object of one's thinking. Two thoughts already exist: the self and its thoughts. A mind with two thoughts is not unified and therefore not in samadhi. Without self-centeredness, a bodhisattva can think without self-motivated purpose. A bodhisattva is not an unthinking block of matter. Thinking still occurs. In fact, a bodhisattva's thoughts are clearer, more expansive, and more profound than those of ordinary sentient beings.

Buddhas and bodhisattvas think and act in response to the needs of sentient beings, and when Buddhas and bodhisattvas think, it is similar to our way of thinking, except that no self-centeredness is involved. Ordinary sentient beings, no matter what they believe, always think with a self involved. It does not matter if their thoughts are good, bad, or neutral.

Although it is impossible in our present condition to think and act without a sense of self and purpose, it is beneficial to understand that it is possible to do so. It will help us in our daily lives. We can be more aware of our thoughts and actions, more aware of how we are motivated by ideas of gain and loss and how we are conditioned by the environment. At these times we can remind ourselves what bodhisattvas are capable of and strive to emulate them. Whenever conflicts arise between ourselves and others or between ourselves and the environment, we can reflect on our mental attitudes. When we realize that we are caught up in our sense of self and with our goal-directed purposes, we can try to move toward a more selfless mentality. In this manner, conflicts will naturally dissipate.

All self-directed thinking derives from information collected by the six senses. The six sense data consist of our sense faculties as well as the objects of the six sense faculties. The internal sense data constitute our bodies and the external sense data make up the environment. All of the sense data are material. No matter how abstract our thinking, we must still use symbols. Our minds cannot move and think unless we interact with the material environment. Hence sometimes people come to the erroneous notion that Buddhism preaches materialism. One can turn the argument around and say that material objects exist because of their interaction with the minds of sentient beings. For example, the external environment does not exist for a person in a dreamless sleep. Moreover, we are unaware of our surrounding environment when our minds are either completely dull or completely on a method of meditation. Only when we are in our ordinary state of mind does the external environment exist for us. Thus one might venture to say that Buddhism preaches a kind of mentalism, that material things exist only because of the movement of the mind.

Materialism and mentalism are opposite extremes, but neither represents the true state of affairs. Both are illusory and can be compared to believing that flowers floating in the sky are real. As flowers in the sky are illusions, so too are the mind and the material world. Neither the mind nor the phenomenal world has true existence. Thus we can reject both materialism and mentalism. Neither the illusory mind of attachment nor the phenomenal world can stand on their own. The illusory mind of attachment exists because it has the phenomenal world to interact with, and the phenomenal world exists because there is a mind that perceives it. Hence, both are illusory.

We would like to reach Buddhahood, or at least know what it is like to be a Buddha. Unfortunately, we seek after Buddhahood with a self-centered mind. In order to attain Complete Enlightenment, we must drop our imaginings and self-attachment, but it is not easy to let go of our selves. It is easy for practitioners to summon up extraordinary effort for short periods of time, but most are incapable of persisting on the path throughout their entire lives. These bursts of effort, courage, and determination are also products of the self-centered mind. Practitioners have a goal, and that goal is to get enlightened. However, most find that getting enlightened is not that easy. Reaching Buddhahood after a few months of hard training is out of the question. Even ridding oneself of the most obvious vexations is not easy. In fact, beginning practitioners often find that they become more acutely aware of their problems, and uncover others they were previously unaware of. It can be disillusioning. Many people turn away from practice when they experience this. They say things like, "I'm not ready to practice yet. I'll wait until I have more strength and determination."

Thus, when we practice, we should do so with an unseeking mind. The more we go after enlightenment or Buddhahood, the further it will recede. Yes, it is important that we have goals. I have said that we should strive to emulate Buddhas and bodhisattvas. These are all goal-directed activities. However, when we are actually engaged in practice, notions and goals are to be left behind. We are to practice with a calm, persistent mind. We are not to concern ourselves with progress or vexations. In this way, progress will naturally occur and vexations will naturally lessen. Practicing with an anxious mind only leads to frustration, tension, and disappointment. Only when we are free from thoughts of purpose and self-centeredness is it possible to experience enlightenment.

Bodhisattva
Maitreya

Then Bodhisattva Maitreya rose from his seat in the midst of the assembly, prostrated himself at the feet of the Buddha, circled the Buddha three times clockwise, knelt down, joined his palms, and said: "O World Honored One of great compassion! You have opened wide the secret treasure for bodhisattvas and have caused the great assembly to deeply awaken from cyclic existence and distinguish between the erroneous and the correct. Your teaching is capable of bestowing the Fearless Eye of the Path to sentient beings in the Dharma Ending Age, causing them to give rise to resolute faith in the great nirvana, and never again to flow within the realm of the turning wheel [of samsara] or hold cyclic views.

"World Honored One, if bodhisattvas and sentient beings in the Dharma Ending Age desire to sail on the Tathagata's ocean of great quiescent-extinction, how should they sever the roots of cyclic existence? In the various cyclic existences, how many types of capacities are there? What are the different kinds of cultivation of Buddha's bodhi? When [bodhisattvas] enter the world of passions, how many expedient methods should they devise to deliver sentient beings? Pray do not forsake your great compassion in saving the world, but cause all practicing bodhisattvas and sentient beings in the Dharma Ending Age to cleanse their wisdom-eyes and illumine their mirror-like minds. May they be completely awakened to the Tathagata's unsurpassed knowledge and vision." Having said these words, he prostrated himself on the

ground. He made the same request three times, each time repeating the same procedure.

At that time the World Honored One said to Bodhisattva Maitreya: "Excellent, excellent! Virtuous man, for the benefit of the multitude of bodhisattvas and sentient beings in the Dharma Ending Age, you have asked the Tathagata about the most profound, secret, subtle, and wondrous truth so that bodhisattvas' wisdom-eyes may become pure, so that all sentient beings in the Dharma Ending Age may permanently sever themselves from cyclic existence, so that their minds may awaken to Absolute Reality, and so that they may possess the patient endurance of the unborn [wisdom]. Listen attentively now. I shall explain it to you."

Hearing this, Bodhisattva Maitreya was filled with joy and listened silently along with the assembly.

Bodhisattva Maitreya asks the Buddha how human beings came to exist. The answer that the Buddha gives to this important question in this sutra has had a great influence on Buddhism. Maitreya does not seek an answer in order to condemn human existence; rather, his goal in asking this question is to urge sentient beings to cleanse their Wisdom-eyes and enjoy the patient endurance of the unborn in the ever-changing world of name and form.

The sutras describe five kinds of vision. The first and most limited kind of vision is through the physical eye. Most sentient beings are at this level. With determined practice, sentient beings can learn to purify their vision so that they may view the world with less prejudice and desire. The second is the development and purification of the heavenly-eye. Beings in the heavenly realms, and those in the human realm who have practiced long and hard over many lifetimes, possess this eye. With it come supernormal powers. Such beings, however, are still subject to birth and death. Third is the Wisdom-eye, which comes when one is free from the cycle of birth and death and of all vexations. Fourth is the Dharma-eye, or Pure Wisdom-eye. This is the level of bodhisattvas, who have transcended samsara yet remain in the world to help sentient beings. When the Dharma-eye is completely purified, the fifth level is reached, that of the Buddha-eye.

The sutra refers to the fourth level, that of the Dharma-eye. In Mahayana Buddhism, the fourth level is subdivided into ten stages, called bhumis, which bodhisattvas pass through as the Dharma-eye is gradually purified. The Dharma-eye at the first stage of bodhisattvahood is not yet pure. At the eighth stage, the Dharma-eye is thoroughly purified. At this level, bodhisattvas have transcended discriminative and illusory thinking as well as any desire to attain Buddhahood or help sentient beings. These bodhisattvas no longer have any notion of accomplishment. There are no goals, no plans, no points of view. They may help innumerable sentient beings, but they will not perceive that they are doing so.

This is the stage of the patient endurance of the unborn, which is the experience of no-vexation and no-wisdom. It is the realization that there is no creation or destruction in the past, present, and future. Patient endurance is not the attainment of wisdom. If wisdom existed, so too would vexation. The common notion is that wisdom arises when vexations disappear and nirvana is attained when samsara is transcended. For the person who sees with the Dharma-eye or Buddha-eye, all such distinctions fall away.

The goal of practice is to purify the Dharma-eye and enjoy the patient endurance of the unborn. To achieve this, the Buddha addresses the origin of human existence and samsara:

> "Virtuous man, all sentient beings [experience illusory] cyclic existence due to all kinds of affection, love, craving, and desire since beginningless time. The different types of births in the world be they from egg, womb, humidity, or by transformation are created by sexual desire. You should know that attached love is the root of cyclic existence. Because there are all sorts of desirable [objects] that enhance and augment the activity of attached love, birth and death proceed in unending succession.
>
> "Desire arises because of attached love. The existence of life comes from desire. Sentient beings' love of their lives [in turn] relies on desire as a base. Therefore, love and desire are the cause, love of life is the consequence. Because the objects of desire [vary], like and dislike arise. If the object goes against one's grasping mind, one gives rise to hatred and jealousy and commits evil karmic deeds. As a result, one is reborn in hell or as a hungry ghost."

Affection arises from attached love, which is interdependent with desire. Attached love and desire are causes and consequences to each other. Together, they give rise to craving, attachment, and all sorts of vexation. Therefore, attached love and desire are the causes for the furtherance of cyclic existence. They compel us to strive for survival and happiness, yet they are the root of all afflictions. There is a story of a lazy person's quest for a means of livelihood. A friend gave him an easy job watching over a cemetery. The man had practically nothing to do. Nevertheless, he quit after a month, complaining, "All those dead people lie around doing nothing night and day, yet I have to sit here and watch them. Why do I have to do all the work?"

His friend replied, "Then where will you find work to make ends meet?" He said he had earned enough money to live for a while. When his money runs out, however, he will undoubtedly look for another job. Even the laziest person desires to survive. Thus it can be said that all sentient beings have desires.

There are physical and psychological desires. Physical desires are limited and can be satisfied, at least temporarily, but psychological desires are unlimited and insatiable, and as psychological desires intensify, so do physical desires. Psychological desires will drive one not only through one's present life but onward through countless more.

Most people do not think about rebirth. They may have other beliefs or they may have no opinion at all about their fate after death. However, the intensity and insatiability of sentient beings' desires generates a force that binds and propels them to further existence in the cycle of rebirths, irrespective of their beliefs or attitudes. This is the force of karma.

Attached love and desire are complementary. Desire indicates an aspiration for future gain. Attached love indicates holding on to something possessed. Karma is created by the force of attached love and desire. On the other hand, without love society could not maintain even a semblance of harmony. Therefore love is both beneficial and deleterious.

The attached love I have been talking about is defiled love, or love that derives from self-centeredness. Undefiled love, or love without attachment, is compassion. Selfish love is narrow in its scope, whereas compassion is limitless. At its crudest, defiled love is focused entirely on the individual. In progressive stages, defiled love can become more expansive, encompassing one's spouse, family, society, or all of humanity. Yet even love for humanity is selfish, because it is limited. Of course, love for humanity is preferable to love that is entirely selfish.

Few of us are capable of loving everyone. Life and experience are centered around the individual. If we do not love our own lives, we would not survive. Therefore, we must start with love for ourselves and gradually expand it to encompass as much of nature and as many sentient beings as possible. Genuine love is selfless giving. There are few people who can give without expecting something in return, whether it be love, wealth, time, or anything else. Many people are capable of altruism, but not completely and not all the time. The Buddhist sutras say that one can give externally and internally. The former is giving money or property, the latter is giving one's time, energy, or life. Donating one's help or talent requires more effort than making a monetary donation, but these types of giving are all defiled. Only when one is completely unselfish does genuine love arise. This genuine love is Buddhist compassion.

Sentient beings have a strong love of life. This love is comprised of two important elements: desire for food and desire for sex. As soon as the body is sufficiently fed, sexual need arises. The desire to have sex not only ensures that other sentient beings will be reborn, but it also drives our own rebirth. If sexual desire is still part of one's karmic force, during the intermediate stage of reincarnation, one will be propelled to be attracted to a copulating couple, thereby giving rise to one's rebirth. Sexual desire during one's life generates a karmic force that has inexorable consequences.

On hearing this, many people might surmise that life in samsara is not that bad. After all, most of us enjoy passionate love and desire. If your goal is to remain in samsara, then your task is quite easy. Continue to love self-centeredly and feed your desires. You will enjoy life after life, but you will also continue to encounter unending afflictions that follows you like your own shadow.

Liberation from samsara requires great effort, and to be liberated yet remain in samsara to help others is more difficult still.

If we can purify our love, then the path to liberation will be easier. However, if the scope of our love remains narrow and our desires remain strong, we are destined to be reborn again and again, and there is no guarantee that we will be reborn as human beings. Passionate love and hate are separated by a fine line and the extent to which some people go to satisfy desires inflicts great harm upon themselves and others. When passionate love turns to hate and desires cause one to act in harmful ways, the karma created by these actions may lead to births in lower realms.

It is not always easy to distinguish between passionate love and hate, between love that is giving and love that is selfish. There is a fable about a wolf and a rabbit. The wolf says to the rabbit, "I love you with all my heart." The rabbit responds, "Thanks, I really appreciate it." The wolf replies, "In that case, stay with me always. I will keep you safe and warm — in my belly!" Although it is a graphic image, similar relationships exist among lovers, friends, and family. No doubt love exists in the beginning of most relationships. Parents love their children. Couples fall in love at first sight. But because of attachment and desire, love can become possessive, stifling, destructive. It can even lead to hatred.

Defiled love is the foundation of samsara. If we cultivate undefiled love, we can slowly stem our desires and passions and reduce the chances of our love turning into something possessive and harmful. If we can do this, then hatred will naturally disappear and we will be able to coexist with others and the environment in greater harmony.

> *"Realizing that desire is detestable, if one desires to leave behind karmic paths and abandons evil and delights in doing good, one is reborn in the realms of gods or humans. If, further, one knows that attachment is detestable, and thus abandons attachment and delights in renunciation, one still stirs up the root of attachment. This results in increased worldly meritorious fruit, which, being samsaric, does not lead to accomplishing the holy path. Therefore, if sentient beings wish to be liberated from birth and death and to*

avoid cyclic existence, they should first sever craving and desire, and eliminate their attached love.

"*Virtuous man, the transformation and manifestation of bodhisattvas [in various forms] in the world are not based on attachment. Out of their compassion, they cause sentient beings to abandon attachment by provisionally taking on all kinds of craving and desire so they can enter birth and death. If sentient beings in the Dharma Ending Age can abandon desire, eliminate love and hatred, permanently sever cyclic existence, and diligently pursue the Tathagata's state of Complete Enlightenment with pure minds, they will attain awakening.*"

Our self-centered love and desire bring other sentient beings into the world. The self-centered love and desire of other sentient beings bring us back to the world after this life. The cycle of samsara is driven by such forces of love and desire.

If self-centered love and desire lead us to commit wrongful actions, the resulting karma may cause us to be reborn in the lower realms of animals, hungry ghosts, or hells. If our actions are beneficial to others and ourselves, we will likely be reborn in the human or heavenly realms. However, even devas of the heavenly realms are motivated by love and desire and are thus subject to the cycle of birth and death.

Attached love and desire continue without cessation because we cling to an idea of self. As long as we are self-centered, we will remain in samsara. Liberation will elude us. It does not matter whether our actions are beneficial or harmful. As long as we are motivated by passionate, self-centered love and desire, we will continue to create karma and be subject to birth and death.

As long as we are habituated with and bond to the self, attached love, and desire, our actions will be defiled no matter how altruistic our motives seem. Yet it is possible through practice to gradually purify these feelings. Desire is the first of the four advance steps to power of ubiquity, desire for practice. The others are diligence and persistence in practice, samadhi, and wisdom. These four ingredients are parts of the Thirty-seven Aids to Enlightenment. Desire is absolutely necessary if one wishes to progress toward enlightenment. One must want to practice. In the beginning there will always be a strong attachment to self, but at least the motivating desire is to become liberated. In choosing the path of practice, we have begun to purify our desire.

Motivation is the key in determining whether desire is pure or defiled. An action is pure when performed solely for the sake of others, without concern for oneself. It is pure even if there is a concept of self behind the action. The actions of parents for their children, for example, can be pure in this sense. On the other hand, if someone helps another in order to win that person's love, the action is not pure. When our actions are motivated by a desire to help others without consideration for personal benefit, desire is transformed into compassion. Although it is not the true compassion of a bodhisattva, it is still good because desire is becoming purified.

Objects of desire may take many forms. We may desire physical things, such as food, clothing, or comfort. We may desire emotional gratification, such as the love of another. We may desire recognition or fame. We may desire good karma in order to ensure better conditions in future lives. There is nothing wrong with having desires. The fulfillment of these examples would not automatically cause one to be reborn in lower realms. But these are not examples of true compassion. If we calculate the benefit we will receive from our actions, it is not compassion. If we practice because we want to transcend samsara and attain Buddhahood, it is not compassion. As long as there are ulterior motives in our minds, no matter how lofty these motives may be, it is not compassion. It is not wrong or bad, but it is self-centered love and desire, not compassion.

We may have passed a wild flower and stopped to admire its beauty and fragrance. The flower may remain in our mind as we walk away. We may even contemplate picking it. In a sense, we have fallen in love with this flower. We have gone beyond enjoying it. Now we want to possess it so that we can enjoy it continuously. We all have a hunger that makes us want to possess something we don't have, and which drives us to hold on dearly to that which we already have.

Similarly, one may have a good experience while meditating, feeling pure and light. In the future that person will likely desire this experience again, and so will continue to meditate. This is yet another attachment. As long as one is attached to spiritual experiences, self-centered love and desire are still present.

Of all the experiences one can have, none brings more happiness than samadhi. The deeper the samadhi experience, the greater the happiness will be and the longer it will last. People who have experienced deep levels of samadhi may remain peaceful and even-tempered for the remainder of their lives. In comparison, the happiness derived from food and sex is coarse and short-lived. Someone who has reached the highest levels of worldly samadhi may feel liberated, but attachment still exists; the person is still motivated by self-centered love and desire, not compassion. It is still samsara. Again, there is nothing wrong with samadhi, but it isn't liberation, and it isn't compassion.

For enlightened bodhisattvas and Buddhas, the forces of self-centered love and desire are replaced by compassion and vows. Compassion manifests when bodhisattvas and Buddhas help sentient beings. Compassion is the action and vows are the motivating force. Bodhisattvas make vows until they reach the eighth bhumi, or stage, of the Bodhisattva Path — the position of non-intentionality. At this stage, they help sentient beings spontaneously. Once they attain the eighth bhumi, bodhisattvas no longer need to make vows. Here's an analogy: you may vow to climb a mountain, but you don't have to repeat the vow once you reach the top.

To vow to be liberated from birth and death because of an aversion to samsara is not enough. To vow to free oneself from vexation is not enough. One must take the vows of a bodhisattva, who is not concerned with liberation but rather with helping other sentient beings toward liberation.

Practitioners on the Bodhisattva Path should make vows for the benefit of others, not for themselves. Bodhisattvas do not vow to reach the Pure Land, but if their vows to help others are accomplished, they will also benefit. By the time we are truly capable of helping others, we will already be more evolved. In fact, it is only when we are awakened that we can truly help others. If we learn to swim well enough to help others from drowning, we will also have liberated ourselves from drowning.

We need vows to motivate ourselves to cultivate compassion in order to help others. In contrasting compassion with love, understand that even with the more elementary levels of compassion we are not concerned with our own benefit; the emphasis is on ultimately helping others toward liberation. On the other hand, although there are many levels of love, some more expansive than others, self-centeredness is always involved.

There are three levels of compassion. The first is compassion that arises from a bodhisattva's relationship with sentient beings. The bodhisattva sees people suffering and vows to help them gain liberation. In this case, there is a subject that feels compassionate and an object of that compassion. Also, the bodhisattva recognizes differences among sentient beings. This is the compassion of a bodhisattva before the first bhumi. The second level of compassion is compassion that arises from the Dharma. The bodhisattva naturally helps sentient beings without distinction or discrimination, but there is still a subject and object involved. This applies to a bodhisattva on the first through seventh bhumi. The third and highest level is where the distinction between subject and object is transcended. This is the compassion of great bodhisattvas and Buddhas and is without limit and conditions. Bodhisattvas on the eighth bhumi and above as well as Buddhas have the greatest power to help others, but for them there are no ideas of sentient beings or compassion. It is only sentient beings who see it as such.

As ordinary sentient beings, it is a given that we possess love, but true compassion is another matter. Even the first level of compassion is hard to attain. As Buddhists, we vow to help others. These vows put us on the path to achieve the first level of compassion. To reach the Dharma level, we need to start ascending the ten bhumis of bodhisattvahood. To reach the highest level of compassion, we must attain at least the eighth bhumi of the Bodhisattva Path.

Bodhisattvas return to the world of samsara to help others by virtue of their vows. They may voluntarily enter the cycle of birth and death and live as humans do, or they may briefly manifest as transformation bodies and then disappear. However, their appearance is not driven by self-centered love and desire, for if it were so, this love and desire would cloud their minds and obscure their wisdom and they would still be subject to the forces of karma. Bodhisattvas appear because of the power of their vows.

Sentient beings are driven by self-centered love and desire and so are concerned with gain and loss. Therefore we suffer vexations. Love, however, is a necessary part of our lives. We must learn to elevate our love, to transform our love for self and others into compassion, which is without limit and distinction.

> "Virtuous man, due to the inherent desire in all sentient beings, ignorance flourishes and increases. Thus [sentient beings] manifest five distinct natures. According to the two obstructions, their hindrances may appear to be deep or shallow. What are the two obstructions? The first is the obstruction of principle, which hinders right views. The second is the obstruction of phenomena, which perpetuates birth and death.
>
> "What are the five distinct natures? Virtuous man, sentient beings who have not eliminated and extinguished these two obstructions are called 'those who have not attained Buddhahood.' Sentient beings who have permanently abandoned craving and desire and have eliminated the obstruction of phenomena, but not the obstruction of principle, can only be enlightened as sravakas or pratyekabuddhas. They are unable to manifest and abide in the realm of bodhisattvas.
>
> "Virtuous man, if sentient beings in the Dharma Ending Age desire to sail on the Tathagata's great ocean of Complete Enlightenment, they should first vow to practice with diligence and sever the two obstructions. When these two obstructions have been subdued, they will be able to awaken to the realm of bodhisattvas. If the obstructions of principle and phenomena are permanently severed, they will enter into the subtle and wondrous Complete Enlightenment of the Tathagatas and consummate bodhi and great nirvana."

Sentient beings experience two kinds of obstructions. The first is the aspect of principle, also known as the noumena, which concerns itself with correct understanding and acceptance of Buddhadharma. The second is the aspect of phenomena, which refers to the actions of body, speech, and mind stemming from our understanding. Not understanding or accepting the concepts of Buddhadharma is an obstruction with respect to principle. Not acting in accordance with Buddhadharma is an obstruction with respect to phenomena. Those who completely remove the two obstructions attain Buddhahood.

In Sakyamuni Buddha's lifetime and for centuries afterward, there were six major religious systems in India. Altogether there were roughly sixty sects, and all were involved with philosophical thinking. Differences among these six schools and the school of Buddhism concerned questions of personal existence, causes and conditions, cause and effect, eternality, and the existence of God. With so many beliefs and theories circulating, it was difficult for many people to accept Buddhism. Buddhist literature was meant primarily to free people from the influence of philosophy and to instill in them faith in Buddha's teachings. Without faith, people will not practice, and without practice there can be no progress.

It is natural to ask questions like, "What existed in the beginning? Why and how did ignorance and desire originate?" Buddhism does not speak of beginnings. Such questions lead nowhere. One person asks, "How did sentient beings originate?" and another answers, "God created them." The first person then asks, "Where did God come from?" and the second person replies, "God always existed." Where does that leave us? The question is merely replaced by more unanswerable questions. Speculations abound. Buddhism refrains from speculating. Similar obstacles arise with the concept of Buddhahood. In Buddhist thought, there is no difference between existence and non-existence. In the sutras there is a story of a person who asked the Buddha what existed in the beginning and what would exist at the end. The Buddha answered, "The banana tree has many leaves that can be peeled off layer after layer, but in the end there is nothing left in the center." It should be the same with practice. Anything in the mind can be an obstruction, and as long as something exists there can be no freedom. We should not seek after or hold onto anything, including Buddhahood.

It is as if, on the path of practice, there is a huge mountain whose summit cannot be seen. You do not know how to cross it, but in the mountain there is a gate — the Dharma gate — and a gatekeeper. The gatekeeper says to all who approach, "To enter, you must leave everything behind: possessions, your body, your mind, and all your attachments." What does this mean? How can one enter a gate without a mind and body? It seems the same as not entering. If you could do this, however, you would discover that there is no door to enter, no mountain to cross. In fact, there is no "you." Liberation is freeing yourself from yourself — from attachment to body, mind, and environment. This is the view, the practice, and the result of Ch'an. If there is no attachment to things inside or outside your mind, there is no more vexation.

People who are highly educated, people who have firm philosophical world views, or people who have deep religious faith, often have strong obstructions with respect to principle. The Dharma says that to practice successfully, eight hurdles must be overcome, the most difficult being a strongly held philosophical view. Removal of the obstruction of principle is accomplished through faith, which can be acquired either through understanding or genuine practice. Faith acquired through intellectual understanding, however, is not strong and enduring. Such faith may remain for a lifetime, but in the next life one will face the same obstruction. Freedom from the obstruction of principle requires faith derived from direct experience — seeing one's self-nature. Seeing one's self-nature will generate unshakable faith in the Dharma and its methods of practice.

Obstructions of phenomena are more difficult to overcome. It is these that keep us in the cycle of birth and death. They are divided into three groups: vexation obstructions, occupational obstructions, and retribution obstructions. Vexation obstructions stem from mental activities. Occupational obstructions stem from our families, jobs, routines, and social lives. Retribution obstructions stem from karma created in the past which prevents one from practicing or understanding the Dharma. Some vexations are noticeable, others aren't. Some vexations seem like obstructions, others do not. Some vexations are heavy, some light.

Heavy vexations overcome reasoning. What we have understood to be correct will either be forgotten or thought to be incorrect. Vexations are lighter when we know we are experiencing them. For example, someone living here at the Ch'an Center was unhappy with me and even yelled at me, but he realized it was his own vexation. This is light vexation. Another person had great respect for me and brought others to the Center. On one occasion I criticized her, and she grew indignant and left. For a while she would have nothing to do with me, but afterward she cooled off and returned. Now she is happy again. It is a sign of progress when a practitioner feels remorse for negative feelings, words, and actions.

Thoughts are like the tides that respond to the pull of the moon's gravity. We feel joy, anger, sorrow, and other feelings in response to the environment. So long as we are attached to such responses, vexations arise. Of the three phenomenal obstructions, vexation obstructions are the most difficult to overcome because any movement of the mind is considered vexation. There are only differences in the degree of vexation. Even if you are happy or in samadhi, it is still vexation.

Those who reach arhatship are free from vexation. Bodhisattvas who have reached the bhumi levels are free from vexation. Actually, bodhisattvas who reach the first bhumi are liberated from gross vexation and are free to be born and leave their lives at will, but they still have intentions of where they want to go and when they want to be born. By the time bodhisattvas reach the eighth bhumi, they are free from such intentions. They have reached the level of non-intentionality.

None of us is completely free from vexation obstructions, but this should not deter or intimidate us. We should not be afraid of vexations or angry that we have them. Knowing we have vexations is already good because vexations arise every moment in everybody. When we are aware of our vexations, they automatically become lighter. The best attitude is not to feel aversion toward, fear of, or sorrow because of vexation. Do not fear that vexations will arise. If you must fear something, fear the possibility that you may not recognize vexations in the first place. Do not worry that vexations will not end. If you must worry, worry about your fear that they will not end.

We can easily see our vexations if our minds are calm. That is good. Problems arise when vexations are too heavy to be recognized. Therefore, on the one hand, vexations can be obstructions to our practice. On the other hand, they can be helpful and encourage us toward higher levels.

The second obstruction of phenomena is occupational obstruction. Your life or job might make it difficult to accept the Dharma or practice. I know someone who works in a Christian faculty organization. He would like to study Buddhadharma with me, but he might lose his job because of it. This is a typical occupational obstruction. Many people would like to participate on retreats, but their job commitments will not allow it. This kind of obstruction is easy to remove if you have strong determination or deep karmic roots. You can always try to change your job or schedule. There was a pig farmer in Taiwan who died. His son and son-in-law took over the business, and because they were involved in killing they stopped coming to the temple. I told them to come anyway and to try to change professions down the road.

Retribution obstruction refers to karmic retribution. This usually refers to sentient beings in the lower realms. Even though some animals understand the Dharma, they cannot practice. Practice requires maintaining a certain posture, and humans are the only species that can do it. In special cases, retribution obstruction refers to humans who are severely disadvantaged and cannot practice. It also refers to people born in areas where there are no Dharma teachers. Where they are born is a consequence of karma, so it is considered a retribution obstruction.

Everyone, to a greater or lesser degree, has noumenal and phenomenal obstructions. It is the nature of being a sentient being. All we can do is persevere in our practice.

"Virtuous man, all sentient beings [intrinsically] actualize Complete Enlightenment. If they meet a good teacher and can rely on

> *his Dharma practice of the causal ground, [their karmic roots for*
> *attainments] will be either gradual or sudden. However, if they*
> *come across the Tathagata's unsurpassable bodhi and engage in the*
> *correct path of practice, they will attain Buddhahood whether they*
> *are of great or small [karmic] roots. If sentient beings, though they*
> *seek a good teacher, meet one with erroneous views, they will not*
> *gain correct awakening. These people are called ones of outer path*
> *nature. This fault is due to the teacher and not to sentient beings.*
> *"The above are the five distinct natures of sentient beings."*

Buddhism speaks of five natures, or categories, that sentient beings
fall into depending on the spiritual path they choose to follow.
Sravakas and pratyekabuddhas comprise the first two natures, both
of which are individual liberation paths. Bodhisattvas and Buddhas
comprise the third and fourth natures, both of which are Mahayana
Paths. These four natures include practitioners who fall within the
realm of Buddhism. The fifth nature refers to those who practice
Buddhism incorrectly or who follow paths outside of Buddhism.
The five natures encompass all sentient beings.

   Buddhism recognizes the validity of other religions. Any
religion that earns the respect, recognition, and faith of the people
and that is beneficial to humanity is a good religion. If a religion has
a long history and finds wide acceptance, it means that humanity
derives benefit from it. Therefore we cannot deny the usefulness of
other religions.

   A widely accepted religion must help maintain the stability of
personal life as well as the harmony of social life. Social life begins
with the family and extends to a society and nation. Religions offer
this stability by giving followers principles and concepts to believe
in and follow. Some religions speak of the power or will of God,
other religions speak of karma. It is difficult to achieve social
harmony without religion, although there will inevitably be oppor-
tunists who think only of personal gain without consideration for
others or for higher principles.

   A successful religion has as its basis a set of principles or
guidelines for behavior, and as its goal personal stability and social
harmony. All religions have a common denominator despite their

differences. They all set moral and ethical guidelines for human behavior. The specific points may differ, but the religions' general structures are similar in that they offer stability, hope, and consolation for their followers.

The differences that do exist among these religions constitute the difference between inner and outer paths from a Buddhist perspective. The conventional meaning of an outer path practitioner is anyone who follows a tradition other than Buddhism. The true meaning of outer path, however, refers to anyone who does not have a clear understanding of one's self-nature and who still seeks personal, material, or spiritual benefit. More to the point, it refers to anyone who is not in accordance with the Buddhist principle of emptiness. By this definition, most Buddhists are outer path practitioners.

The outer path includes the vast majority of human beings. Outer path followers can be divided into two main groups. The first consists of those people who cannot or do not accept Buddhism. Such people are unable to enter the inner path of Buddhism because their karma and beliefs lead them elsewhere. The second consists of those people within Buddhism whose karmic roots are not strong, who still pursue material and spiritual benefit for themselves. However, since they are already familiar with and accept Buddhist principles, it is easier for them to eventually move toward the inner path.

Thus, in the strict sense the outer path's definition, all sentient beings — with the exception of sravakas, pratyekabuddhas, bodhisattvas, and Buddhas — are outer path followers. The four inner path natures include practitioners who have reached the saintly stages of Buddhism. Among Buddhists, how many can claim this achievement? However, through practice Buddhists can eventually enter the inner paths, so we should neither feel discouraged nor consider "outer path" to be a derogatory term. It is not shameful to fall under this category.

Where sentient beings fall with respect to the five natures depends on the principles of cause and consequence (karma) and causes and conditions. It depends on what we have done and where our interests have been throughout our innumerable lifetimes.

Some have had extensive contact with Buddhadharma and have practiced a great deal; others have had little contact with Buddhadharma and have not practiced at all.

There are those who have had a lot of contact with Buddhism and have practiced extensively, but who do not have expansive hearts. They have not sincerely generated great vows to help other sentient beings. They strive to liberate themselves from suffering, not the whole of humanity. These are inner path practitioners of the individual liberation vehicle. These practitioners lack the strength to help others because of their karma. Here is an analogy. A young boy who is a strong swimmer is swept into a wide, deep river with two men who cannot swim. The men beg the boy to save them, but he cannot. He is too small, too weak. He may want to help them, but he is unable to do so. Likewise, the practice and karma of people only seeking their own liberation are not deep enough for them to help innumerable others. Eventually, with time and practice, they can move toward the Bodhisattva and Buddha Paths, just as the boy swimmer will grow into a strong young man who can save others from drowning. They are where they are because of past actions, but they do not have to remain that way forever.

Bodhisattvas and Buddhas are inner path practitioners because of their karmic nature. In terms of their practice, there are quantitative as well as qualitative differences. In Ch'an there is sudden enlightenment and gradual enlightenment. From a wider perspective, there is nothing superior about sudden enlightenment or inferior about gradual enlightenment. Here is another analogy. Suppose I have a five pound ball of steel in my bag and you have a one ounce spike of steel in yours. Both objects are steel, but yours is sharp as a needle and easily pokes a hole through the bag for everyone to see. People will say that the spike is superior because it leads to quick breakthroughs. My steel ball is invisible, but it's heavy. It may take longer, but it too will break through the bag. Same result. In fact, the ball will make a larger hole than the spike. The spike represents instantaneous enlightenment practice, whereas the ball represents gradual enlightenment practice. Gradual path followers direct their practice toward building a wide foundation, whereas sudden path followers direct their practice toward making breakthroughs.

One can say that people with Buddha karmic nature have sudden karmic nature, whereas people with bodhisattva karmic nature have gradual karmic nature. From the point of view of karma, one is not better than the other. Karmic nature is the consequence of whatever we have done in the past. We cannot place a value on karmic nature. Large-framed people may be stronger than small-framed people, but that does not make them superior. Strength is not the only desirable quality. There are situations where a small-framed person has an advantage. Similarly, we should not judge people according to which of the five different categories they fall into.

Although people who seek greater truths and spiritual levels will always set out seeking the highest, sometimes they end up on outer paths. This is because actions from previous lives push people in different directions. There is a story which tells of a monk who had just left home to seek a famous old Ch'an master who lived far away. He traveled thousands of miles. One day he saw an old monk in farmer's clothes tending a field and asked about the master's whereabouts. The old monk asked, "Why do you want to find him?" The young monk answered, "I want to be close to him and study with him." The older monk asked, "Would you like to study with me?" The young monk looked him over and was not impressed. He had an image of what a Ch'an master should be like and this man did not meet his standard, so he answered, "Not especially." The farmer monk replied, "In that case, I wouldn't look for that master. He's worse than I am."

The young monk did not realize that the old farmer was the Ch'an master he had been searching for. Disappointed, he sought advice elsewhere and people told him to live alone in the caves of distant mountains, eat wild grass, and wear only leaves for clothing. Living this natural way, they said, was befitting of a great practitioner. He did this for three years, without making progress. Living alone in this manner, he realized that he would never know if he made a breakthrough. Eventually he left, found the farmer master, and studied with him.

The point of this story is that this monk's karma led him to spend three years in the mountains practicing outer path ways but because he had strong inner path karma, eventually he came back to the master. If the outer path karma had been stronger, he would have had powerful personal experiences while in the mountains and would have been satisfied with that type of practice. He would never have found the master and would have abandoned Ch'an practice.

The erroneous views of outer paths stem from attachment, especially to gain and loss. For example, in one's practice one may develop supernormal powers, such as the ability to see across great distances, hear sounds beyond human range, or read minds. Such powers are great temptations. Those exposed to these powers who do not stray from their practice are rare. Most ordinary people would latch onto and misuse such powers because of greed and attachment to worldly benefits.

When I was practicing in the mountains, someone visited me. His father was dying, and he wanted my help. I told him I could make vows, transfer merit, and recite sutras. These things could help, but I could not guarantee that his father would recover. The man, however, wanted me to help in a direct way. I told him that I did not have such powers and that it was his father's karma that would dictate how things would turn out. The man went to another group who claimed to have supernormal powers, and when he arrived they said, "We were expecting you and already know about your father's situation. Give us $5000 and we'll take care of everything." He complied. Two months later his father died, and he demanded his money back. They scolded him, saying, "Because of our rituals your father was reborn in the heavens. You should thank us." He demanded proof. A man in the group performed some rituals. Then his voice changed to match the father's, and he chastised the son. The son was deeply moved and stayed with the group as a true believer.

We may consider this person gullible, but many skeptics have been converted by such cultic groups because some people do have supernormal powers. But if you follow such paths, even for the rest of your life, it does not mean that you will never turn back to Buddhadharma. It only means that at that time and stage of your practice, your karma led you in that direction. After that stage passes, your karma may lead you back to Buddhadharma.

If you are properly grounded in Buddhadharma, you will realize that there are many mysterious and wonderful phenomena and powers in the world, but that in the end they are of no genuine benefit. The benefit from the development of these powers might seem great, the advice based upon them might seem reliable, but such powers are transient. It is like borrowing money from the bank. You must always pay it back, with interest. To progress on any path, the effort must come from you. Any other way would be contradictory to the principle of cause and consequence. The goal of Buddhist practitioners is to practice and follow Buddhadharma and gradually move from the outer to inner path.

> *"Virtuous man, with great compassionate expedient methods, a bodhisattva enters the world to expand and mature [the minds of] the unenlightened. He manifests in various forms, amidst favorable or adverse situations so that he may work together with sentient beings in order to guide them to Buddhahood. In so doing, he relies entirely on the power of his pure vows made since beginningless time.*
>
> *"If sentient beings in the Dharma Ending Age can arouse the supreme thought of [awakening to] great Complete Enlightenment, they should make the pure great vow of bodhisattvas, declaring: 'May I, from now on, abide in Buddha's Complete Enlightenment, and may I, in my search for a good teacher, not meet outer paths and practitioners of the Two Vehicles. With their practice based on this vow, they will gradually sever all hindrances. When all hindrances are exhausted, their vows will be fulfilled. They will then ascend the pure Dharma hall of liberation and actualize the wondrous, august citadel of great Complete Enlightenment."*
>
> At that time, the World Honored One, wishing to clarify his meaning, proclaimed these gathas:
>
> Maitreya, you should know
> that sentient beings
> cannot attain great liberation

because of their craving and desire,
which cause them to fall into
the cycle of birth and death.
If they can sever like and dislike,
along with greed, anger, and delusion,
regardless of their difference in nature,
they will all accomplish the Buddha Path.
The two obstructions will also be permanently severed.
After correct awakening is attained
by meeting a good teacher,
one accords with the bodhisattva vow
and abides in the great nirvana.
All bodhisattvas in the ten directions,
relying on the great compassionate vow,
manifest the appearance of entering birth and death.
Practitioners now and
sentient beings in the Dharma Ending Age,
should diligently sever all attached views.
Then they will return to
great Complete Enlightenment.

I have already spoken about outer path practitioners. Pratyeka-buddhas and sravakas are followers of the individual liberation (Two Vehicles) path. In this section I will talk about bodhisattvas, followers of the Mahayana path.

All bodhisattvas make four great vows. They vow to help all sentient beings, to remove all obstructions and vexations, to master endless approaches to Dharma, and to attain supreme enlightenment. It is important that people who decide to follow the Bodhisattva Path take these four vows. It may seem that the vows are impossible to fulfill, but we must remember that before we have firmly generated the bodhi mind we are like seeds that have yet to sprout. We may not be able to carry out the vows; we may not be aware of the full meaning of the vows; we may not realize the necessity of following the Bodhisattva Path toward Buddhahood. Nonetheless we should take the four great vows.

Most people are not confident in themselves. They will not set goals that are too high because they feel they will be unable to reach them. Instead, they will set small goals and try to accomplish things one step at a time. As they reach each step, they will re-evaluate their progress and decide whether or not to set another goal. A person who is unsure of his or her intelligence and ability to do well in school, for example, may vow to graduate from high school. Having completed that stage, he or she may decide to try college and then graduate school.

Taking such measured steps is normal and good. After all, a person's life span, abilities, and merit (accumulated from previous karma) are limited. One may not be able to accomplish everything one sets out to do. However, taking one step at a time, it is difficult to gauge how far someone will go. One may reach a certain level and then stop, satisfied with where one is or too tired to go on. In general, those with good karmic foundations will have the confidence to set high goals right from the beginning.

It is unrealistic to assume that everyone will achieve the goals they set for themselves. There can be only so many presidents or billionaires. Human life is short and the obstacles are many. In making goals of this nature, it is probably better to take a step-by-step approach. However, one should not take the same approach when following the Bodhisattva Path and studying Buddhadharma. Deciding to go a little way and then figuring out what to do from there is the incorrect attitude when it comes to practice. Your worldly desires are limited to this lifetime, but the practice of Buddhadharma is endless. It spans countless future lives. Thus we are not limited by time or our present conditions and situations. There are no obstructions or difficulties that cannot eventually be overcome. Some may reach Buddhahood quickly. Others may take numberless eons. Since there is an endless amount of time in which to practice, however, we can have complete confidence that each and every one of us can reach the highest level.

I once had a friend who was not at all intelligent, but he made a vow that if he could get into a university, he would graduate. He said, "It may take me eight years instead of four, and I may have to study twice as much as everyone else, but I know I can do it." This kind of confidence is admirable. It is the kind of confidence needed to do well as a practitioner. We may feel we do not have good karmic roots or much merit, but it doesn't matter. If we are willing to work hard now, then we are already sowing the seeds for change in the future. Everyone knows the story of the turtle and the hare. The hare was by far the faster animal, but the turtle didn't care. It set its sight on the goal and went for it at its own pace. Similarly, practitioners — followers of the Dharma — should not become disillusioned. Set your aim for the highest goal and persist.

It is equally important not to take a lazy attitude and think that if there is limitless time, then one can enjoy oneself now and begin to practice at some future time. People cannot predict or guarantee where or what they will be in the future. Now we are human beings and have encountered the Dharma and see that it is something worth following. It is best to begin now, while we are in a good position to do so, and lay the foundation for a stronger and better practice in the future.

Of course, at the onset of practice, one cannot expect to carry out the vows as they are spoken. It would be impossible to help innumerable sentient beings in a single lifetime. However, in successive lifetimes, one's ability and influence will grow and widen until more and more sentient beings are reached. Therefore do not be concerned at the present time about whether or not you are helping innumerable people. Set the goal in your mind and begin to practice.

Another vow is to master limitless ways of approaching the Dharma. A bodhisattva uses many expedient means to help sentient beings. For the individual, only one method may be necessary, but there are innumerable beings with varying capacities. To help them it is necessary to employ a variety of tools. For example, I am teaching in America, so I must learn to communicate in English. When I studied in Japan I had to learn Japanese. Language is one tool. There are many others.

Naturally, anyone taking the great vows should gauge his or her abilities and act accordingly. In helping sentient beings, for instance, it would be wise to begin with those who are around you — family, friends, and acquaintances. If someone disregarded those who are dear to him and then talked about helping all sentient beings, starting with ants and roaches, he would be thinking in an inverted way. The sutras say that we should first aim to help those who are in a similar position as we, and from there expand outward to the best of our abilities.

In the chapter of the "Universal Door" in the *Lotus Sutra* it is explained that bodhisattvas manifest in innumerable incarnations to help all sentient beings. Bodhisattvas will assume forms and characteristics most suitable for helping a particular being. In this way they are able fully to convey the Dharma, bringing benefit to all sentient beings in whatever conditions they may be in.

We who are born in the human realm are in a unique and special position. We can communicate to others what we have learned about the Dharma. To the extent that we do this we can be considered incarnations of bodhisattvas. We may not see ourselves as such, but indeed we are already treading the Bodhisattva Path.

Typically those who place faith in bodhisattvas look to them for help and rely upon them. This is normal for people who do not have sufficient confidence in themselves. Genuine practitioners, however, should not only accept the guidance and help of bodhisattvas, but should also use what they have gained to help other sentient beings. I encourage practitioners to communicate — to the best of their abilities — what they have learned from the Dharma to others. This is the way of a bodhisattva.

Bodhisattva of
Pure Wisdom

Then the Bodhisattva of Pure Wisdom rose from his seat in the midst of the assembly, prostrated himself at the feet of the Buddha, circled the Buddha three times clockwise, knelt down, joined his palms, and said: "O World Honored One of great compassion! You have broadly expounded to us inconceivable things which we have never seen or heard before. Because of your excellent guidance, our bodies and minds are now at ease and we have gained great benefit. For the sake of all practitioners of the Dharma who have come here, please expound again the nature of the Dharma King's complete and fulfilling enlightenment. What are differences in the actualization and attainment between all sentient beings, bodhisattvas, and the World Honored Tathagata? [Pray teach us] so that sentient beings in the Dharma Ending Age, upon hearing this holy teaching, may follow and conform to it, be awakened, and gradually enter [the realm of Buddhahood]." Having said these words, he prostrated himself on the ground. He made the same request three times, each time repeating the same procedure.

At that time the World Honored One said to the Bodhisattva of Pure Wisdom: "Excellent, excellent! Virtuous man, for the benefit of sentient beings in the Dharma Ending Age, you have asked the Tathagata about the distinct progressive stages [of practice]. Listen attentively now. I shall explain them to you."

Hearing this, the Bodhisattva of Pure Wisdom was filled with joy and listened silently along with the assembly.

> *"Virtuous man, the intrinsic nature of Complete Enlighten-*
> *ment is devoid of distinct natures [as described before], yet all*
> *different natures are endowed with this nature [of Complete*
> *Enlightenment], which can accord and give rise to various*
> *natures. [Since these two natures are non-dual], there is neither*
> *attainment nor actualization. In Absolute Reality, there are*
> *indeed no bodhisattvas or sentient beings. Why? Because*
> *bodhisattvas and sentient beings are illusory projections. When*
> *illusory projections are extinguished, there exists no one who*
> *attains or actualizes. For example, eyes cannot see themselves.*
> *Likewise, this nature is intrinsically impartial and equal, yet there*
> *is no 'one' who is equal.*
>
> *"Because sentient beings are confused, they are unable to*
> *eliminate and extinguish all illusory projections. Because of the*
> *illusory efforts and activities of those who extinguish and those*
> *who do not extinguish [vexations], there manifest distinctions. If*
> *one can attain accordance with the Tathagata's quiescent-extinc-*
> *tion, there is in reality neither quiescent-extinction nor the one*
> *who experiences it."*

In these paragraphs the Buddha speaks of the distinctions between
sentient beings, Buddhas, and bodhisattvas from the standpoint of
non-distinction. From the Buddha's perspective, it is only because
sentient beings discriminate that distinctions arise. The Buddha
himself makes no distinctions among beings. However, it is impossible for us to conceptualize this directly, so in order to talk about
non-distinction we must make distinctions.

Distinction and non-distinction are based on the Buddhist
concept of nature. Nature in this sense is not the environment
around us but rather the fundamental essence of things. According
to Chinese thought, there are two facets of this essential nature:
that which is common or shared among all things and that which is
different or unique. For example, all birds have certain shared
characteristics that identify them as birds — they have feathers,
beaks, wings, etc. Yet there are many different species, each with its
unique adaptations and behaviors. Some eat meat, some eat seeds,
some live in forests, some live near water. Furthermore, there are

different varieties within each species, and if we look closely enough we will find that each individual bird has its own unique qualities.

Distinctions between people and things arise from their individual natures, and the lack of distinction arises from their common nature. It is impossible to ignore differences. For instance, men and women can say anything they want about the sexes being equal, but only women can bear children. One cannot take distinctions that exist and turn them into non-distinctions. Everything in the world has its own place, its own characteristics. We cannot reduce the world to one undifferentiated mass.

It is because things are different that there can be interaction between them. A married couple once complained to me that they fight too much. I told them that if a baby cries, it means it is healthy and strong but in need of something; if it never cries, something is probably wrong. Similarly, if a couple argues, it is a sign of health. At least they are making clear what their problems are.

The world works in just such a manner. When different things come into contact, they either blend together or grate against each other. Either way, something new is produced from the interaction. It is because of differences between things that interactions take place. Nothing stays the same. Everything is in a dynamic process of constant transformation. Distinctions, however, are never apart from non-distinction. No matter how different two birds may be, they are still birds. Within distinction there is non-distinction.

About thirty years ago I watched a Chinese man sit next to an American woman at a lecture. She moved away, and he followed because he wanted to speak to her. She turned around and called him a jack-ass. Perhaps in the United States at that time Americans considered Asians ignorant. Now, when I return to Taiwan, some people say, "Why do you waste your time teaching Americans? They're too stupid to learn Buddhadharma." People always make distinctions based on differences and have been doing so for ages.

I have been talking about distinctions from a conventional standpoint. The sutra, on the other hand, speaks of the intrinsic and essential nature, or self-nature, of things. This self-nature has no distinctions whatsoever. It is undifferentiated and unmoving. This is difficult to grasp, so I will use a crude analogy. Substances exist in one of three states: solid, liquid, or gas. Water can be steam, liquid, or ice, depending on conditions. However, its molecular composition remains the same. Its essence remains the same even though its appearance changes. The essential nature that the Buddha speaks of is also unchanging. Phenomena change and interact, but essential nature does not. Phenomena arise and perish through causes and conditions. They are impermanent. They "exist" only in transformation and interaction with other phenomena. They have no real existence in and of themselves. That is why the Buddha calls them empty illusions. Just as liquid, steam, and ice are different manifestations of water, so living beings are of one essential nature.

Saying that all things are the same does not mean that everything is identical. Differences appear to arise between things because of causes and conditions. Fundamentally, however, there are no distinctions. All sentient beings are fully endowed with the nature of Complete Enlightenment. Yet, sentient beings are deluded. We allow ourselves to be influenced by our habitual patterns of fixations and surrounding environment. When the surrounding environment interacts with our senses, our habitual patterns of fixations stir up and we make distinctions. Intellectually, one may accept that there are no distinctions in the world, but as a result of delusion and attachment one cannot help but get caught up in them. We are swayed by conditions and are thus transformed and changed. Therefore, we too are illusory, just like everything we experience and everything that can be known — bodhisattvas and sentient beings alike. Therefore, the Sutra states, "In Absolute Reality, there are indeed no bodhisattvas or sentient beings. Why? Because bodhisattvas and sentient beings are illusory projections."

The Buddha was compassionate in telling us that there originally is no distinction. But even our perception of non-distinction is impure and with distinctions. If we think self-nature is something that we can find or gain, then we have already made distinctions and will be unable to experience it. We will be caught in deluded thinking again. We must see the non-distinction that is presently in the midst of distinction. This is the essential nature the Buddha speaks of.

"*Virtuous man, all sentient beings since beginningless time have deludedly conceived 'self' and that which grasps on to the self; never have they known the succession of arising and perishing thoughts! Therefore, they give rise to love and hatred and indulge in the five desires.*

"*If they meet a good teacher who guides them to awaken to the nature of pure Complete Enlightenment and to recognize these arising and perishing [thoughts], they will understand that it is the very nature of such rising [thoughts] that causes toils and anxieties in their lives.*

"*If, further, a man permanently severs all toil and anxiety, he will realize the dharmadhatu in its purity. However, his understanding of purity may become his obstruction and he will not attain freedom and ease regarding Complete Enlightenment. This is called 'the ordinary man's accordance with the nature of enlightenment.'*

"*Virtuous man, all bodhisattvas realize that this very understanding is a hindrance. Although they sever themselves from this hindrance of understanding, they still abide in this realization. The realization of hindrance is yet another hindrance. Therefore they do not have freedom and ease. This is called 'the bodhisattva before the stage of the first bhumi's accordance with the nature of enlightenment.'*

"*Virtuous man, 'attaining' illumination and realization is a hindrance. Thus a great bodhisattva is constantly in realization without abidance, where the illumination and the illuminator simultaneously become quiescent and vanish. For instance, if a man beheads himself, there exists no executioner after the head has been severed. It is the same with eliminating various hindrances with a mind of hindrance: when the hindrances have been eliminated, there is no eliminator. The teachings of the sutras are like the finger that points to the moon. When one sees the moon, one realizes that the finger is not the moon. Likewise, the various teachings of all Tathagatas in instructing bodhisattvas are also like this. This is called 'the bodhisattva above the stage of the first bhumi's accordance with the nature of enlightenment.'"*

The Bodhisattva Path can be divided into three levels. The first describes bodhisattvas who are still at the level of the common person. That is the level of the "Ten Faiths." The second describes bodhisattvas who are at the level of the "Ten Abidances," the "Ten Practices," and the "Ten Transferences." The third describes bodhisattvas who are at the stage of the "Ten Bhumis," or ten grounds. Actually, one can speak of a fourth level consisting of people who have not even heard of Buddhadharma. Thus, in a sense there are four levels.

Those people who have not yet heard of Buddhadharma, or who are aware of it but lack faith in it, have not attained the first level of the Bodhisattva Path. They still have a strong sense of self, of who they are and what belongs to them. What they believe to be the self is actually the progression of thoughts through the mind, a progression which creates the illusion of a solid and enduring entity. Most people think a self consists of a body and its needs in conjunction with one's ideas, opinions, views, and feelings. People form their likes and dislikes toward themselves, other people, and things on these bases. If things go right and they get what they want, they feel good. If their desires are not satisfied, they feel badly.

The body and mind have needs. You may long for a life with no responsibilities and worries, but if you were to eat and sleep and do nothing else for the rest of your life, I doubt you would be happy. You would long for something to do to keep yourself occupied. If the mind is not occupied, it feels uncomfortable. The same is true for the body.

I knew a woman who had to take care of a wealthy couple's child and dog. The couple lived far away, so the woman was away from her own home, family, and friends most of the time. All she did was look after the baby and dog. She told me she was going crazy with boredom, so I told her that I once spent six years alone in the mountains. She asked, "Didn't you go crazy? What did you do to pass the time?" From the woman's point of view, what I did for six years was incomprehensible.

Realizing that their bodies and lives change constantly, some people wonder, "If the body always changes, can I really call it myself?" They conclude that there must be something else other than the body that is the self — a spirit or soul. But is this spirit or soul the self? If we look, what we find is a series of seemingly connected thoughts. But they are always changing. At which point do we say, "This thought is me, this is myself?" Can we point to something clear and substantial and say that it is the self thinking these thoughts?

The person who accepts all that has been said up to this point is ready to accept the Buddhist view that the body and mind come together through the combination of causes and conditions. The person who accepts Buddhadharma is ready to practice. Through practice one can gradually come to the realization of what the Dharma teaches: that the body and mind are not permanent; that everything changes from moment to moment; that nothing can be called "self." These are the three seals of Dharma. Realizing this, such a person can become free of attachment. To most, this freedom would be the final destination of practice, but if one feels that one has left behind vexations and attained freedom, that is also an obstruction.

In the course of practice, you may experience a feeling of ease and freedom from physical discomfort and desire. At this point you may mistakenly believe you have attained liberation. This is quite common among practitioners. At first they do not have any experiences. Then they experience the sensation of physical lightness, comfort, peacefulness, and purity. These are obstructions that block the practitioner from liberation.

Someone asked me what liberation felt like. I answered, "When you attain liberation there is no attachment to feeling. If you have some kind of feeling, you have not attained liberation."

Then the person quoted a line from the *Diamond Sutra:* "Non-abiding, the mind arises." She thought that non-abiding referred to liberation, and the mind arising suggested that there was still feeling present.

I answered, "If there is a feeling of the state you are in, then that is abiding, and therefore you have not attained liberation. It is impossible to explain what liberation feels like. You must experience it yourself." Many people cannot comprehend this. They think the feeling of purity and freedom is already non-abiding, liberation. These are, in fact, obstructions, and such people are still at the first level of the Bodhisattva Path.

The second level refers to the next thirty steps of the Bodhisattva Path consisting of the Ten Abidances, the Ten Practices, and the Ten Transferences. At this level, although bodhisattvas are in the position of sages, and are aware that feelings of purity and freedom are not liberation, they are attached to the understanding that these feelings are not liberation. This attachment too is an obstruction.

It is impossible for an ordinary person to discern what level a practitioner is at, but for a Ch'an master or an advanced practitioner it takes only one or two sentences to know the nature of another's mind. For instance, if one asks, "Have you experienced enlightenment?" and another answers, "Well, I can't say for sure, but it felt like it," that person is still at the first level.

A long-time practitioner who felt that he had had an enlightenment experience ten years earlier told me of his experience. He asked if I would certify it as such, so I asked him, "As far as fame, self-benefit, or sex are concerned, how do you feel?"

The man answered, "My mind is always free. At all times I am detached, but my body still has needs." This person is still at the first level of practice.

There is a story from the Ch'an historical record that is considered a kung-an. Master Weishan (771-853) asked two disciples, "A trillion lions appeared simultaneously on the tip of a single hair. How was this possible?" For the average person, this would be ridiculous, but for the disciples who had been practicing, this was not such an outrageous idea.

The first disciple, Yangshan (807-883) (who later formed the Wei Yang school), replied, "A strand of hair has two tips on it. Which tip are you talking about?"

The other disciple replied, "There is no before or after, no this end or that end. How could you ask such a question?"

Some might think the second disciple smart, but Yangshan shook his head no. So Master Weishan asked him, "What do you say about this?" Yangshan stood up and left. The master turned to the other disciple and said, "You are finished. Your lion has been cut in half. It is a dead lion!"

The second disciple said there was no before or after, no above or below, but he still had a middle — the present. He was still attached to an idea of totality and so was at the second level. Ch'an advocates passing through the first and second levels and going directly to the third level arrive at sudden enlightenment. On the third level of the Bodhisattva Path, the enlightened person and the illumination from the wisdom of the enlightened person both disappear. Here, illumination does not refer to a special state of mind, but rather to the every function and action of a truly enlightened being. If you feel you are enlightened and that through your great wisdom you can save sentient beings, then you are, at best, at the second level.

When one arrives at the third level, the highest mountain and lowest valley are the same. From the point of view of a satellite in space, the highest point in the Himalayas is actually the lowest point. Everything is inverted. The satellite views from top to bottom. How can one say which is high or low? The *Lotus Sutra* speaks of Bodhisattva Never Disparaging, who sees all sentient beings as Buddhas. He sees himself as a common man and everyone else as a bodhisattva who, in asking him for help, is in fact helping him toward liberation.

What level bodhisattvas are at depends on their mental states. If they think everyone is being saved by them, then they are discriminating between subject and object. Therefore they are still at the first level. If in their minds they do not feel that way, they are at the second level.

For people at the third level, there is no sense or trace of enlightenment, no sense that they are enlightened beings, no sense of the illumination of their wisdom. Others may see them as enlightened beings, but that is the point of view of others, not their own. At this level they do not have vexations or wisdom.

At the third level there is no need to sever vexations because there is no such thing. There is no seeking wisdom because there is no such thing. There is no need to become a Buddha because there is no such thing.

A monk asked a Ch'an master, "What is a Buddha?"

The master laughed and said, "Find me a Buddha and I'll beat him to death with a stick and feed him to the dogs!" The master is at the third level because he has no attachment to an idea of Buddha. At the beginning of the first level, we must still believe that there are vexations to sever, liberation to attain and Buddhas to become. Thus, there is no point in our trying to imagine what the third level may be like.

> "Virtuous man, all hindrances are themselves [the nature of]
> ultimate enlightenment. Having a [correct] thought or losing it is
> not different from liberation. Conglomeration and dispersion of
> dharmas are both called nirvana. Wisdom and stupidity are
> equally prajna. The Dharma accomplished by bodhisattvas and
> that by outer path practitioners are both bodhi. Ignorance and
> true suchness are not different realms. [The threefold discipline of]
> sila, samadhi, and prajna and [the three poisons of] greed, anger,
> and delusion are all pure activities. Sentient beings and the world
> they live in are of one Dharma-nature. Hells and heavens are all
> Pure Lands. Regardless of [their distinct] natures, all sentient
> beings have [intrinsically] accomplished the Buddha Path. All
> vexations are ultimate liberation. [The Tathagata's] ocean of
> wisdom which encompasses the whole dharmadhatu clearly
> illuminates all phenomena as empty space. This is called 'the
> Tathagata's accordance with the nature of enlightenment.'
>
> "Virtuous man, all bodhisattvas and sentient beings in the
> Dharma Ending Age should at no time give rise to deluded
> thoughts! [Yet], when their deluded minds arise, they should not
> extinguish them. In the midst of deluded concepts, they should not
> add discriminations. Amidst nondiscrimination, they should not
> distinguish true reality. If sentient beings, upon hearing this
> Dharma method, believe in, understand, accept, and uphold it
> and do not generate alarm and fear, they are 'in accordance with
> the nature of enlightenment.'
>
> "Virtuous man, you should know that these sentient beings
> have made offerings to hundreds of thousands of millions of
> Buddhas and great bodhisattvas as innumerable as the grains of

*sand of the Ganges, and have planted the roots of all merits. I say
that such people will accomplish the [Buddha's] Wisdom of All
Aspects."*

At that time, the World Honored One, wishing to clarify his
meaning, proclaimed these gathas:

*Pure Wisdom, you should know
that the nature of perfect bodhi
is without attainment or actualization.
It is without bodhisattvas or sentient beings.
However, when there is enlightenment
and unenlightenment,
there are distinct progressive stages.
Sentient beings are obstructed by understanding.
Bodhisattvas [before the first bhumi]
have not left behind realization.
[Once] they enter the first bhumi
there is permanent quiescent-extinction
with no abidance in any form.
Great enlightenment, being complete,
is called 'pervasive accordance.'
If sentient beings in the Dharma Ending Age
do not give rise to deluded thoughts,
the Buddha says that they are
bodhisattvas in this very lifetime.
Having made offerings to countless Buddhas
as innumerable as the sands of the Ganges,
their merits are perfected.
Though expedients are many,
all are called in accordance with wisdom.*

Concluding his answer to Bodhisattva of Pure Wisdom, the Buddha
expounds the principle of non-discrimination. All hindrances and
obstructions are identical with Complete Enlightenment and the
highest bodhi. Vexations are bodhi, samsara is nirvana. One must
realize, however, that this is the perception of the Buddha, not that
of ordinary sentient beings.

It would be unwise for ordinary sentient beings to adopt the

views of a Buddha without having had the direct experience of
enlightenment. We must still recognize the differences between
unenlightened people and bodhisattvas. We should understand that
because of our vexations we are immersed in samsara; because they
have no vexations, Buddhas and bodhisattvas have transcended
samsara. That is our understanding, the conventional understanding
of ordinary sentient beings.

It is impossible for ordinary sentient beings to understand
what the Buddha knows. We can try to understand intellectually
that vexation and bodhi are identical, but to truly understand it we
must start from the beginning and walk the Buddha Path of practice. Eventually we can progress and come to know what the
Buddha perceived. This is the safest way. If we were to start by
proclaiming that vexations are bodhi, samsara is nirvana, and
sentient beings are the same as Buddhas, then we would quickly and
easily give rise to wrong thinking and to inverted views about the
Dharma.

In Buddhist texts we often come across the words "hindrances" and "obstructions." One may say that hindrances and
obstructions are those things that prevent us from doing what we
want to do and accomplishing what we wish to accomplish. We
might blame hindrances on any number of things, such as the
environment or our lack of ability, but there is really no one and
nothing to blame but ourselves.

An American woman told me about her pilgrimage to holy
places in India. She does not speak any of the Indian languages, and
many of the places she visited are very difficult to reach. She had to
traverse long distances along perilous roads and paths. She was
warned that many people each year who attempt these pilgrimages
die from mud slides, storms, accidents, and diseases. It was a dangerous trip, yet this woman went. She is no superwoman. She is
similar to everyone here. All she possessed was the determination
and will to accomplish her goal, and so she did.

Anyone can do what this woman did. People like her are not
special. They have not received special grace from the gods. They
are not protected by deities or guardian angels. They are ordinary
people who set their minds on doing something and then do it.

Other people who think they cannot do such things view these people as special or extraordinary. These admirers could do the same, but they feel hindered, obstructed, incapable, unworthy.

There is a Chinese fable about a man who lived in the mountains and worked in the fields. Directly in front of his house was a mountain that blocked his way. No matter what he wished to do, he had to walk around the mountain to get to where he wanted to go. One day he made up his mind to move the mountain. People laughed at him and told him it was a futile endeavor, but he persisted. He said the magnititude of the undertaking did not concern him; he would move the mountain rock by rock. He had the rest of his life, and his children and their children could continue the job if they wished to.

Here is another story, to illustrate that determination need not be on such a grand scale. I have a disciple in Taiwan who, for a few years, expressed the strong desire to become a monk. Just recently he told me he was getting married. I asked why. He said that for years he had been in love with a particular woman and wished to marry her and no one else. She, however, would not return his love. He decided that if he could not have this woman, he would become a monk. Even while he lived at the temple, he continued to write to her. Through the years they stayed in contact and remained friends. A while back she was in a serious car accident and was hospitalized for several months. He visited her every day. She fell eventually in love with him.

Obstructions exist only in our own minds. We are unable to accomplish things because we think that we do not have the ability, understanding, confidence, or determination. It is because we think such things that we do not succeed or even try to succeed. We feel that we are inferior and give up before we even begin. If we refuse to let ourselves be influenced by negative ideas, set a goal, and work towards it, we will be successful. We may not accomplish the highest goal we set, but we will achieve something close to it. Something is better than nothing or not having tried at all.

Many people lack determination and persistence. They go down one path, become discouraged, and try another. This process go on and on, and these people never take one path to its final destination. They spend their lives giving up, until they are too old to try at all, and through it all, they try to convince themselves that they will succeed the next time. For these people there will never truly be a next time. Their negative thoughts stop them as soon as they start down a path.

At other times, people act as if they are wearing blinders. It seems their vision is blocked or clouded by demons, but these demons are not external beings. If they were, they would be easy to deal with. These demons are created by their own minds. They are the demons of doubt and lack of determination. These are the demons that keep us from achieving our goals.

The Buddha differs from us in that he does not let his mind block him from what he wants to do. We may blame things on the weather, our family and friends, our job, our age or our physical condition, but they are all excuses. People are always telling me they cannot practice and meditate because of this and that. They are convinced that it is something external that prevents them from practicing. The fact is, if they truly had the determination to practice, nothing would stop them. They do not practice because they are obstructed by their own minds. Any other reason is an excuse.

The sutra says that obstructions are identical with enlightenment. This is true, but it is not meaningful to the unenlightened. I have said that through the practice of meditation one can elevate one's wisdom. Someone who heard me say this told me that he did not need to meditate because he learned by making errors — that the mistakes themselves were the key to wisdom. In making mistakes and suffering, this person learned not to repeat such actions. I replied that what he did was good, but if he had practiced meditation, then he might not have made those mistakes in the first place. He need not have paid the price of learning the hard way — by experiencing mistakes and the suffering that comes from them.

Through meditation we can learn to avoid making mistakes. We may not know this from our vantage point, but we can study the teachings of great practitioners to see that it is so. Without their experience and without the teaching and guidance of those who have traveled the path of practice, it would be virtually impossible for us to make the journey ourselves. The path is difficult enough even for those who have the good fortune to study under a master's guidance. It was true for the ancients and it is true for us. For some people it is difficult or even impossible to begin right away with meditation. These people must go through much hardship and become more wholesome, complete human beings before beginning to meditate.

The obstructions mentioned in the sutra are not just mental obstructions. They also refer to karmic obstructions. Karmic obstructions may manifest in any number of ways. Your environment or job may make it difficult for you to practice meditation well. A karmic obstruction can be anything in your life that limits your body and mind. For instance, in Taiwan I lectured one Saturday to an audience of roughly sixty people. Of those sixty, only four were men. One of the men asked why it was so. I said that perhaps it was because many men in Taiwan work all week long and set aside Saturdays for chores and errands. The men at the lecture did not have heavy karmic obstructions.

Why, then, does the sutra say that obstructions are identical to enlightenment? On one level, obstructions provide us with the opportunity to accumulate merit and to increase our determination. In spite of obstructions — mental or karmic — we can still persist in our practice. This is not easy. It requires strength, will, inner faith, and confidence. We can either be like grass or bamboo. If you place a rock on a patch of grass, the grass will die. If you do the same to bamboo, it will snake around the rock and continue to grow and flourish. It will even generate new shoots. The rock does not hinder the bamboo. If we can persist in our practice, we will be stronger when hindrances and obstructions arise.

In the Buddha's past lives, when he was a bodhisattva, there was one person in particular who routinely appeared and made it difficult for him to practice. Life after life he gave the Buddha problems. After the Buddha had achieved Complete Enlightenment, he praised this man and said that without the hindrances he created, it would have taken him much longer to reach Buddhahood.

There is a saying that a person who practices should be like a stupid mosquito trying to draw blood from an iron bull. The mosquito's efforts are in vain, yet it persists. We should be as persistent in our practice. If we give up and try something else, or if we rationalize our failure, we will get nowhere. We must come to realize that it is the self who wishes to practice and the self that creates these problems. If we persist, these problems or obstructions will disappear. When obstructions disappear, the self-centeredness will be gone as well. We could also say it the other way. We practice until the self is gone. When the self disappears, all obstructions will be gone too. There cannot be a self that is free from all obstructions. If there is a sense of self, then there are also obstructions. There cannot be obstructions without a self to create and experience them, because the self is an obstruction. This is non-discrimination of the highest order.

The sutra speaks of many paired opposites — nirvana and samsara, wisdom and ignorance, vexation and bodhi — and says they are all the same. To the unenlightened, this is unimaginable. To the enlightened, it is just so. To realize what the enlightened perceive we must practice and persist through all hesitations and difficulties. We should not let our minds of doubt weaken and deter us. Furthermore, we should not be afraid of or worry about karmic obstructions. They provide us with opportunities to change and improve ourselves. If we trip and fall over of these obstructions, it is all right. We should get up and continue on and try to learn from it. If we fall again, we should get up again, no matter how many times it takes.

We should realize that whenever we feel blocked, it is our own minds that block us. If we cannot understand this, it will be difficult to remove any obstruction. Once we realize that the obstructions are in our minds, it becomes easy to remove them. Do not fear karmic obstructions. They help us in our practice. They provide us with the impetus to grow.

It may seem I have contradicted myself in these paragraphs and in so doing have confused you. It's quite all right. View it as an obstruction and use it to grow.

Bodhisattva
at Ease in Majestic Virtue

Then the Bodhisattva at Ease in Majestic Virtue rose from his seat in the midst of the assembly, prostrated himself at the feet of the Buddha, circled the Buddha three times clockwise, knelt down, joined his palms, and said: "O World Honored One of great compassion! For our sake you have extensively clarified the different ways of according with the nature of enlightenment and caused the enlightened minds of the multitude of bodhisattvas to be illuminated. Hearing your perfect voice, we have gained great benefit without cultivation.

"World Honored One, a great city has four gates. People coming from different directions have more than one entrance. Likewise, all bodhisattvas who embellish the Buddha Lands and attain bodhi do so by means of more than one single expedient method. Please, World Honored One, broadly expound to us all the expedient methods and stages as well as how many types of practitioners there are, so that bodhisattvas in this assembly and sentient beings in the Dharma Ending Age who aspire to the Mahayana may quickly attain enlightenment, and roam and play in the Tathagata's ocean of great quiescent-extinction." Having said these words, he prostrated himself on the ground. He made the same request three times, each time repeating the same procedure.

At that time the World Honored One said to the Bodhi-
sattva at Ease in Majestic Virtue: "Excellent, excellent! Virtuous
man, for the benefit of the multitude of bodhisattvas and sentient
beings in the Dharma Ending Age, you have asked the Tathagata
about such expedient methods. Listen attentively now. I shall
explain it to you."

Hearing this, the Bodhisattva at Ease in Majestic Virtue was
filled with joy and listened silently along with the assembly.

"Virtuous man, unsurpassable wondrous enlightenment
pervades all ten directions. From it arise the Tathagatas and all
dharmas, which are equal and identical to one another and of the
same substance. [Likewise], the various methods of cultivation are,
in reality, not different [from one another]. Though there are
countless expedient methods for becoming attuned to the nature of
enlightenment, if one categorizes them according to their different
natures, there are three kinds.

"Virtuous man, if, after awakening to pure Complete
Enlightenment, bodhisattvas with pure enlightened minds engage
in the cultivation of stillness, they will cleanse and settle all
thoughts. Becoming aware of the agitation and restlessness of
consciousness, they will cause their wisdom of stillness to manifest.
Their bodies and minds, [which will be realized as adventitious]
guests and dust will be permanently extinguished. Inwardly they
will experience lightness and ease in quiescence and stillness.
Because of this quiescence and stillness, the minds of all Tathagatas
in all ten directions will be revealed like reflections in a mirror.
This expedient is called samatha."

Representing all bodhisattvas, Bodhisattva at Ease in Majestic Virtue
raises a question. Even though the ultimate goal for all bodhisattvas
is the same, he asks the Buddha to explain the many different gates
through which each one can enter into Complete Enlightenment.
The Buddha concurs, saying that the Buddhadharma is indeed
universal, that there are no differences to be distinguished within it.
Nonetheless, the methods of practice and gates of entry are innumerable. If one were to classify the methods, however, they would
fall into three categories. The first is *samatha*, the second, *samapatti*,
and the third, dhyana.

Samatha is a method of gradual practice and enlightenment. Its purpose is to help practitioners progress from mental confusion to concentration to the stage of no-mind. Ch'an Master Yongjia Xuanjue (665-713) said that the practice of samadhi begins with *samatha. Samatha* aims at directly stilling the mind.

People who have just started to practice always encounter difficulties. Either their minds are scattered and they cannot calm down, or they become tired and drowsy, or they are too eager and generate a variety of illusory sensations. If such people have good teachers or a solid theoretical understanding of practice, they can free themselves from these obstacles. However, if they do not have a firm understanding or someone to properly guide them, they may begin to think they are in a better position than they really are and subsequently fall into truly demonic states.

There is a difference between karmic obstructions and demonic obstruction. Karmic obstructions arise from one's negative karma created in the past. They manifest when causes and conditions are ripe or because of intense practice, which you may say "speeds up" their time of manifestation and dissolution. Demonic obstructions are forces external to oneself. They also manifest because of serious practice, especially when one is deriving power from the practice. To put it simply, if one is about to jump out of the palm of Mara — to be free from samsara — Mara would get pretty angry and nervous! Therefore, depending on the practitioner's level of practice, either Mara would send his retinues, to distract or harm the practitioner, or he would go himself — as in the case of Sakyamuni Buddha. Practitioners often ask me what they should do if they find themselves in either one of the situations. Usually, I tell them to ignore whatever arises in their minds or to view whatever arises as empty. However, to view things as empty is difficult for people. Therefore, one should thoroughly familiarize oneself with the teachings of conditioned arising, or causes and conditions, and learn to integrate this understanding in one's life. To view experiences as empty means not to attach to them. In fact, only when one has a firm understanding of emptiness can one ignore whatever arises in one's practice and keep on with the practice. This is not self denial. It is a direct way of dealing with situations that arise during practice. In fact, it is precisely the practice of stilling the mind, or *samatha*.

When I was in Japan, I visited a Soto temple. When I asked the teacher what methods he taught, he said *shikantaza*, which means "just sitting." So I asked, "What do you keep in your mind?" He answered, "Nothing. Not to have one thought in one's mind is our method." Then I asked, "Can you really keep from having any thoughts in your mind?" He replied, "No, but whenever a thought arises you just ignore it and check whether your posture is correct."

With *shikantaza*, one is concerned only with sitting. Thoughts may arise in your mind, but you just forget about them. It is especially important not to take an opposing attitude towards thoughts. The purpose of the method is to free your mind from everything that occupies it. Thoughts that appear are not to be bothered with. You simply let them go and check your posture. It is an excellent method. Practitioners who use *shikantaza* sit well in a physical sense. They don't slouch or lean to one side.

There are sayings in the Ch'an sect that illustrate this principle. It is said that when you sit firmly on your cushion, keeping an upright posture, you can beat all thoughts to death. If you can refrain from being attached to thoughts which enter your mind while remaining conscious and alert, you will experience your Dharmakaya coming alive. In other words, you will see your Buddha-nature. In fact, *shikantaza* is not a "method." You don't try to deal with your vexations. You simply sit upright, and eventually all vexations leave the mind of their own accord.

Keeping your mind quiet is comparable to a windy day on a lake. As long as there is wind, there are waves, but when the wind disappears, so do the waves. When the mind becomes pure and still, it disappears; then there is no mind and body. There is nothing that comes out of the interaction between body and mind. You are calm and stable. When everything is clear, there are no vexations. This is wisdom. It is no different from the Buddha's mind.

To ignore problems when they arise, at least in the context of practice, is *samatha*. It is not easy to do. On the other hand, you should not ignore problems in everyday life. Most people seek to avoid or escape problems. They may get drunk, or look for some kind of excitement, or try to block their mind from dwelling on problems. You can overcome problems temporarily with these methods, but it is not "ignoring" in the *samatha* sense. *Samatha* is a meditation method. During meditation, problems that arise in your mind are thoughts and should be ignored. Ignoring them does not mean blocking them; rather, you note them and then drop them. You do not let wandering thoughts go on and on. You do not let yourself fall asleep on the cushion. Allowing thoughts to continue and falling asleep are not ways of "ignoring problems." You should check your posture and maintain mindfulness. The aim of *samatha* is to still the mind directly, to control the mind and its thoughts. The aim is not to build more barriers or to become lazy.

If you practice *samatha* correctly, eventually your mind will rest on one subject, that is, thoughts may still arise, one after the other, but they will all be the same thought. If, in fact, the mind stops on one thought and no longer moves, it is samadhi. While one practices *samatha*, there is no contact with the environment or other people. You are in meditation, with your mind on one thought.

There are subtle levels of movement and thought pattern in our consciousness. Prior to a deep enlightenment experience, all thoughts are governed or tainted by self-cherishing, self-referential notions. In the course of meditation practice, we can be aware of these movements and patterns. We will also be aware of the agitation and restlessness of out thoughts. In fact, all these movements are caused by our self-attachments nurtured by our discriminating mind — the sixth "consciousness". There is a clear distinction between what the sutra states, "becoming aware of the agitation and restlessness of consciousness" and of mere movement of thought. A practitioner can only be aware of the agitation and restlessness of consciousness after his or her mind is quite settled, free from wandering and scattered thoughts. When one's thoughts have subsided, one will realize that all thoughts arise from the activity of the sixth consciousness; whatever we are experiencing at this very moment is just this mind! There is absolutely nothing graspable or fixed about it. Only when both the coarse movements of thought and the subtle movements of consciousness are both still can wisdom manifest. This is the practice of *samatha* according to *The Sutra of Complete Enlightenment.*

> *"Virtuous man, if, after awakening to pure Complete Enlighten-ment, bodhisattvas with pure enlightened minds realize the nature of mind and realize that the six sense faculties and sense objects are illusory projections, they will then generate illusion as a means to eliminate illusion. Causing transformations and manifestations among illusions, they will enlighten illusory sentient beings. By generating illusions, they will experience lightness and ease in great compassion. All bodhisattvas who practice in such a manner will advance gradually. That which contemplates illusion is different from illusion itself. Nevertheless, contemplating illusion is itself an illusion. When all illusions are permanently left behind, the wondrous cultivation completed by such bodhisattvas may be compared to the sprouting of seeds from soil. This expedient is called samapatti."*

At a higher level there is *samapatti*, which literally means "equally arriving." It is a stage where bodhisattvas do not depart from *samatha* and samadhi, yet they still interact with the world. They are in a state of stillness, which is *samatha*, but they continue to perform functions, among them compassionate acts for sentient beings. When one practices *samapatti* well, there is nothing inside or outside one's mind, yet the existence of objects is not negated. One still responds to the environment. It is like a mirror which does not move, yet myriad reflected images can appear before it. The aim of *samatha* is to place the mind at a point of perfect stillness and quiescence. *Samapatti* practice is not restricted to stillness and quiescence. Any illusory condition can be reflected. An illusory condition is anything that can be perceived by the senses.

The Buddha says that the six consciousnesses, the sense facul-ties, and the objects perceived by consciousness are illusory. These acts of consciousness arise from the mind of vexation. All phenom-ena arise because of the grasping and discriminating mind. In Ch'an, a mind free from grasping and discrimination is an unmoving mind. The unmoving mind is Buddha-nature, the intrinsic nature. There is also an external environment, which refers to the sense faculties and their associated sense objects. These three things — the mind of vexation, intrinsic nature, and the environment — are illusory manifestations. We can speak of them and experience them, but they have no real existence.

We can say that Buddha-nature is the foundation of the mind and the external environment, but from the point of view of Buddhadharma, the environment is the consequence of our moving mind. Our minds "move" toward things that attract us, away from things that repel us, back and forth, back and forth. Our minds are constantly mobilized by a series of reactions. It is because of the mind of vexation that an environment exists. It is commonly said that although our physical and mental world is illusory and transient, the world of Buddha-nature is genuine. *The Sutra of Complete Enlightenment* takes a different stance. It agrees that the mundane truths are transient, but it says that the ultimate truth of Buddha-nature is also illusory.

These three illusions — the physical world, the mental world, and Buddha-nature — arise so that beings who take illusions to be real can be freed from them. Thus *samapatti*, a method of illusion, helps beings free themselves from illusions.

In the sutra, a condition of lightness and ease is described. Great compassion is always related to the condition of lightness and ease. What is meant by lightness is that there are no burdens or vexations whatsoever. Ease signifies non-obstructedness and the state of stillness. Great bodhisattvas do not feel burdened by the fact that they have vowed to deliver innumerable sentient beings. They experience lightness and ease. To feel burdened suggests pressure, and would mean that a bodhisattva was still holding on to a self. If there was still a self, the weight of vexations would also be there. Thus, the bodhisattva would never be in a state of lightness and ease.

The experience of lightness and ease can be achieved both through *samatha* and *samapatti*. However, there is an important difference between the two practices. With *samatha* there is no interaction with sentient beings. You practice by yourself. With *samapatti*, you use various expedient illusions to help illusory beings in their illusory environments. In the process you cultivate great compassion, from which comes lightness and ease. Bodhisattvas who use the method of *samapatti* and help other beings enhance their own practice.

Practitioners should keep in mind the fact that nothing is real — not the mind, nor the environment, nor the Buddha. If the Buddha's mind were real, then the mind and the nature of sentient beings would also be real. The attainment of a peaceful state through practice is ultimately unreal, but you can call it real from our perspective. From an enlightened point of view, the sutra and meditation are illusory, yet they help illusory sentient beings.

> *"Virtuous man, if, after awakening to pure Complete Enlightenment, bodhisattvas with pure, enlightened minds grasp on to neither illusory projections nor states of stillness, they will understand thoroughly that both body and mind are hindrances. [Awakening from] ignorance, their [minds] will be illuminated. Without depending on all sorts of hindrances, they will permanently transcend the realms of hindrance and non-hindrance and make full use of the world as well as the body and mind. They will manifest in the phenomenal world [without any obstructions], just as the sound of a musical instrument can travel beyond [the body of the instrument]. Vexations and nirvana will not hinder each other. Inwardly, they will experience lightness and ease in quiescent-extinction. They will accord with the realm of quiescent-extinction in wondrous enlightenment, which is beyond the reach of body and mind and the reach of self and others. All sentient beings and all life are only drifting thoughts. This expedient method is called dhyana."*

In the *Lankavatara Sutra* it is said that genuine Buddhadharma is apart from words and language. Words and language encompass all means of expression, whether they be sounds, gestures, symbols or anything else that can be transmitted or received by the senses. The same sutra also says that genuine Buddhadharma is apart from all mental activities — thoughts and feelings. Therefore, no matter what we think, feel, say, or do, none of it is genuine Buddhadharma.

Whether our minds are scattered, one-pointed, or unified does not matter. They are still impure minds. Only when there is no-mind — no self-centered activity — can it be said that the mind is pure. This is dhyana, or Ch'an.

Once on a return flight to Taiwan via Korea, I sat next to an American missionary. He was reading a magazine article that described the various religions in Korea. He asked me what religion I practiced. When I told him, he thought it somewhat amusing. He pointed to a picture of a Korean Buddhist monastery that housed a thousand Buddha statues and asked, "This is your religion?" When I nodded yes, the man laughed softly. "These statues are made of wood. Do you believe they are God?" I replied, "To tell you the truth, I don't believe in any god." He asked what I believed in and I said, "I don't really believe in anything." "Then what use do these statues have?" he asked. I answered, "There are people who benefit from these statues, so Buddhism makes use of them." On another page the article talked about Catholicism, so I pointed to a picture of a crucifix and asked, "This is your religion, is it not? Do you believe that this cross is God?" The man thought about it and said, "God cannot be represented by objects and forms. The cross is only a symbol." So I replied, "In that case, we are in agreement. The cross as well as Buddha statues have their uses for people who need them." The missionary said, "No, it's not the same. The cross symbolizes God's love for humanity, but when people prostrate to wooden statues, that's worshipping false idols." I said, "The sutras don't say anything about false idols, and they don't say prostrating is evil." He said, "The Bible says that bowing down to statues and false idols is a sin." Realizing the futility of the discussion, I said, "You base your beliefs on the Bible. I base mine on the sutras. You are Catholic, and I am Buddhist. We may never agree on certain issues, but it doesn't mean one is right and the other wrong."

A short time later I spoke with an elderly Catholic priest and he told me that, on the highest level, God is formless. God does not require people to pay respect or have adoration for Him. It is natural for God to have boundless love for people, but it is not necessary for people to love God back, because it is understood that people are basically ignorant. The need to love is for people, not for

God. I said, "According to your interpretation, Catholicism is very similar to Buddhism."

These stories point out that words, language, symbols and ideas are subjective. They can be twisted, changed, tossed aside, and picked up again. They are therefore unreliable. All opposition between religions comes from the different words and beliefs of different people. Who is correct? No one. In the third category of practice — dhyana — all concepts, forms, and descriptions are transcended. If we want to reach the dhyana level, we must leave behind form, language and thoughts.

As the plane was landing, I said to the missionary, "I do not deny the existence of God. Likewise, Buddhas exist for Buddhists. As for myself, however, I don't believe in them." "How can you be a Buddhist and not believe in Buddha?" he asked in disbelief. "For people who understand Buddhadharma, my statement would not come as a surprise. Buddhas were people of the past. Whether they exist today is irrelevant. A Buddhist with sufficient practice would not be attached to Buddhas. But most Buddhists also find this difficult to grasp."

Once when I held a retreat in Taiwan, one of the participants was an elderly, devout Buddhist. I told the participants, "There's no Buddha, no bodhisattvas, no Pure Land, no deities. Put all such ideas out of your mind. Just ask yourself where you came from before this life and what you are at this moment!"

The old man came to me and told me he had to leave. When I asked him why, he said, "For over thirty years I've been practicing with the support of Buddhas and bodhisattvas. I have gotten through hard times believing that in some future time I will become a Buddha or bodhisattva. Now you are telling me none of it exists. If I believe you, then I must conclude that I've wasted half of my life. I can't do that, so I'm leaving." And he did.

Apparently this man never read *The Sutra of Complete Enlightenment*, or if he did, then he did not understand it. The sutra is filled with Buddhas, bodhisattvas, and Pure Lands. It talks of deities, methods of practice, and many other things. But when you reach the dhyana level, there is nothing. Dhyana in this sutra describes the sudden enlightenment method. To successfully practice the sudden enlightenment method, there can be no attachments. To be enlightened, you must leave everything behind, including your self. Only in leaving behind your self can you perceive your Buddha-nature, the nature of emptiness.

The sutra speaks of Buddhas, bodhisattvas, and Pure Lands because there are different levels of practice. We must use our bodies, our mental activities, and our external environments to practice to attain various levels of samadhi. To attain the highest level of enlightenment, however, we must leave it all behind. In terms of gradual practice, we can view the body, mind, and external environment as causes and conditions that help our practice. In terms of sudden enlightenment, however, the body, mind, and external environment are illusions, hindrances to our practice, and to reaching dhyana.

There is no such thing as the mind. The mind is what arises when the environment interacts with our body. The body, as well as the environment, is illusory. Therefore, the interaction that comes from it — mental activity — must also be illusory. Through mental activities we can perform virtuous or unwholesome actions, but Ch'an cannot be acquired through knowledge, learning, the Buddha's wisdom, or through one's own experience and wisdom. If you think the Buddha can bring you to Ch'an, then you are depending on external conditions. If you think your own wisdom and knowledge can bring you to Ch'an, then you are relying on internal conditions. You have to leave behind all dependencies. Only then can you enter Ch'an.

> "Virtuous man, these three Dharma methods are intimately in accordance with Complete Enlightenment. Tathagatas in all ten directions accomplish Buddhahood through these means. The myriad expedient methods used by bodhisattvas in all ten directions, whether similar or different, depend on these three activities. At the perfect actualization of these practices, one accomplishes Complete Enlightenment.
>
> "Virtuous man, if, in his practice on the holy path, a person teaches, delivers, and succeeds in guiding hundreds of thousands of millions of people into arhatship and pratyekabuddhahood, he

cannot be compared with someone who, upon hearing these Dharma methods of the unhindered Complete Enlightenment, practices accordingly for even an instant."

At that time, the World Honored One, wishing to clarify his meaning, proclaimed these gathas:

*Majestic Virtue, you should know
that the unsurpassable mind of
great enlightenment is intrinsically non-dual.
Even though the various expedients
that accord with it
are limitless in number,
the teachings of the Tathagata are
altogether three in kind.
Quiescent and still in samatha,
[the mind] is like a mirror
reflecting myriad images.
Samapatti, wherein all is seen as an illusion,
is like a bud growing gradually.
Dhyana is quiescent-extinction,
[yet, its functions are] like the sound
of a musical instrument.
These three wondrous Dharma methods
are all in accordance with enlightenment.
The Tathagatas in all ten directions
and the great bodhisattvas
achieve Buddhahood through them.
Perfect actualization of these three
is called ultimate nirvana.*

Sometimes during retreat people ask for my blessing because they feel they cannot practice well enough by themselves. They think that I can empower them. To some I answer, "Sure, no problem, I will help you." I say this to people who are just beginning to practice. I tell more experienced people to work on their own and not rely on outside help. I say, "If you were hungry, would you ask me to eat for you?" This is the second stage of practice. At the third stage, people who have gotten results from the practice may feel proud or overconfident. They think they can be their own teachers. These people I scold and criticize. I tell them their actions are befitting of ghosts and demons, not humans. I do this to help them detach themselves from their good meditation experiences.

Any attachment, even to previous meditation experiences, is a hindrance to practice. Of course, progress comes from our meditation experiences, but once the meditation experience is over, it should be dropped. Some people hold onto these memories and feel content with their past accomplishments. This is attachment. Chances are, if the person has another meditation experience, it will be of the same nature and at the same level.

If practitioners do not become attached to such experiences, they will not perceive them as being signs of progress. In this way they will be free to progress further. Leaving all such experiences behind is a state of non-hindrance. Sometimes, unfortunately, practitioners who get a taste of this experience of non-hindrance develop a dislike for the world. They become apathetic. This is not Ch'an either.

Genuine Ch'an is not being attached to anything inside or outside the mind; there is neither desire for nor aversion from anything. You do not perceive your body, mind, and external environment as things which can help your practice. Neither do you see your body, mind and external environment as hindrances to practice. This is a true Ch'an state.

Ordinary people view their bodies and minds as their own, but practitioners at the dhyana level have no attachment to body and mind. If sentient beings need your help, then you will help them. In effect, your body and mind will belong to them, not to you. They will benefit from your body and mind, your words and actions. Practitioners at the dhyana level still think, speak, and act, but they do so in response to the needs of others, and their actions stem from wisdom, not subjective discrimination. These people are neither inactive nor pessimistic. They are active, and their actions are positive.

The sutra uses the analogy of music to describe the dhyana level of cultivation. Music is not bound by the body of the instrument, yet it is created by the instrument. Similarly, practitioners need to be separate from body, mind and external environment in order for wisdom to manifest. Yet, at the same time, it is within the body, mind, and world that wisdom does manifest in order to benefit sentient beings.

The body, mind, and world are illusory, and illusion is considered vexation. Advanced Ch'an practitioners, however, have no attachment or aversion to vexation. Even though they live in a world of vexation, their minds are always unmoving, always quiescent. Therefore, to them, vexation is bodhi and samsara is nirvana. This is the third level of practice — dhyana, or Ch'an.

Bodhisattva
Cleansed of All Karmic Obstructions

Then the Bodhisattva Cleansed of All Karmic Obstructions rose from his seat in the midst of the assembly, prostrated himself at the feet of the Buddha, circled the Buddha three times clockwise, knelt down, joined his palms, and said: "O World Honored One of great compassion! You have broadly expounded to us such inconceivable things as the practices of all Tathagatas of the causal ground, and have caused the assembly to gain what they have never had before. Having seen the Buddha's arduous toil through kalpas as innumerable as the grains of sand of the Ganges, and his efforts in practice unfold as if they were in but an instant of a thought, we bodhisattvas feel deeply fortunate and joyous.

"World Honored One, if the intrinsic nature of this enlightened mind is pure, what caused it to be defiled, making sentient beings deluded, perplexed and unable to enter it? Pray let the Tathagata thoroughly expound and reveal to us the nature of dharmas so that this assembly and sentient beings in the Dharma Ending Age may use [your teaching] as a guiding vision in the future." Having said these words, he prostrated himself on the ground. He made the same request three times, each time repeating the same procedure.

At that time the World Honored One said to the Bodhisattva Cleansed of All Karmic Obstructions: "Excellent, excellent!

Virtuous man, for the benefit of this assembly and sentient beings in the Dharma Ending Age, you have asked the Tathagata about such expedient methods. Listen attentively now, I shall explain it to you."

Hearing this, the Bodhisattva Cleansed of All Karmic Obstructions was filled with joy, and listened silently along with the assembly.

"Virtuous man, since beginningless time all sentient beings have been deludedly conceiving and clinging to the existence of self, person, sentient being, and life. They take these four inverted views as the essence of a real self, thereby giving rise to dual states of like and dislike. [Thus], based on one delusion, they further cling to other delusions. These two delusions rely on each other, giving rise to the illusory paths of karma. Because of illusory karma, sentient beings deludedly perceive the turning flow [of cyclic existence]. Those who detest the turning flow [of cyclic existence] deludedly perceive nirvana, and hence are unable to enter [the realm of] pure enlightenment. It is not enlightenment that thwarts their entering; rather, it is the idea that 'there is one who can enter.' Therefore, whether their thoughts are agitated or have ceased, they cannot be other than confused and perplexed.

"Why is this? Because the original-arising ignorance has been [falsely perceived as] one's own master since beginningless time, therefore all sentient beings are unable to give rise to the wisdom-eye. The nature of their bodies and minds is nothing but ignorance. [This ignorance which does not eliminate itself may be illustrated] by the example of the man who does not take his own life. Therefore, you should know that people get along with those who like them and resent those who contradict them. Because like and dislike nurture ignorance, sentient beings always fail in their pursuit of the Path."

In this section, the Buddha addresses three questions commonly asked by people who practice or study Buddhadharma. First, when did sentient beings first become impure and ignorant? Second, what is the cause of this ignorance and impurity? Third, why does this ignorance and impurity last indefinitely?

Buddhadharma often says that all sentient beings are intrinsically Buddhas and that Buddhas see no distinction between themselves and sentient beings. These statements may confuse people new to Buddhism. If this is so, they may ask, then why are we not Buddhas right now? Have we ever been Buddhas? If we have been Buddhas in the past and then later became ignorant, it seems Buddhahood is not reliable. Perhaps sentient beings who become Buddhas will again fall into ignorance and impurity at a later time. If this is true, why should anyone practice?

First, it is incorrect to say that sentient beings were once Buddhas. Rather, it is true to say that the intrinsic nature of sentient beings is identical to Buddha-nature. Since beginningless time, there has been no separation of or distinction between the Buddha-nature of sentient beings and that of Buddhas. On the other hand, since beginningless time, sentient beings have been ignorant, and so they do not recognize or understand this fundamental principle. We do not perceive our Buddha-nature. Therefore, we are ignorant and unaware of our ignorance.

The Sutra goes on to say that Buddha-nature and ignorance are one and the same and have been so since beginningless time. Our ignorance has always been with us, but it too is Buddha-nature. Take the analogy of ice and water. Imagine that the ice at the Earth's poles has been ice since the beginning of the planet's history. Although it is and always has been ice, its nature is no different from the water flowing in the oceans. In the same way, sentient beings have the same nature as Buddhas, yet they are unaware of it. Scientists say that at some time in the future the polar caps may melt. Likewise, sentient beings may melt their ignorance and become enlightened, and when they do they will realize that the nature of ignorance and the nature of wisdom are one and the same.

This analogy of water and ice, however, raises an interesting question. Logic dictates that if ice can become water, then water can also become ice. If we extend this analogy to our discussion, then it suggests that Buddhas can again become ignorant. According to Ch'an, nirvana and samsara both exist and do not exist. They exist from the perspective of sentient beings because sentient beings are attached to a sense of self and hence cling to form and appearance.

Samsara and nirvana do not exist from the perspective of a Buddha because a Buddha is not attached to a sense of self and is independent of form and appearance. The Buddha, however, can utilize form and appearance for the benefit of sentient beings. A Buddha can make use of samsaric and nirvanic dharmas according to the needs of sentient beings. Therefore, just as water can freeze again, a Buddha can also appear to become a sentient being. However, there is a difference between us and Buddhas. We are sentient beings because of our karma and impurity — we have no choice. Buddhas choose to manifest as sentient beings through their wisdom.

The impurity that we have been talking about stems from our attachment to four signs: the self, the person, other sentient beings (as well as non-sentient forms), and life. Self, person, and sentient beings are spatial signs. Life, the temporal phenomenon, arises when the first three signs interact with one another. The sutra goes into a detailed explanation of the four signs or characteristics in subsequent paragraphs. The Buddha also addresses these signs from two different perspectives: from the standpoint of ordinary sentient beings and from the point of view of bodhisattvas on the path of practice. For now, however, we will look at these signs in relation to ordinary sentient beings.

To illustrate the four kinds of signs or phenomena, let's say that a young man and woman meet and fall in love. If the feelings of this couple are mutual and sincere, then it is unlikely that they will be in love one day and out of love the next. Usually when people fall in love, they wish to remain in love forever, even over the course of many lifetimes. People in love do not care if religions view such great attachment unfavorably. They wish only to stay in love and would be willing to endure anything as long as love remains. Here, three of the four signs of attachment are present: selves that fall in love, individuals who are beloved, and the desire for this love to persist. If through their love the couple raises a family, which in turn gives rise to future families, and so on through many generations, then the attachment to the phenomenon of sentient beings is also satisfied.

I once asked someone if he wanted to become a monk. He said, "It is not that I do not want to become a monk, but my father would like to have some grandchildren." So I suggested that he have children and then become a monk. He responded positively to this suggestion, but I assured him that he would never leave home after having children. He, too, would want to see his children grow and have families so that he could enjoy his own grandchildren. This is life for sentient beings, and it is seemingly without end.

These four signs, the self, the person, sentient beings, and life are illusions and arise and perish because of causes and conditions. One holds on to signs as if they are real due to one's attachment to self. There can be no self alone. The self manifests through interaction with other beings and forms.

Attachment can be of two kinds. It can be directed primarily towards outer objects, relationships, or events, or it can be self-centered. I know of a mayor who is over fifty years old and has never been married. However, his attachments are hardly any fewer than those of married people. His love is the city and he treats it as if it were his own child. This is the first kind of attachment, an attachment to a worthy cause. Those whose attachment is of the second kind care little for others, yet they are deeply bound to themselves. They feel no sense of duty to causes or commitment to other people. They live their lives without direction. Of the two, the first kind of attachment is preferable.

Impurity and delusion arise because of attachment to the four signs. There are two related explanations for what sustains impurity and delusion indefinitely. When the self is erroneously taken to be eternal, attachment arises not only to the present self, but also to the future self. As people make plans and prepare for the future, they create karma. At the end of their lives, the accumulation of karma will lead to further births so that the consequences of such karma may be experienced. This process continues without end. Because people are always attached to an idea of a future self, they will accordingly continue to create karma that will lead to future retribution.

The second explanation pertains to practitioners of inner and outer paths who seek to reach Buddhahood, nirvana, or any kind of heavenly realm. These people feel aversion to the world and a corresponding desire to escape its suffering. Practitioners on outer paths who seek to reach a heavenly realm can do so through the accumulation of merit, but their stay in these worlds is ultimately limited, for departure is unavoidable once the energy of their previous practice is exhausted. Similarly, those who seek Buddhahood as an escape from the world may gain entrance into a kind of expedient, temporary Pure Land. Though such practitioners may feel that they have achieved nirvana, they too will have to leave the heavenly realm once the power of their practice wanes. Upon their birth in an ordinary world, these people will immediately yearn to return to the heavenly realm. They will then work lifetime after lifetime on Earth to accumulate sufficient merit to gain respite in the heavens. Thus they do not transcend attachment and remain impure indefinitely.

It is attachment that creates impurity and delusion, and it is through attachment that they are sustained. If sentient beings are to become Buddhas, then there can be no attachments, no seeking, and no goal.

> *"Virtuous man, what is the sign of the self? It is that which is experienced in the minds of sentient beings. Virtuous man, for instance, when a man's body is well coordinated and healthy, he forgets about its existence. However, when his four limbs are sluggish and his body unhealthy and unregulated, then with the slightest treatment of acupuncture and moxa he will become aware of the existence of the self again. Therefore, the self manifests when experience is felt. Virtuous man, even if this man's mind experienced the realm of the Tathagata and clearly perceived pure nirvana, it would be but the phenomenon of the self.*
>
> *"Virtuous man, what is the sign of the person? It is that which is experienced in the minds of sentient beings. Virtuous man, he who awakens to the self no longer identifies with the self. This awakening, which is beyond all experience, is the mark of the person. Virtuous man, both what is awakened to and the awakening are not the self. Thus, even if this man's mind were perfectly awakened to nirvana, it would be but the self [because] as long as there is even the slightest trace of awakening or striving in the mind to realize the principle, it would be the sign of the person.*

"Virtuous man, what is the sign of sentient beings? It is the experience which is beyond self-awakening and it is that which is awakened to in the minds of sentient beings. Virtuous man, if for example a man says, 'I am a sentient being,' we know that what he speaks of as 'sentient being' refers neither to himself nor another person. Why is he not referring to his self? Since this self is sentient being, it is not limited to his self. Since this self is sentient being, therefore it is not another person's self. Virtuous man, the experiences and awakenings of sentient beings are all [traces of] the self and the person. In the awakening beyond the traces of the self and person, if one retained the awareness of having realized something, it would be called the sign of sentient beings.

"Virtuous man, what is the sign of life? It is the mind of sentient beings that illuminates purity, in which they are aware of what they have realized. Karmic [consciousness] and wisdom cannot perceive themselves. This is comparable to the root of life. Virtuous man, when the mind is able to illuminate and perceive enlightenment, it is but a defilement, because both perceiver and perceived are not apart from defilement. After ice melts in hot water, there is no ice to be aware of its melting. The perception of the existence of the self enlightening itself is also like this."

These paragraphs describe practitioners who have made progress, but who remain attached to illusions that correspond to the four signs of the self, person, sentient being, and life. These illusions confront practitioners who lack proper guidance and can lead to erroneous ideas and attitudes concerning their realizations. Such people may come to believe that they are enlightened or have attained nirvana.

The four signs described by the text actually refer to one thing — the self. The four signs describe the self from four perspectives. These four signs give to the self its impression of solidity and existence. In truth, the self only exists in relation to its continuing interaction with other beings, objects, and events. Self refers to whatever is experienced by the mind; it constitutes and is constituted by mental experience. This includes not only the simple awareness of one's body, but also the experience of one's Buddha-nature. The second sign, the person, is the source of one's experience of self. More concretely, it is the ground of wisdom, because it is through wisdom that Buddha-nature is experienced. Self is what the mind of the sentient being experiences, and the person is what makes the experience possible. The first two signs can be thought of as Buddha-nature and wisdom, respectively.

The third sign, sentient being, is neither Buddha-nature nor wisdom. How is this so? At a certain level of practice, one may experience Buddha-nature and realize that all sentient beings are the same as the Buddha but still have the notion that sentient beings need deliverance. The *Platform Sutra* says, "All sentient beings in my self-nature have to be delivered." But Buddha-nature makes no distinction between others and oneself. The third characteristic is not wisdom because if one's attainment were truly great, one would see all sentient beings as Buddhas who are not in need of deliverance. Therefore the characteristic of sentient being arises at that level of practice where one makes a distinction between oneself and sentient beings who need to be saved.

All three signs are grounded in the self, but each identifies the self from a different perspective. In the first sign, the self identifies with Buddha-nature, in the second with wisdom, and in the third with a sentient being among other sentient beings needing deliverance. At the third stage, while there is a perception that sentient beings are within one's self-nature, they are still distinct from oneself.

The fourth sign, life, refers to the ongoing functioning of wisdom through time. To use the analogy of the sutra, the boiling water of wisdom takes time to melt the ice block of suffering. In our practice it takes time for wisdom to dispel the vexations within self-nature. In this context, vexations of self-nature have special meaning. They refer not specifically to our own vexations but rather to the vexations of sentient beings perceived to exist within Buddha-nature. Once Buddhahood is attained, sentient beings are no longer perceived to exist. Until then, they are perceived as vexations within self-nature. The light of wisdom melts away these vexations.

Practitioners who gain partial realization are prone to believe that their enlightenment is profound and complete. This belief in their own enlightenment sets them apart, in their own minds, from other sentient beings, thus betraying their attachment to illusion. The four signs are still present, and therefore the self is still solid and firm. This is why Ch'an says that people who believe in their own enlightenment are not really enlightened.

In the course of practice your mind may become calm and clear in all aspects, and you may feel that you are in possession of great wisdom, capable of acting correctly in every situation. On one retreat a student told me that she didn't want to meditate anymore. She just wanted to talk. I invited her to the interview room and she said, "I'm very happy. It's as if, in one instant, the whole world brightened up. I looked out of the window and everything was so beautiful. The birds, flowers, and everything else are part of myself. I feel beautiful. I believe I've really gotten into it." I asked her to tell me what she had "gotten into" and she replied, "Isn't this what you call enlightenment?" When I told her it was illusion, she became unhappy. "I've made such tremendous progress, and now you tell me it's just an illusion!" I told her that it is precisely this desire for enlightenment that creates such illusions.

On another retreat one of the participants stopped coming to the meditation hall. I sent a couple of people to look for him and they found him in the woods. He was extremely happy. He had brought back a small dried twig, which he respectfully offered to me. "I've gotten it!" he exclaimed. I took the twig and threw it out the window. He became angry and complained that his realization was a precious thing, one that he had worked hard in getting.

In both anecdotes, the students had worthwhile experiences after practicing diligently for some time. Enlightenment, though, is not a possession you can hold onto like a jewel. The mind experiences something that it takes to be enlightenment, but it is just the self in a happy state. It is not necessarily the narrow, selfish ego. It may even be the unified self. But it is not Buddha-nature. Buddha-nature is empty of all characteristics. These feelings are illusory expressions of a larger sense of self gained through hard practice. To feel that everything in the universe is part of you may be a noble sentiment, but it is not enlightenment.

Some years ago in Taiwan I was visited by a monk who had heard I was teaching Ch'an in America. The monk said, "Since you are enlightened, I want to tell you something." When I told him I was not enlightened, he said, "Oh, don't be so modest. We can talk frankly. Do you know who I am?" I answered, "No, I don't." "Well," he said, "I am the Bodhisattva Manjusri." "Really," I said, "How do you know that?" He replied, "Originally, I didn't know it. I had been practicing in a mountain hut for four years. Nothing much happened, but about six months ago, I started writing. I wrote so fast I could finish a book in one night. If I were not Manjusri, how could I have written this?" He then showed me a manuscript he had written. It was not completely meaningless — one could make some sense out of some of the paragraphs — but there was no continuity. I told him, "It seems to me that you have been taken in by a spirit." Indignantly, he packed up his manuscript and left.

This monk took his experience as a sign not only of enlightenment but as proof that he was the manifestation of a great bodhisattva. Because he lacked proper guidance, he fell into Ch'an sickness. If he had ever read *The Sutra of Complete Enlightenment*, he obviously did not understand it.

If during practice you feel the rising and manifestation of wisdom, consider it a natural phenomenon that accompanies practice. True wisdom, if and when it arises, comes undetected and unannounced. It occurs without self-consciousness, just as ice is not aware that it is melting in hot water. The wise person has no special feeling of being wise.

The third sign, sentient being, is associated with people who have a great sense of mission and responsibility for helping others. It can be positive, but the problem with this attitude is that it separates oneself from others who need to be saved. To say, "I must go out and save sentient beings," is attachment. Enlightened beings do not perceive sentient beings as apart from themselves. On the other hand, if we say that there are no sentient beings to save, that too is an erroneous view.

The *Avatamsaka Sutra* says that saving sentient beings is like fishermen bringing in fish with their nets. The fish that are too small slip through while the larger ones are caught. In other words, those who have grown enough through practice will be saved and the others will slip through. Some may be strong enough so that they do not need to be hauled in by a bodhisattva. They can reach the other shore on their own. Like fishermen, bodhisattvas practice their trade. On the way, sentient beings may be saved, but it is the natural result of practice.

The fourth sign is life. Normally, when we speak of life we are referring to the physical phenomenon. Here we are referring to the life of one who has practiced and become enlightened. This kind of life also has an historical dimension because the acts of enlightened people persist through time. When enlightened beings are helping others, we see their wisdom. When there is no situation calling for that wisdom, the wisdom does not manifest. Such people are not attached to material things, including their own bodies. They continue to nurture and cultivate their wisdom, but because there is still an attachment to the notion of helping others, these bodhisattvas have not attained ultimate enlightenment. The block of ice has not fully melted. There is a residue of self — not the self of ordinary sentient beings, but a Dharma self, still dwelling in relativity. With final enlightenment, wisdom falls away, and with it the need to save others. This is the absolute state of Buddhahood.

> *"Virtuous man, if sentient beings in the Dharma Ending Age do not understand these four characteristics [of the self], even after cultivating the Path diligently for many kalpas, [it is still] called practicing with attachments and they will not be able to accomplish the fruition of sainthood. Therefore, this is called [cultivating] the True Dharma in the Dharma Ending Age. Why? Because they mistake the various aspects of the self for nirvana, and regard their experiences and awakenings as accomplishments. This is comparable to a man who mistakes a thief for his own son. His wealth and treasure will never increase. Why? Because if one grasps onto the self, one will also grasp onto nirvana. For him, the root of grasping onto the self is [merely] suppressed and [seemingly]*

there is the appearance of nirvana. If there is one who hates the self, that one will also have hatred for birth and death. Not knowing that grasping is the real [source of] birth and death, hatred for birth and death is [also] not liberation.

"How does one recognize the Dharma of non-liberation? Virtuous man, if sentient beings in the Dharma Ending Age, while cultivating bodhi, have partial actualization [of Complete Enlightenment] and think they are already pure, then they have not exhausted the root of the trace of the self. If someone praises his Dharma, it gives rise to joy in his mind and he wants to liberate the praiser. If someone criticizes his achievement, that gives rise to hatred in his mind. Thus one can tell that his attachment to the phenomenon of the self is strong and firm. [This self] is hidden in the storehouse consciousness. It wanders in the sense faculties and has never ceased to exist.

"Virtuous man, these practitioners, because they do not eliminate the phenomenon of the self, cannot enter [the realm of] pure enlightenment. Virtuous man, if one truly actualizes the emptiness of the self, there will be no one there who can slander the self. When there is a self who expounds the Dharma, the self has not been severed. The same holds true for sentient beings and life.

"Virtuous man, sentient beings in the Dharma Ending Age speak of illness [in their practice] as the Dharma. They are pitiable people. Though diligent in their practice, they only increase their illness and are consequently unable to enter the [realm of] pure enlightenment.

"Virtuous man, because sentient beings in the Dharma Ending Age are not clear about these four signs [of the self], when they take the Tathagata's understanding and conduct to be their own practice, they will never reach accomplishment. Some claim that they have had actualizations though they have not; some claim that they have had realizations though they have not. When they see others more advanced than themselves, they become jealous. Because these people have not severed their grasping onto the self, they are unable to enter the [realm of] pure enlightenment.

"Virtuous man, sentient beings in the Dharma Ending Age who wish to accomplish the Path should not seek awakening

*through increasing their knowledge by listening [to the Dharma].
This will only further strengthen their view of the self. Instead,
they should strive to diligently subdue their vexations! They should
generate great courage to attain what they have not attained and
sever what they have not severed. In all circumstances, they should
not give rise to craving, hatred, attached love, arrogance, flattery,
crookedness, envy, and jealousy. Then, the affection and grasping
between the self and others will be extinguished. [When they can
do this], the Buddha says that they will gradually reach accomplishment. Furthermore, they should seek good teachers so that
they will not fall into erroneous views. However, if they give rise
to hatred and love in their minds while seeking [a good teacher],
they will be unable to enter the ocean of pure enlightenment."*

At that time, the World Honored One, wishing to clarify his
meaning, proclaimed these gathas:

*Cleansed of All Karmic Obstructions,
you should know that sentient beings,
because of their attachment to and love of self,
have been bound in the illusory turning flow
[of cyclic existence] since beginningless time.
Without severing the four signs [of the self],
bodhi will not be attained.
With the mind harboring love and hatred,
and thoughts carrying flattery and crookedness,
one is full of confusion and perplexity,
and cannot enter the citadel of enlightenment.
To return to the realm of enlightenment,
desire, anger, and delusion must first be eliminated.
When attachment to the dharma [of nirvana]
no longer exists in the mind,
one can gradually reach accomplishment.
This body is originally non-existent
so how can love and hatred arise?
A practitioner should also seek a good teacher
so as not to fall into erroneous views.
If hatred and love arise in the quest,
he will not accomplish [enlightenment].*

In previous paragraphs the Buddha spoke of attachment to the four kinds of signs: the self, the person, sentient beings, and life. The Buddha also described how practitioners can experience these attachments through different levels of cultivation and the problems that can occur when practitioners are attached to the four signs. He also gave solutions to these problems.

I will divide my discussion of these topics into three sections: first, how attachment to the self manifests in practitioners' behavior; second, how experienced practitioners conduct themselves in order to progress; third, what attitude practitioners should cultivate in the course of their practice.

People who have had good results from practice and who have practiced for many years may feel that they have reached the stage of pure wisdom, where attachment to self is terminated and nirvana is attained. Actually, people who think they have become enlightened really have not, because they still possess a sense of a self that needs to be enlightened or has become enlightened.

Enlightenment is not an object, a feeling, or a place. Were enlightenment any of these, it would be limited and thus illusory. There can be no wisdom as long as enlightenment is seen as an objective and as long as there exists a self to benefit from it.

You may think you understand what I have said and feel confident that you would not be misled by "false" enlightenments, but it is difficult for a beginner to appreciate the joy that results from these experiences. Suppose after diligent practice you experience the feeling of self disappearing and nirvana being attained, and suppose that you also experience transcendent bliss. Have you really entered nirvana? Since there is still a sense of self that enters nirvana, the achievement is not genuine. So powerful is this experience, however, that it is likely to mislead all but the most experienced practitioner.

This is the first example of misconceptions that result from attachment to the self. Here is a second example. Suppose, through practice, you reach the stage where self-centeredness seems to vanish and the method of practice dissolves. You feel relaxed, free, unified with the universe, yet unconcerned with its relationship to you. You are outwardly calm. But here, too, self still exists, no matter what you feel.

You may assert that you understand nirvana, that you have seen the Dharmakaya of the Buddha and that you have attained final wisdom. If I attempt to contradict you, you will likely try to overcome me in argument. You are strongly attached to your achievement and will be frustrated that I do not believe what you say. You will claim that I am in no position to judge your realization. To make matters worse, another person may affirm your claims, perhaps because this other person feels that your description of nirvana accords perfectly with that given in the sutras. This other person may say that he has also experienced such realization, so he is in a position to affirm your claims. This will make you happy. You will embrace the other person and call him your true Dharma friend.

What kind of liberation could practitioners possibly possess when they respond to praise with delight and to insult with frustration? If this is so, their nirvana seems faulty. But even if this incongruity is brought to their attention, they will likely answer: "I respond to praise and criticism in different ways, but not for myself. I am free from the self, so I don't care one way or the other; but in order to uphold the dignity of the Buddhadharma, I censure those who contradict the Dharma and praise those who are in accordance with it." One cannot argue with people who seem to have all the answers! However, it is not difficult to ascertain the validity of their experiences. If they claim to have entered nirvana and speak of their wisdom, then they have not entered nirvana. Nirvana is achieved only when both samsara and nirvana disappear and are seen as dreams, when there are no more feelings of happiness and sorrow, when the mind is stable and tranquil.

It may be easy to accept samsara as a dream, but the sutra says that enlightenment is a dream as well. If nirvana and samsara are equally illusory, then it seems we are fighting to leave one dream only to enter another. Actually, enlightenment as such is not a dream, but the concepts of enlightenment and its attainment are. Thus practitioners are living in the dream of samsara with a concept of enlightenment that is nothing more than an object of desire. Once they reach enlightenment, enlightenment is no longer a dream. In fact, it ceases to exist. When genuine enlightenment is attained, it cannot be said to be present.

Practitioners are comparable to mountain climbers trying to scale a glass mountain. The mountain is steep and slippery and the mountaineers are barefooted. To add to the difficulty, the mountain is covered with oil. Every time the mountaineers make an effort to climb, they slip back down. Persistently they try again and again, but to no avail. In the end, utterly exhausted, they collapse and let go of all grasping. Instantly they find the mountain gone. They realize that all of their efforts were a dream — there was no need to climb and no progress to be made. In the dream, however, the mountain did exist, and if the mountaineers had not attempted the impossible, they would not have awakened. Thus it is necessary to try to leave samsara and achieve nirvana, even though both are illusory. If in the course of your practice you experience enlightenment as what I have described above, then you should know that you are still dreaming.

Thus far we have described practitioners who feel that they have achieved enlightenment in relation to an existing self. In the third example, we will examine the equally false reverse perspective. In this case, practitioners assert that they are indifferent to praise and blame, to the affairs of the world, and even to their own practice. They perceive that there is neither nirvana nor a self that enters nirvana and that everything is meaningless illusion. This attitude can be dangerous. Practitioners in the previous examples may still be able to attain the heavenly states of dhyana after death. At the very least, these practitioners will probably keep practicing to preserve their experiences. But practitioners of the third example will be tempted to stop practicing. If they persevere, they will likely enter the formless heavens; but if they cease practicing because they feel that nothing matters, they may contemplate suicide or engage in evil activities and fall into lower realms after death.

There are two important rules that practitioners should follow to maintain a correct attitude toward practice. First, one should not claim to have attained enlightenment. Second, one should make enlightenment or nirvana the goal of practice. It is important that you not claim that you have already achieved enlightenment. It may be all right for people who are enlightened to confirm the fact if they are asked, but they should never boast. There are two ways to determine if you have experienced genuine enlightenment. The first is to consult someone whose practice is more advanced than yours. The alternative is to attempt to discern whether your experience is the same as that described in the sutras. This method is recommended only when the first way is not possible because it is easy to misinterpret the sutras. The proper approach is to rely on the traditional explanations of the sutras when gauging your experience. The wrong approach is to use your own experience to interpret the sutras.

It is common for serious practitioners to make an incorrect association between their experiences and enlightenment. Rather than reaching enlightenment, they become affected by a special kind of pride. In order to avoid the misconception of false enlightenment, serious practitioners must remain alert to such pride. This advice is pertinent to practitioners who actually believe that they have entered nirvana. At least these people are serious practitioners. However, people who make this claim without even having experienced false enlightenment merely demonstrate that they have not practiced. They are not serious practitioners.

The second rule, to take enlightenment or nirvana as the goal of practice, obliges practitioners to read the sutras and Buddhist literature as much as possible in order to understand the nature of the goal and the path that leads towards it. However, it is important not to become bound by the teachings of the sutras, otherwise they will become an obstacle to practice. Nor should one simply study the sutras to acquire information and to impress others.

There are two extremes. Meditators may wish for enlightenment so intensely that they may believe themselves to be enlightened before they really are. Alternatively, meditators may give too much credence to what they have read and heard about the nonexistence of enlightenment. They may think there is no enlightenment because the Buddha, the sutras and their masters tell them so. They may say, "I really don't care about enlightenment, but all the same I will continue to practice." This is not a satisfactory attitude because these practitioners will become lazy and never generate sufficient energy or diligence in their practice.

A goal is as important in the practice of Buddhadharma as it is in any other activity. If practitioners do not care what happens in the future, they will never achieve anything significant. We must believe that enlightenment is something worth striving for and that we are presently bound to samsara by ignorance. On the other hand, we must not become overly zealous in our attempt to accomplish the goal of reaching enlightenment. It will cause anxiety that in turn will stifle practice.

A patriarch once said that the practice of Dharma should commence with the perfection of *dana*: the giving of offerings to the Three Jewels (the Buddha, Dharma, and Sangha). When the patriarch made this statement, a man in the audience said, "The Three Jewels are identical to my self-nature. Likewise everything that I offer is not other than my self-nature. In other words, I offer self-nature to self-nature. Therefore, it follows that I offer my whole mind to you. Whatever you want I shall think of and I will offer those thoughts to you."

The patriarch said, "It is good that you offer your mind to me, so from this moment onward, when you eat, consume only the food of the mind. When you drink, drink only the water of the mind. When you walk, traverse only the roads of the mind. When you speak, utter only words of the mind. When you sleep, sleep only the slumber of the mind. When you can do this, you have indeed made the full offering to me. However, if this is not possible for you, then you must make physical offerings like everyone else."

The questioner was still in the realm of the illusory mind and could not truly offer his self-nature. Just as the questioner still had to make physical offerings, so too one who is not enlightened must still strive to attain nirvana. Now I will talk about ways to overcome obstacles encountered in practice. Two rules must be followed to overcome any obstacle. First, you must work hard. Second, you must study with those who have a genuine understanding of Buddhadharma.

Vexations arise according to the intensity of practice. The idea is to quell vexations at all times. When there are no vexations, you will be able to practice without paying attention to anything that arises in your mind. When vexations are present, you must deal with them swiftly. If your practice is strong, you will be able to tell when such disturbances are about to arise and prevent them from taking hold. If your practice is weak, you will not be able to foretell when vexations are about to arise and will be unable to control them once they do. If your practice is mediocre, you will sometimes be able to recognize imminent vexations. For instance, some people who feel the onset of problems may tell their friends to leave them alone because they foresee a bad mood.

There are many kinds of vexations. Some are brought about by physiological problems, others by psychological problems. If you know such problems are about to arise, you can try to stop them from occurring, or at least dampen their intensity. If a problem cannot be resolved, it may have to be endured. Inevitably some people will try to escape from their problems.

The easiest type of vexation to recognize before its full arising is anger. One past resident would hit the wall when he was angry, sometimes until he broke it or injured himself. The pain in his fist would take his mind off his vexations.

The best way to tame vexations is to prevent them from arising and becoming strong. Once they arise, they are best tamed by vigorous practice. In such cases the best practice is prostration. After prostrations, anger, greed, and sexual desire lessen, particularly if one prostrates until fatigue sets in. The practice of prostrations is also suitable for almost everyone.

What is most important, however, is to practice and study diligently, preferably with a good teacher. This is the best way to overcome obstacles encountered on the path.

Bodhisattva of
Universal Enlightenment

Then the Bodhisattva of Universal Enlightenment rose from his seat in the midst of the assembly, prostrated himself at the feet of the Buddha, circled the Buddha three times clockwise, knelt down, joined his palms, and said: "O World Honored One of great compassion! You have with no hesitation explained the faults in practice so that this great assembly [of bodhisattvas] has gained what it never had before. Their minds are thoroughly at peace and they have gained a great, secure, and steadfast [teaching as a guiding vision for their practice].

"World Honored One, sentient beings in the Dharma Ending Age will gradually be further away from the days of the Buddha. The sages and saints will seldom appear, while the heretical teachings will increase and flourish. What kind of people, then, should sentient beings seek to follow? What kind of Dharma should they rely on? What line of conduct should they adopt? Of what faults [in practice] should they rid themselves? How should they arouse the [bodhi] mind so that the blind multitude can avoid falling into erroneous views?" Having said these words, he fully prostrated himself on the ground. He made the same request three times, each time repeating the same procedure.

At that time the World Honored One said to the Bodhisattva of Universal Enlightenment: "Excellent, excellent! Virtuous man, you have asked the Tathagata about such methods of practice which are able to impart to all sentient beings, in the Dharma Ending Age, the Fearless Eye of the Path so that they will be able to accomplish the holy path. Listen attentively now. I shall explain it to you."

Hearing this, the Bodhisattva of Universal Enlightenment was filled with joy and listened silently along with the assembly.

"Virtuous man, sentient beings in the Dharma Ending Age who wish to arouse the great mind should search for a good teacher. Those who wish to practice should look for one who has correct views in all aspects. Such a teacher's mind does not abide in characteristics. He has no attachment to the realms of sravakas and pratyekabuddhas. Though [expediently] manifesting worldly afflictions, his mind is always pure. Though displaying misdeeds, he praises the practice of purity and does not lead sentient beings into undisciplined conduct and demeanor. If sentient beings seek out such a teacher, they will accomplish unexcelled perfect enlightenment.

"If sentient beings in the Dharma Ending Age meet such a teacher, they should make offerings to him even at the expense of their lives, not to mention their food, wealth, spouse, children, and retinue. Such a teacher always reveals purity in the four modes of conduct. Even if he shows misdeeds and excesses, disciples should not give rise to pride and contempt in their minds. If these disciples do not entertain evil thoughts of their teacher, they will ultimately be able to accomplish correct enlightenment. Their mind-flowers will blossom and illumine all Pure Lands in the ten directions."

Sakyamuni Buddha once remarked that the depth of a Buddha's wisdom and the extent of his merit are ascertainable only by those who have also reached Buddhahood. Similarly, it is true that a master's level of practice can be assessed only by another master. A student, consequently, cannot measure the extent of a master's attainment. The most a student can do is to become acquainted with the correct view of Buddhadharma and be certain that the master teaches this view.

Three fundamental principles make up the right view of Buddhadharma: causes and conditions, cause and consequence, and the middle way. Buddhadharma explains that all things, being illusory and without self-nature, are completely dependent on causes and conditions for their appearance. Cause and consequence are inextricably connected over time, such that no action in the past, present, or future can be separated from its corresponding cause and consequence. Lastly, all extremes, such as clinging to existence or emptiness, are false and erroneous. Thus the only recourse is the middle path, which remains free from all attachments.

Students must be wary of false views. For example, some hold the view that there are eternally existent dharmas or phenomena. Theists, for example, hold that there exists an eternal soul that is subservient to an omniscient God. Others believe that the dharmas of cause and consequence are unrelated through time. They say that events occur randomly. Materialists recognize cause and consequence only in relation to actions in the physical world, where the relationship between a consequence and its cause is experimentally verifiable. They deny the notion of a karmic principle of cause and consequence that permeates all planes of existence.

Anyone whose teachings are consistent with the correct view of Buddhadharma has met at least the minimum requirement of a true teacher. Hence, in selecting a teacher, students should concern themselves only with the correct view. They should not become preoccupied with a teacher's character and conduct.

Usually, however, a teacher's character and conduct are students' primary preoccupation. They typically make judgments based on what they see as inconsistencies between a teacher's words and actions. This causes problems. If there are any discrepancies between a teacher's avowed standards and his or her behavior, practitioners will gradually come to perceive only the teacher's failings and possibly abandon the teacher, if not the practice.

Teachers are always subject to criticism by their students. Enlightened teachers need not remain in society, yet they do so to help guide others out of delusion. Enlightened teachers are still human, and they still have weaknesses. Like anyone else, they must eat, urinate, defecate, wear clothes, and sleep. Some people stare wide-eyed at teachers and exclaim, "How can they be masters? I'm just like them!" For this reason, some teachers prefer to hide their personal lives. Students rarely see them sleeping, eating, using the bathroom, or in informal situations. Teachers are seen only sitting on a proper seat wearing magnificent robes, looking pure and somber.

Although teachers may appear to suffer from the same failings as their students, it should be remembered that the minds of true teachers are pure. Were they impure, there would be inconsistencies in their understanding of the Dharma. Some people consider me to be a master, but I am quick to point out that I am human, just like them. On one retreat while everyone was participating in the evening service, I dropped a bell. I was tired, and my reactions were slow. I remember thinking that it is best for old teachers to retire because the body ceases to listen to the commands of the mind.

If students see apparent carelessness in their teachers, they may proceed to imitate them. This is not proper practice. It would be foolish if students judged me by my coordination. It would be even more foolish if they imitated my behavior and dropped bells every time they were performing ceremonies. Even if teachers lie, steal, drink alcohol — even if they do so in full view of their students — they should still be judged by their teachings. The teachers themselves will reap the consequences of their actions. Their actions have nothing to do with the students, and if they are good teachers, they will scold students who imitate their undesirable habits. I would not tolerate my students dropping things all the time. The point is, one should rely on the Dharma and not the person. In fact, this is one of the four reliances that the Buddha taught. The other three are: to rely on the meaning not on the words, to rely on wisdom not on consciousness, and to rely on ultimate not on expedient means.

Most students cannot understand this, so trouble arises. It is worst for those students who are unclear about the purpose of practice and who study with teachers only because others do. Instead of paying attention to the teachings, they focus on the teachers' conduct and imitate it, thinking it is the path to progress. This is foolhardy. They will have to reap the consequences of their actions, too, but because their minds are not clear, they will suffer far more. If a teacher curses, they curse. If a teacher drinks alcohol, so do they. Blind and clueless, they do not grasp the correct view, and their karmic burden grows ever heavier.

The moral problems we hear about among Buddhist teachers and their students in the United States are not something new to Buddhism. They have arisen ever since the time of Sakyamuni Buddha. Throughout the history of Buddhism, there have been frequent debates about which is more important: holding the correct view or adhering to the precepts. There is an aphorism in the Ch'an tradition that instructs the practitioner to prize the correct view over the precepts. However, if students were to put this into practice, they would probably break the precepts all the time! This aphorism is not meant for students, but rather for the students' view of the teacher. Students should pay attention to and put into practice the teachings, not the character and conduct, of their teachers.

As far as enlightened practitioners are concerned, their action and behavior should be in accordance with their experience, because enlightenment is not an acquired knowledge. Their enlightenment experience is revealed through the way they behave and interact with the environment. If they still break the major precepts after such an experience, by killing, stealing, sexual misconduct (or sexual conduct for monks), or taking intoxicants, then they are either not truly enlightened or their experience is too weak. Small glimpses into our self-nature, where attachments temporarily drop away, really do not count as enlightenment experiences. It would be much better, both for themselves and others, to forget about the experience, not cling to it, and move on. They should deepen and mature their realizations under another teacher. This is not to say that they should not teach others. Practitioners who are not enlightened, yet have correct views, can and should teach and propagate Buddhadharma. If everyone waited until they were enlightened to teach others, Buddhadharma would become extinct. They should teach but they should be humble and continue with their own practice.

Teachers' faults are symptoms of their own weaknesses or illnesses. It would be stupid for students to desire to contract a teacher's illness. Students' efforts should be geared to finding teachers whose teachings accord with Buddhadharma. Thereafter, students should apply the teachings to their lives and to their lives alone. If you can achieve this, then you have achieved a great deal.

> *"Virtuous man, the wondrous Dharma that is actualized by this good teacher should be free from four kinds of faults. What are these four faults?*
>
> *"The first is the fault of contrivance. If a man says: 'I exert myself in all kinds of practices based on my intrinsic [pure] mind in order to seek Complete Enlightenment,' this is a fault, because the nature of Complete Enlightenment is not 'attained' by contrivance.*
>
> *"The second is the fault of allowing things to be as they are. If a man says: 'I neither wish to sever birth and death nor seek nirvana. There are no conceptions of samsara and nirvana as truly arising or perishing. I allow everything to take its course with the various natures of dharmas in my quest for Complete Enlightenment,' this is a fault, because the nature of Complete Enlightenment does not come about through accepting things as they are.*
>
> *"The third is the fault of stopping. If a man says: 'In my quest for Complete Enlightenment, if I permanently stop my mind from having any thoughts, then I will attain the quiescence and equality of the nature of all [dharmas],' this is a fault, because the nature of Complete Enlightenment does not conform with the stopping of thoughts.*
>
> *"The fourth is the fault of annihilation. If a man says: 'In my quest for Complete Enlightenment, if I permanently annihilate all vexations, then my body and mind, not to mention the illusory realms of sense faculties and dust, will ultimately be emptiness and utter nothingness. Everything will be [in the state of] eternal quiescence,' this is a fault, because the nature of Complete Enlightenment is not annihilation.*
>
> *"One who is free from these four faults will know purity. To discern these faults is to have the right discernment. To have other discernments than these is called erroneous discernment."*

These paragraphs speak of four "faults," or erroneous views, that can befall teachers of the Dharma. The faults correspond to attitudes towards practice. Most of us probably think that the attitudes described in the sutra — contrivance, leaving things as they are, stopping thoughts, and extinction or annihilation — are either indicative of high attainment or prerequisites for attaining high levels of practice. However, from a Ch'an point of view, people with such attitudes fall short of high attainment and are not true Dharma teachers. They teach false Dharma. Discerning students should avoid them.

The first fault, contrivance, is the erroneous view that Complete Enlightenment is the result of practice. It implies that enlightenment originally does not exist and can only be made to appear through practice. People who have this view might also believe that everyday actions — like eating, walking, and talking — are separate from Complete Enlightenment because they are not what are normally considered "methods of practice."

The goal of practice is not to become enlightened and attain Buddhahood. It is necessary for practitioners who need motivation to have this as their goal, but it is not true Buddhadharma. We are all intrinsically Buddhas. If we were not, then it would be impossible to attain Buddhahood no matter how hard we practiced. It is impossible to polish coal and expect to obtain gold; one must start with gold ore. We are all Buddhas, but we must refine and polish ourselves in order to reveal our true nature.

In the beginning stages of practice, it is correct to say that we practice to attain Buddhahood, because we cannot progress on the Buddha Path without making effort. On the other hand, we must realize that practice does not create Buddhahood, just as refining gold ore does not create gold. Practice merely allows our Buddha-nature to manifest.

The points of view of Buddhas and sentient beings are quite different. We see others, including Buddhas, as being sentient beings. If a Buddha walked by, we would just see another person. A Buddha, however, would see everybody as already being a Buddha. A Buddha would not say, "If you sentient beings practice hard, you may someday become like me!" *The Sutra of Complete Enlightenment* speaks from this point of view. It says that a teacher who actively seeks Buddhahood suffers from a fault.

The second fault, leaving things as they are, is to allow things to take their natural course. Some teachers may say that since samsara and nirvana are the same, there is no need to practice. Striving to reach nirvana is just one more attachment, because everyone is already a Buddha. Samsara will naturally become nirvana. People with this attitude may abandon practice and even Buddhadharma. This is another erroneous view. True, enlightenment is not separate from ignorance, but is impossible to realize that without practicing.

Practitioners stuck at this level as well as teachers who advocate this interpretation of the teachings are said to have fallen into the cave of nothingness. They may practice, but they say they do so solely for the sake of practicing, with no guideline or direction. What appears to be energetic practice is really aimless wandering. If the captain of a ship put his whole heart into exercising his skill as a sailor, but ignored warnings of icebergs, I doubt anyone would have much confidence in him.

Teachers with a nonchalant attitude give the impression that they are enlightened. They may say, "Vexation is bodhi and bodhi, vexation," but they do not realize that such insight is gained only with profound enlightenment. Without deep enlightenment experience, such talk is merely throwing around words and empty posturing. For ordinary sentient beings, vexation is vexation and not bodhi. Nirvana and samsara are different, too. One who thinks that there is no cycle of birth and death is like the foolish ship captain who is oblivious of icebergs. Teachers with such an attitude will lead students down the wrong path.

The third fault is stopping, or not moving. This is characterized by the apparent absence of vexation, where the mind is completely unperturbed. This condition applies in general only to advanced practitioners. It refers to those samadhi states where wisdom does not manifest.

Buddhadharma speaks of the three poisons — greed, anger, and delusion — as the root of all vexations. Greed often masks itself as pleasure and enjoyment, feelings not usually associated with vexation. Vexation caused by delusion often goes unnoticed as well, because the mind is unaware of the source of the vexation. It is only with anger that vexation is easily recognized. However, any movement or reaction of the mind — pleasant or unpleasant — is vexation.

Practitioners strive to get to the point where the mind does not move under any circumstances. This is difficult to do. First, one must be serious about practice. Second, one must never stray from the method. Third, one must enter samadhi. In samadhi, the mind is unmoving. But if a person reaches the point where the mind is unperturbed and claims, "I've got it!" then there is a problem.

There is a story about an old woman who provided food and lodging to a Ch'an monk for three years while he practiced diligently. One day, she instructed her daughter to take the monk's meal to him, and affectionately embrace him. The next day the old woman brought food to the monk and asked, "How did you find my daughter?" The monk answered, "Like a dry piece of wood leaning on a cold rock." The old woman picked up a broom, beat the monk, and yelled, "Instead of making offerings to a Ch'an master, I've been wasting my time and effort on a corpse!" She chased the monk away and burned down the hut.

The monk suffered from the illness of stopping the mind. Through practice his mind had reached the point where it dwelled in non-motion, but he falsely believed that this condition was enlightenment. The mind of such a practitioner never moves and is not disturbed, but a teacher would be able to diagnose his stopped mind for what it really is: a dead-end state.

In practice, in order to achieve a true enlightenment stage where you are genuinely alive, you must first pass through a stage of great death — the stage of the non-moving mind. The illness of stopping the mind is to stay in this death-like state. Some practitioners who have not gone beyond this stage have proclaimed themselves masters and gurus, and this is a problem. They are not ready to be true Dharma teachers.

Complete Enlightenment is neither exclusively movement nor non-movement. Enlightenment is in the midst of both. To say that enlightenment can only manifest in a stopped mind is erroneous. In an enlightened state, there is no movement driven by the sense of self in the mind, yet it still contemplates and illuminates; the mind still gives rise to functions. Without contemplation and illumination, a stopped mind is a dead-end state, a rock soaking in cold water.

The fourth fault is annihilation. It is not the same as the third fault of stopping. Stopping means that the mind does not move and that the sense consciousnesses do not arise. Once the mind moves again, however, the sense faculties begin to function once more. Annihilation means ceasing to exist. This fault happens at a more advanced stage than stopping. I sometimes describe the path of practice as going from scattered mind to one mind to no-mind. One mind corresponds to samadhi, in which there is no distinction, no differentiation, and the mind does not move. With annihilation, however, the mind no longer exists. Senses no longer function. Vexations and wisdom no longer exist. Nothing exists. Some would say such a person has entered nirvana. Others would say this person has ceased to exist.

However, one does not have to actually experience annihilation to have this fault. It is also a sickness to hold the erroneous view that annihilation is true Buddhadharma and the goal for practice. In the dhyana state there are three realms: the realm of desire, the realm of form, and the formless realm. Practitioners who experience the formless realm have no perception of bodily existence, mental existence, or the phenomenal world. Nevertheless, to become attached to this sense of liberation from phenomena is a great obstacle.

How can students tell if a teacher is affected by one or more of the four faults? The truth is that students are usually not at a level of practice where they are able to pass judgment on their teachers. The teacher must, through introspection, see if he or she suffers from any of the four illnesses. On the other hand, it is possible for a teacher to be aware of the four faults, to teach about and warn against them, and still not be able to detect them in him or herself. The most that students can do in this situation is rely on what was said in previous paragraphs. The paragraphs I have just commented on are meant for teachers, not students.

> "*Virtuous man, sentient beings in the Dharma Ending Age who wish to cultivate themselves should, to the end of their lives,*

make offerings to virtuous friends and serve good teachers. When a good teacher approaches them, they should sever arrogance and pride. When the teacher leaves them, they should sever hatred and resentment. Be it a favorable or adverse condition that [a teacher] brings them, they should regard it as empty space. They should fully realize that their own bodies and minds are ultimately identical with all sentient beings', and are the same in essence, without difference. If they practice in this way, they will enter the [realm of] Complete Enlightenment.

"Virtuous man, when sentient beings in the Dharma Ending Age are unable to accomplish the Path, it is due to the seeds of love and hatred towards themselves and others since beginningless time. Thus they are not liberated. If a man regards his foes as he would his parents, without duality, then all faults will be eliminated. Within all dharmas, self, others, love, and hatred will also be eliminated.

"Virtuous man, sentient beings in their quest for Complete Enlightenment in the Dharma Ending Age should give rise to the bodhi-mind, saying: 'I will lead all sentient beings throughout boundless space into ultimate Complete Enlightenment. In [the realm of] Complete Enlightenment, there is no realizer of enlightenment, and [the signs of] self, others, and all characteristics are left behind.' Giving rise to such a mind, they will not fall into erroneous views."

At that time, the World Honored One, wishing to clarify his meaning, proclaimed these gathas:

> *Universal Enlightenment, you should know*
> *that sentient beings in the Dharma Ending Age*
> *who wish to seek a good teacher*
> *should find one with correct views*
> *whose mind is far away from the Two Vehicles.*
> *The Dharma [he actualizes] should be free*
> *from the four faults of*
> *contrivance, stopping, allowing things*
> *to be as they are, and annihilation.*
> *Approached by the teacher, they should*
> *not be arrogant and proud.*
> *Left by the teacher, they should not be resentful.*

When witnessing different conditions
displayed by the teacher,
they should regard them as precious rare occurrences,
like a Buddha appearing in the world.
[They should] break not the rules of discipline and demeanor
and keep the precepts forever pure,
lead all sentient beings into
the ultimate Complete Enlightenment,
be free from the signs of the self,
person, sentient beings, and life.
When relying on correct wisdom,
they will transcend erroneous views,
actualize enlightenment and enter parinirvana.

The concluding section of this chapter of the sutra deals with the proper attitudes and prerequisites for those on the path. In particular it deals with the relationship between students and teachers.

It is important that students unconditionally respect their teachers and make offerings to them. People who have been accepted as students by teachers should not become attached to their good fortune as though it were a medal of honor. On the other hand, if teachers refuse to instruct certain people, the rejected students should not be insulted or respond in resentment. This is the proper attitude for students. Teachers should not feel joy or pride when students seek their guidance; nor should they feel unhappy if students leave to study elsewhere. This is the proper attitude for teachers.

Maintaining such an attitude of equanimity is not easy. Ordinary people will find it difficult to be impartial when they consider their own merits. They might be reluctant to see their faults for what they are, or they might discredit their genuinely good traits. Although outwardly different, pride and self-deprecation are really the same thing. Self-deprecation usually stems from a feeling of insecurity or worthlessness. Insecurity can be negative if it leads one to conclude that it is impossible to accomplish anything. Insecurity can also be positive. It can help one to strive toward goals, attain wealth, fame, or self-respect.

If people succeed in their goals, they may feel special or better than others. This is pride. Here is an example: The boss of a company lectures the employees, saying, "You want a raise? Consider this. You wouldn't be working here if it weren't for me. It's my intelligence and effort that make it possible for you to have work. When you reach my level, then come talk to me about a raise." This is a proud boss.

Spiritual teachers can also be proud. A master might say, "I've practiced for many years and have followed many masters in my time. Now I've reached my ultimate attainment. You students, however, have not reached that stage. You're far from my level and must go a long way before you achieve what I have already achieved." This is not proper conduct for a true teacher.

Some Ch'an masters might act like dictators, but it is not proof that they are proud. The question is whether the teachers feel pride within themselves. Once I was riding with two of my students, a husband and wife. They asked, "Have you had any problems lately?" I answered, "As far as I am concerned, there are no problems." The woman said, "I always knew you were a proud man. Everyone has problems. As the saying goes, unless you've been through it, you can't understand what the problem is. So how can you avoid problems?"

My student perceived that I was proud. That was her assessment, but here is my explanation: If I set out to accomplish something, the obstacles I encounter do not seem like problems. They're part of the process. If there is something I cannot accomplish, I don't waste my time trying to do it. Thus nothing seems like a problem to me. Is this pride? It depends on how you look at it. To truly see pride and insecurity in someone, you must also look at the motivation, not just the action.

Suppose as many people came to the Ch'an Center as go to other popular centers. I might say, "Before, I couldn't compete with these other groups, but now I'm catching up with them." This would be pride because I'm competing with and comparing myself to others. You should not compare yourselves to others. It is not necessary. If you compare, you'll either feel superior or inferior.

In ancient China there was a search for the most beautiful woman in the land, whose name was Xisi. Her beauty was comparable to that of Cleopatra. Xisi underwent long training in the arts of walking, applying make-up, singing, playing musical instruments, and speaking. Another woman in the same area named Dongsi was jealous. She imitated Xisi's every move, look, and mannerism, but it didn't work. The more she imitated Xisi's walk, the clumsier she appeared. The more make-up she applied, the worse she looked.

Learn not to compare yourselves to others. Almost everyone at one time or another will say, "I am no good." But really you are only hoping that someone will praise you and point out your good points so that you can feel better. In ordinary people, pride and insecurity are to be expected. It is the extremes that are dangerous. If you feel totally useless, then your insecurity becomes a major problem; you might even do harm to yourself. If you are bloated with pride to the point where you feel god-like, then you might turn into another Hitler, Stalin, or Mao Zedong.

A Ch'an master, on the other hand, is more likely to show pride than insecurity, because no one could become a master if he or she were insecure. Someone who felt insecure would say, "How can I be a master and teach others when I'm not good enough myself?" Such a person has no confidence.

Self-respect, however, is a normal and healthy feeling to develop in the course of practice. Indeed, you should experience it. Self-respect is a sign that your faith in yourself is growing stronger. As a result of practice, you gradually come to see things that others may miss, and from this recognition springs compassion. You become more tolerant of other people's shortcomings because you see them in yourself.

For both students and teachers, the most important thing is to attend to practice and be free of attachment — attachment to self, others, and external phenomena. To be free of attachment while practicing the Dharma is the foundation for helping oneself and others. Attachments will inevitably lead to erroneous views.

The sutra speaks of two kinds of learned teachers: those who are virtuous and those who, despite being learned, have a bad influence on others who study with them. As I discussed earlier, there are three main principles of the correct view of practice, and it is important that teachers adhere to these principles. Bad teachers might say that worldly phenomena are eternal and independent and deny the emptiness of causes and conditions; or they might incorrectly teach the principles of karma and cause and consequence; or they might be extreme in their views and teachings and not keep to the middle way. Many people have difficulty determining whether a teacher is virtuous or non-virtuous. They do not know which path is correct. It is difficult to know if a teacher is virtuous, in the West as well as in the East. Many practitioners go from one teacher to another, like tourists on a Dharma circuit. They lack faith in their teachers. They study with one master for a while, hear something good about another, and move on.

Someone once asked a Dharma master, "How many teachers have you had?" When he found out that the master had had only one teacher, he said, surprised, "Only one? How can you learn the Dharma from only one teacher? How long have you practiced with this teacher?" The master said thirty years, and the person expressed pity for him for spending so much time with only one teacher. The Dharma master said, "The fact that I have studied with one teacher for thirty years is a minor accomplishment, but if I had studied with thirty teachers for one year apiece, then I would not even call myself a practitioner!"

Many people try to collect teachers like trophies. Here in the United States I've met many such people, but they are found in the East as well. In Taiwan we use a term for them which can be rendered gypsies for lack of a better translation.

I once asked a Chinese student how many teachers he had studied with. He replied, "You name the master, and I probably studied with him," and then he rattled off names of teachers, both living and dead, from many traditions.

"How can you learn anything when you move from one teacher to the next as often as you do?" I asked.

He said, "Have you ever watched bees? They go from flower to flower and collect the nectar from each one. In the same way, I go from master to master and extract the 'essence' of their teachings and incorporate it into my own being."

"Excellent!" I said. "You take their essence and leave behind the less desirable aspects. You should be more outstanding than any of them."

"That's what I'm aiming for," he replied, "but I can't say I've accomplished it yet."

"So you've studied with masters of many traditions. If you were to die right now, where would you go?"

"I'm surprised you asked that," he said. "You should know that all the myriad dharmas reduce to one. If I were to die at this moment, my Pure Land teacher would chant for me, my Ch'an master would give me a kung-an, my Vajrayana teacher would bless me, and so on. I only need a little bit of help from each of them. All dharmas reduce to one, so there is no problem."

"That was well said," I responded. "But suppose there were four boats ready to take off for a distant destination. If you had one foot in each of two boats and each hand holding onto the other boats, what would you do when they all launched and took different routes?"

"I'd be in trouble," he replied, "but I don't like your analogy. In the *Avatamsaka Sutra*, Bodhisattva Manjusri told Sudhana to learn from other masters. He ended up studying with fifty-three teachers."

"Yes, but he was fortunate to have met the right teacher the first time. Furthermore, it was Manjusri who sent Sudhana to another master. Sudhana didn't take it upon himself to leave. In every case, it was the master who advised Sudhana to go to another teacher. Was this the case with you?"

"No," he said. "If I were to stay with a master for a long time, he wouldn't want me to go. So I take it upon myself to leave."

I answered, "If a master has that attitude, then he is not virtuous."

"Then there isn't a single virtuous master alive today," he said.

"Now you're more wrong then ever," I replied. "Some of the names you mentioned I recognize, and they are virtuous and learned. In accepting you as a student it shows they see that you are worthy. You should be grateful."

"Obviously," he said, "you don't know how these people really are. They don't teach you everything, and they always hold back the most special Dharma for themselves."

"If that's true," I told him, "then your previous comment about collecting their 'essence' is wrong. You haven't been like a bee at all, but rather like a fly collecting garbage!"

Since ancient times those who became accomplished in the Dharma practiced with one teacher for a long time. If you recognize a good teacher, then stay and study with that person. There may come a time when this master sends you to another teacher, perhaps to practice a special method. That is fine. Often enough, practitioners who are sent away by masters return later on.

There are people who study under various teachers in different traditions without ever finding one they can call master. In Japan I met a man who wanted to become a monk, but he was unable to choose a master because he saw shortcomings in all of them. He particularly objected to some priests being married, even though this is the custom in Japan. I suggested that he study under a particular Shingon master who was not married, but he said, "He may be single now, but later on he may decide to marry."

"With that attitude," I said, "you'll never know if teachers are good enough until they're dead. Students shouldn't judge teachers by their own standards. Practitioners should learn from and concentrate on a teacher's virtues, not weaknesses. Use the fundamental principles of rightview and the three principles of precept, samadhi, and wisdom in Buddhism to find a virtuous master, and when you do, respect and make offerings to that teacher."

Bees see fragmented rather than smooth images. Their vision is different from ours. In the same sense, as students we have a point of view that is confused and distorted. We should not rely on our own viewpoints when judging the virtues and weaknesses of teachers. It is worse to anticipate faults in teachers before they even exist.

In Taiwan there was a monk who had four devoted lay disciples. After ten years, the monk became a layman again and married. Nonetheless, his lay followers continued to consider him their master. People said that it was wrong to make offerings to a layman, but the lay disciples did not care. They said that his getting married was no concern of theirs. He introduced them to the Dharma, and for this they were grateful. These students had the proper attitude.

As far as making offerings to teachers is concerned, we must remember that we cannot place material value on the teachings and guidance we receive. Virtuous teachers have few material needs, yet it is important for our practice that we express our gratitude, and this often takes material form. Making offerings is highly regarded in the sutras.

Making offerings to teachers is like feeding grass to cows. The cow eats your grass, but then it produces milk to nourish you and others. The grass is not nutritious to humans, but transformed by a cow it becomes nutritious. When you make offerings to a teacher, you are giving something to the Dharma. Your material gift may be transient, but its benefit is lasting and unlimited. In making offerings, you gain not only merit, but your determination to cultivate the Dharma is planted like a seed that will no doubt grow. The more you offer, the more your determination will grow.

The offerings you make depend on your capacity and situation. Until you are a bodhisattva, do not make offerings that might endanger your life or livelihood. Great bodhisattvas can offer anything to the Dharma, including their own lives. The important thing is what you feel in your heart and mind when you make offerings.

A person once said to me, "I always think about you and want to make offerings to you, but you live such a simple life and seem to have everything you need. Since it's what is in the heart that is important, I will make an offering within my heart. Is that sufficient?" I said, "The fact that I have enough to live on is my concern. Making offerings is your concern."

If you look at the altar in the main hall at our temple, you see that every day we make offerings of fruit, vegetables, and flowers. The Buddha statue never eats the food or smells the flowers, but this should not concern us. What should concern us is that we want to make offerings, and that we continue to want to make offerings.

Bodhisattva of
Complete
Enlightenment

Then the Bodhisattva of Complete Enlightenment rose from his seat in the midst of the assembly, prostrated himself at the feet of the Buddha, circled the Buddha three times clockwise, knelt down, joined his palms, and said: "O World Honored One of great compassion! You have broadly expounded expedient methods for attaining pure enlightenment so that sentient beings in the Dharma Ending Age may receive great benefit. World Honored One, we have already awakened. Yet after the nirvana of the Buddha, how should sentient beings in the Dharma Ending Age who are not awakened dwell in retreats to cultivate this pure realm of Complete Enlightenment? Which of the three kinds of pure contemplation are foremost within the [cultivation of] Complete Enlightenment? May the great Compassionate One bestow great benefit upon this assembly and sentient beings in the Dharma Ending Age." Having said these words, he prostrated himself on the ground. He made the same request three times, each time repeating the same procedure.

At that time the World Honored One said to the Bodhisattva of Complete Enlightenment: "Excellent, excellent! Virtuous man, you have asked the Tathagata about such expedient methods for the sake of bringing great benefit to sentient beings. Listen attentively now. I shall explain them to you."

Hearing this, the Bodhisattva of Complete Enlightenment was filled with joy and listened silently along with the assembly.

"Virtuous man, whether during the time of the Buddha's stay in the world, after his nirvana, or in the declining period of the Dharma, sentient beings with Mahayana nature who have faith in the Buddha's mysterious mind of great Complete Enlightenment and who wish to cultivate themselves should, if they live in a monastic community with other practitioners and are occupied by various involvements, examine themselves and engage in contemplation as much as circumstances permit in accordance with what I have already taught.

"If they are not occupied by various involvements, they should set up a place for practice and fix a time limit: 120 days for a long period, 100 for a medium period and 80 for a short period. Then they should dwell peacefully in this pure place. If the Buddha is present, they should hold correct contemplation of him. If the Buddha has entered nirvana, they should install his image, generate right mindfulness, and gaze at him as if he were still living in the world. They should adorn [the sanctuary] with banners and make offerings of flowers and within the first twenty-one days make obeisance to the Buddhas in all ten directions with utmost sincere repentance. Thus they will experience auspicious signs and obtain lightness and ease [of the mind]. After these twenty-one days, their minds should be well collected.

"If the retreat period overlaps with the three-month summer retreat [of sravakas], they should adhere to and abide with the retreat of a pure bodhisattva instead. Their minds should stay away from the [ways of] sravakas, and they do not have to be involved with the community at large. On the first day of the retreat, they should say this in front of the Buddha: 'I, bhikshu or bhikshuni, upasaka or upasika so-and-so, in the bodhisattva vehicle, will cultivate the practice of quiescent-extinction and together enter [with other bodhisattvas] into the pure abode of Absolute Reality. I will take the great Complete Enlightenment as my monastery. My body and mind will peacefully abide in the

Wisdom of Equality. The intrinsic nature of nirvana is without bondage. Without depending on the sravakas, I now respectfully pray that I can abide for three months with the Tathagatas and great bodhisattvas in all ten directions. For the great cause of cultivating the unsurpassed wondrous enlightenment of a bodhisattva, I will not be with the community at large.'

"Virtuous man, this is called the retreat manifested by the bodhisattva. At the end of the three kinds of periods of retreat, he is free to go unhindered. Virtuous man, if practitioners in the Dharma Ending Age go into retreats on the Bodhisattva Path, they should not accept [as authentic] any experience which they have not heard [from the Tathagata]."

There are two main types of practice: practice in daily life and practice during a specific time and at a specific place — as in a retreat.

Many people have spoken to me about the problems of maintaining their practice. One practitioner said, "I've been listening to Dharma lectures for years, and I've practiced hard, but it seems that when vexations arise, I'm unable to get rid of them. Perhaps practice is useless."

Another person said, "Every day I have to manage two hundred people and give them assignments. If I don't do my job, they won't know what to do. If they have problems, they come to me. Their problems become my problems. This is too much for me."

A woman told me, "I'm sixty years old. During my life I've helped many people. Now I feel it's time for me to practice seriously. But I can't let go of the people that I've helped. I'm nagged by thoughts and dreams that I should continue to help them. How can I practice if I have to care for all these others? I must practice alone, but it's so difficult."

I believe these three examples are relevant to many people. I doubt that most of you are able to make vexations go away the moment they arise, and although you shouldn't let other people's problems cause you vexation, how many of you can claim to have this ability? Ideally one should be like a glass filled with colored water. No matter what the water may look like, the glass remains unaffected. But if you were faced with the kinds of problems mentioned above, could you remain unaffected like that glass? Even if you could only do it sometimes, that would be good. Most people, however, are like a piece of cloth, absorbing the paints and stains that fall on it. Most people, when confronted by a problem that has nothing to do with them, make it their own.

Many people are like the sixty year-old woman who is unable to give up her old habits and the surroundings she is familiar with. She lacks determination. Some people feel that they cannot yet put down responsibilities of family or work. But if they cannot put aside these things while practicing, they cannot truly practice.

If someone who was mentally unbalanced were to spit in your face, how would you respond? You might tell me now that you would not be upset because you would realize that the person was unaware of his or her actions, but if it really happened, would you be so calm and clear? In fact, I saw something like this happen. A crazy person beat a man on the street. The man went to the police and complained, but the policeman said, "That guy is crazy."

So the man said, "Then he should be locked up." The policeman responded, "He was in an asylum, but they released him."

"Then he should be put back in because he's still insane," said the man.

"Don't be so angry," said the policeman. "He can't help himself. He's insane."

The man could not be appeased. If he had the right attitude, he would have understood that the problem belonged to the insane person, and he would not have been bothered by the turn of events. He would have remained free of vexations.

I point out these things to show you that, in general, daily practice is insufficient. It is difficult to reach a level of purity and peace strictly through daily practice. We live in the midst of confusion and agitation, so it is difficult to achieve the kind of tranquillity that allows the mind to remain unbothered by external events. This is why one or more periods of sustained practice each year are essential. If you are serious about practice, it is necessary that you devote an extended amount of time to intensive practice sometime during your life.

If you do not practice daily, you may not be able to maintain enthusiasm for practice, and without periods of extended practice, it is impossible to experience even a brief period of true peace. Daily practice is useful for two reasons: it maintains your interest in and enthusiasm for practice, and it reminds you that you are a practitioner. This constant reminder helps you to realize how inappropriate and foolish it is to be vexed by life's ups and downs. However, a deeper sense of peace can only be experienced through intensive practice over an extended period of time.

Because of the relative importance of daily and intensive practice, I found it necessary to give three different answers to those who complained to me about their difficulties. To the first person, who was discouraged by the persistence of his vexations, I said it was good that he recognized his inability to transcend vexations. It meant that he was practicing well. If he had been practicing poorly, he would not even have noticed his vexations. Thus he had virtuous karmic roots. I said to him, "You are like someone who has eyes to see and a brain to think, but whose arms and legs don't listen to commands. You see a pile of dung in front of you, yet you are unable to avoid walking into it." Having an idea of what is about to happen is better than blindness or ignorance. The blind person cannot see at all, and the ignorant person sees but does not understand. It takes someone who has practiced for a while to recognize vexation.

When I related this to the person, he was reassured, but he asked, "Will there ever be a time when I am unaffected by vexations?" I told him that it was possible to transcend vexation, but it was impossible to say when it would happen. I told him that he had to continue to practice. In this way, vexations would gradually lessen and not disturb him.

Practitioners deal with vexations in three stages. First, they recognize and identify vexations. This is the beginner's stage. Second, they deal with their vexations. When a vexation arises, they are clear about the nature of the problem and how it arose. They do not feel resentment toward the vexation. They simply accept it, and then they repent the action that caused the vexation and try not to let it happen again. Third, vexations arise only once and then disappear, never to return again. Further vexations arise, but they too disappear and never return. Problems are terminated piece by piece. Most people, when they begin to practice, hope that all their vexations will immediately end forever. This is impossible for beginners. Only practitioners whose karmic roots are profound and whose merits are immensely virtuous are capable of such complete and immediate attainment. Such practitioners are already bodhisattvas.

Beginning practitioners should not be disillusioned when intense vexations arise. It is like weeding a garden. The day after you weed, the weeds are already growing again. One must weed again and again. If one's attitude is to let the weeds grow, then soon the garden will be overrun and will never be cleared. The same is true of vexation. However, if we never cease in our efforts, then there will be times when our minds are clear and undisturbed by vexation. For those who say that it's useless to strive to cut off vexations, I say this: "Since you are going to get dirty again, there is no point in bathing anymore." I doubt you would go along with that kind of logic. Just as you bathe to keep your body clean, so should you meditate regularly to keep your mind clear.

To the man who manages two hundred people, I said, "You should practice Ch'an in daily life. You have the perfect opportunity in your work environment to practice the Bodhisattva Path. My recommendation is that you meditate two hours every day, longer on Sundays, and attend two week-long retreats each year. Then you will easily be able to deal with any problems that arise at work, and you will see them as an opportunity to practice Ch'an."

If what you do in daily life is for the benefit of others, then everything in daily life is the practice of Ch'an. Serving and helping is an essential part of Ch'an practice. We should treasure any opportunity to practice, even in difficult situations. With this attitude, we will see people with problems as bodhisattvas who are giving us an opportunity to practice.

To the sixty year old woman, I said, "You understand the importance of Ch'an practice. I advise you to put away everything else and direct all your effort to practice. Without sufficient practice, the help that you give to others will be limited, regardless of how much effort you put into it. But if you practice, there will be no limit to the help you can give to others. This is why I tell you to make practice your first priority."

Becoming a great practitioner is not easy. You begin as an ordinary person with all of the problems, difficulties, and doubts that ordinary people have. From there you must strive, always trying harder and harder, until you reach your goal. This is the only way for a true practitioner.

> "*Virtuous man, if sentient beings practice samatha, they should first engage in perfect stillness by not giving rise to conceptualization. Having reached the extreme of stillness, enlightenment will come about. Such stillness [acquired] in the beginning [of practice] pervades a universe from one's body, as does enlightenment. Virtuous man, when enlightenment pervades a universe, a single thought produced by any living being in this universe can be perceived by these practitioners. When their enlightenment pervades hundreds of thousands of universes, the same condition prevails. They should not accept [as authentic] any experience that they have not heard [from the Tathagata].*"

This paragraph addresses the practice of *samatha*. *Samatha* means stilling the mind. When the mind stills to the point where thoughts cease to arise, then the body, mind and universe disappear. This is bodhi. Bodhi is being clearly aware of everything.

Bodhi, as it is described here, has three distinct levels. As the mind gradually stills, you will first be aware of each of your thoughts as they pass in succession. Second, you will be aware of the thoughts of every sentient being in this universe. Third, you will be aware of the thoughts of every sentient being in every other universe. At the second level, awareness is better described as illumination and is analogous to the way a camera records all that is in front of it without making distinctions. The third level differs from the second level in that distinctions are made between this and that, but without the attachments that beset the ordinary mind. At this level, an enlightened bodhisattva will see clearly and without attachment and will be able to make distinctions based on wisdom to help sentient beings.

The last line of the paragraph admonishes us not to cling to anything that one does not hear from the Buddha. Hearing is not to be understood in its usual meaning. Conventionally speaking, hearing means listening to teachings of the Buddha. Hearing the Dharma can lead one to have faith in and understanding of the Buddha's teachings, but it is not enough. One must also practice, for only through practice can one directly experience the true meaning of the Dharma. This realization clears away all doubts and is beyond intellectual understanding. The hearing that the Buddha refers to in this paragraph refers to direct realization. Anything else is illusion.

There are people who come to hear me lecture, but they do not practice. Many of them eventually stop coming to the Ch'an Center, saying that all I do is repeat myself over and over again, and that it does not help them in any way. There are others who listen and also practice, but who still have problems. For those people, reciting the Buddha's name does not bring one-mindedness, contemplating emptiness does not bring obstructionless clarity, and counting breaths does not calm the mind. The first group of people has some level of faith and understanding, but it's not firm. The second group has gone on to practice, but this does not guarantee firm faith in and progress on the Buddha Path either. Such people are still in the midst of vexation. At least, however, these people have a chance of gaining realization. Faith and understanding alone are not enough.

> "Virtuous man, if sentient beings practice samapatti, they should first be mindful of the Tathagatas in all ten directions and the bodhisattvas in all worlds. Relying on various methods, they will diligently cultivate samadhi in gradual steps, bearing hardship. They should make great vows [to save sentient beings] and thus ripen their seeds [of Complete Enlightenment]. They should not accept [as authentic] any experience that they have not heard [from the Tathagata]."

As I have said before, samapatti literally means equal holding and refers to holding both samatha (chih, stillness) and vipassana (kuan, contemplation) in the mind. The mind is not moving, yet it is clearly aware of the object of contemplation. This sutra expounds Mahayana *samapatti*, which has at its base the motivation to save sentient beings. In order to be correctly practicing Mahayana *samapatti*, one must have the compassionate vows of the bodhisattva at the forefront of one's mind while cultivating the deepening levels of samadhi. As in the paragraph on *samatha*, the last sentence of this paragraph should be interpreted to mean: Do not believe in anything that does not come from direct experience and realization.

> *"Virtuous man, if sentient beings practice dhyana, they should begin with methods of counting. [Gradually] they will be clearly aware of the arising, abiding, and ceasing of each thought, as well as the state before the arising of a thought, the state after the arising of a thought, and the scope and number of these thoughts. Further on, they will be aware of every thought, whether walking, standing, sitting or lying down. By gradually advancing still further, they will be able to discern a drop of rain in hundreds of thousands of worlds as if seeing, with their own eyes, an object used by them. [Again], they should not accept [as authentic] any experience that they have not heard [from the Tathagata]."*

Although this paragraph seems identical to the paragraph on *samatha* practice, it is subtly different. The paragraph on *samatha* speaks of being aware of every thought in one's mind as well as in the minds of every sentient being throughout innumerable universes. The paragraph on *samapatti* emphasizes experiencing the compassionate vows of the bodhisattva while cultivating samadhi. This paragraph explains what one should do on mastering the levels of *samatha* and *samapatti*. There are two parts to this paragraph: one deals with the practitioner and the other with the world and other sentient beings.

The word "count" in this paragraph describes what one has to do with respect to oneself and others. One must be clearly aware of one's every thought, but on a deeper level than that explained by *samatha*. *Samatha* requires that one be aware of each successive thought. Dhyana goes a step further. Namely, with each thought one should be aware of its "life span": its arising, abiding, changing nature, and annihilation. In every bodily position — described by the terms walking, standing, sitting, and lying down — one must be aware of the four parts that constitute each thought that arises in the mind.

To be clearly aware of thoughts as they arise in succession in the mind is already a major accomplishment in one's practice. To be aware of the four stages that every thought goes through is extremely difficult to master. However, it is a worthwhile method to practice. Seeing thoughts as they pass in succession is like watching a movie, but seeing the stages of each thought is like slowing the movie down and carefully observing the nature of each frame.

After one has mastered the ability to watch the arising, abiding, changing, and perishing nature of each thought in one's own mind, one must then clearly perceive the same process in the minds of every other sentient being throughout every universe. At that time, one would be aware of every occurrence everywhere — a drop of water in another world would be as clear as if it were before one's eyes.

It seems that this paragraph does not talk about helping sentient beings, but at this stage of accomplishment it is not necessary to mention it. Helping others becomes spontaneous. Seeing vexations in others is the same as seeing vexations in oneself. Such beings who can do this are bodhisattvas of the highest order. They do not simply perceive the world with clarity like a mirror reflecting images. They are actively engaged in the world, fulfilling their compassionate vows.

It is clear that one can be aware of one's own thoughts, but I will explain how it is possible to be aware of the thoughts of others as well. First you must reach the stage where body and mind are unified. Ordinarily we are aware of others through our sense organs. We see light waves with our eyes and hear sound waves with our ears. Our capacity, however, is dull, limited, and coarse.

Scientists have proven that brain waves can be detected. When the mind is functioning, waves are emitted. Thoughts carry energy, so if the mind is sufficiently still and clear, these thoughts can be detected. When the mind is clear, the six senses become keenly powerful, and one becomes capable of sensing and knowing things that would ordinarily go by undetected.

The capacity of people with unified bodies and minds is still limited, however. They may be aware of the thoughts and feelings of those who are within range, but for them to know the thoughts of all sentient beings in all universes is impossible. To reach this stage, body, mind, and universe must disappear. In other words, all attachments must fall away. At this point, the six senses are purified, and one can know the thoughts of all sentient beings simultaneously. In the Mahayana tradition, such a practitioner would be a bodhisattva on the first bhumi level or higher.

> *"These are the foremost expedient methods in practicing the three contemplation techniques. If sentient beings thoroughly practice and master all three of them with diligence and perseverance, it will be called, 'Tathagata appearing in the world.' In the future Dharma Ending Age, if sentient beings with dull capacities who wish to cultivate the Path are unable to gain accomplishment due to their karmic obstructions, they should zealously repent and always remain hopeful. They should first sever their hatred, attachment, envy, jealousy, flattery, and crookedness, and pursue the unsurpassable mind. As to the three kinds of pure contemplation, they should practice one of them. If they fail in one, they should try another. They should steadily strive to attain realization without giving up."*

At that time, the World Honored One, wishing to clarify his meaning, proclaimed these gathas:

> *Complete Enlightenment, you should know*
> *that all sentient beings*
> *seeking to tread on the unsurpassed Path*
> *should first enter a retreat.*
> *They should repent their beginningless*
> *karmic obstructions for twenty-one days*
> *and then engage in right contemplation.*
> *Experiences that they have not heard about*
> *   [from the Tathagata]*

should not be accepted [as authentic].
In samatha one practices perfect stillness.
In samapatti one upholds right mindfulness.
In dhyana one begins with clear counting.
These are the three pure contemplations.
Those who practice them with diligence
are called "Buddhas appearing in the world."
Those with dull capacities who are not accomplished
should repent zealously of all the misdeeds
they have created since beginningless time.
When all obstructions are extinguished,
the realm of Buddhahood appears.

If one practiced these three contemplation methods successfully, then it would be as if the Tathagata were appearing in the world. This can be interpreted in two ways: first, on accomplishing these contemplations, one personally sees the Tathagata; second, on accomplishing these contemplations, others see the Tathagata in the practitioner.

On the other hand, practitioners who do not have keen capacity and who are mired in vexation should repent their past actions. Repentance is best done through prostration practice. Prostrating helps to alleviate heavy karmic burdens, thus making it easier to practice contemplation methods.

The sutra says that if practitioners are unsuccessful in cultivating one of the three contemplation methods, then they should try another. This is possible, but it should be emphasized that one should try *samatha* first, *samapatti* second, and dhyana third. These are deepening levels of cultivation, and if one is unsuccessful in practicing *samatha*, it is doubtful that one will be successful in practicing the other two. My advice is if you have difficulty with the first contemplation method, then practice repentance instead.

The sutra has its reasons for saying what it says, however. It can be interpreted this way: If one can gain accomplishment in one method, then one can gain accomplishment in all three methods. All methods of practice are interrelated.

Bodhisattva
Foremost In Virtue and Goodness

Then the Bodhisattva Foremost in Virtue and Goodness rose from his seat in the midst of the assembly, prostrated himself at the feet of the Buddha, circled the Buddha three times clockwise, knelt down, joined his palms, and said: "O World Honored One of great compassion! You have broadly revealed to us and sentient beings in the Dharma Ending Age such inconceivable things. World Honored One, what should this Mahayana teaching be named? How should one receive and observe it? When sentient beings practice it, what merit will they gain? How should we protect those who keep and recite this sutra? What will the extent of the benefit be if one spreads this teaching?" Having said these words, he prostrated himself on the ground. He made the same request three times, each time repeating the same procedure.

At that time the World Honored One said to the Bodhisattva Foremost in Virtue and Goodness: "Excellent, excellent! Virtuous man, for the benefit of the multitude of bodhisattvas and sentient beings in the Dharma Ending Age, you have asked the Tathagata the name and merit of this teaching. Listen attentively now. I shall explain it to you."

Hearing this, the Bodhisattva Foremost in Virtue and Goodness was filled with joy and listened silently along with the assembly.

> *"Virtuous man, this sutra is expounded by hundreds of*
> *thousands of millions of Buddhas as innumerable as the grains of*
> *sand of the Ganges. It is esteemed by all Tathagatas in the past,*
> *present, and future. It is the refuge of all bodhisattvas in all ten*
> *directions. It is the pure eye of the twelve divisions of the Buddhist*
> *scriptures.*
>
> *"This sutra is called the Dharani of Complete Enlightenment*
> *of the Mahavaipulya Teaching. It is also called the Sutra of the*
> *Ultimate Truth, the Mysterious King Samadhi, the Definitive*
> *Realm of the Tathagata, and the Distinctions within the Intrinsic*
> *Nature of the Tathagatagarbha. You should respectfully receive and*
> *observe it."*

Sakyamuni proclaims that he is not the only Buddha speaking these words. He is joined by innumerable Buddhas from the past, present, and future. Therefore *The Sutra of Complete Enlightenment* is spoken in every world and universe, not just ours. It is thus protected by all Buddhas of all universes. It is in this sutra, as well, that all bodhisattvas take as their refuge. Sakyamuni calls it the most important of all Buddhist sutras, one that every bodhisattva and Buddha has to understand and practice. Moreover, when practitioners attain Buddhahood, these are the words which they will expound.

The Sutra of Complete Enlightenment is called the "pure eye of the twelve divisions of the Buddhist scriptures" because it serves as the basis of understanding all other sutras, whether they be gathas, prose, analogies, or descriptions of Buddhas' past lives. The sutra is called the Mysterious King Samadhi because it expounds the highest samadhi and those teachings that are most subtle. It is called the Definitive Realm of the Tathagata because the sutra can only be fully understood by Tathagatas. It is called the Distinctions within the Intrinsic Nature of the Tathagatagarbha because it is from the intrinsic nature of Complete Enlightenment that all differentiation arises. The Tathagatagarbha itself is unmoving, yet the merit intrinsic in it manifests in innumerable ways.

> *"Virtuous man, this sutra reveals only the realm of the Tathagatas*
> *and can only be fully expounded by the Buddha, the Tathagata. If*
> *bodhisattvas and sentient beings in the Dharma Ending Age rely*

on it in their practice, they will gradually progress and reach Buddhahood.

"Virtuous man, this sutra belongs to the sudden teaching of the Mahayana. From it sentient beings of sudden [enlightenment] capacity will attain awakening. This sutra also embraces practitioners of all other capacities who engage in gradual cultivation; it is like a vast ocean which allows small streams to merge into it. All who drink this water, from gadflies and mosquitoes to asuras, will find fulfillment."

Some sutras stress that teachings of sudden enlightenment can only benefit those who already have the karmic potential for sudden enlightenment. Sentient beings without this karmic potential would be unable to practice according to such sutras, but *The Sutra of Complete Enlightenment* is different because beings of all potentialities can receive benefit by practicing according to its teachings. The sutra is described as a great ocean that accepts all streams. Gadflies, *asuras*, or titans can all gain satisfaction from hearing the teachings of the sutra.

There is also a deeper meaning to this ocean analogy. Because the water comes from the one ocean, whatever amount different sentient beings draw from it will be of the same taste. Therefore if someone directly experiences the teachings of this sutra, then no matter what his or her potential, he or she will see what the Buddha sees. The depth and breadth of the experience may vary, but its essence is the same.

"Virtuous man, if there were a man who, with the purest intentions, gathered enough of the seven treasures to fill a great chiliocosm and gave them all as alms, he could not be compared to another man who hears the name of this sutra and understands the meaning of a single passage. Virtuous man, if someone teaches hundreds of sentient beings as innumerable as the grains of sand of the Ganges such that they attain arhatship, his merit cannot be compared to that of an expounder of half a gatha of this sutra.

"Virtuous man, if a man hears the name of this sutra and has faith in it without any doubt, you should know that he has sown the seeds of merit and wisdom not with just one or two

Buddhas; indeed he has cultivated roots of goodness and heard the teaching of this sutra from Buddhas as innumerable as the grains of sand of the Ganges. Virtuous man, you should protect all practitioners of this sutra in the Dharma Ending Age so that evil demons and heretical practitioners will not disturb their bodies and minds and cause them to regress."

The Buddha makes several points here. First, he speaks about the merit gained by listening to and gaining understanding from this sutra. If you just hear the name of this sutra, then your merit is greater than if you had given away an uncountable amount of treasure as alms. Even greater is your merit if you understand a sentence of its teachings.

Second, helping innumerable beings to reach arhatship does not compare to teaching even so much as half a gatha of this sutra to someone. Sakyamuni is extolling the virtues of Mahayana, which teaches that in order to reach Buddhahood, one must take the great compassionate vow of the bodhisattvas.

Third, it states that those who hear the sutra now must have heard it innumerable times before from previous Buddhas, and that those who have firm faith in its teachings must have practiced with countless Buddhas.

Fourth, the Buddha beseeches the bodhisattvas and disciples in the assembly to help and protect future practitioners who take this sutra as their guide. Practitioners should be guided in such a way that they not diverge from the path or regress in their practice. The sutra then continues by naming a number of these protectors in the assembly:

At that time in the assembly, the Fire Head Vajra, the Wrecking Vajra, the Nila Vajra, and other vajra [guardians] numbering eighty thousand, together with their retinues, rose from their seats, prostrated themselves at the feet of the Buddha, circled him three times clockwise, and said in unison: "World Honored One! If in the Dharma Ending Age there are sentient beings who practice this definitive Mahayana teaching, we will guard and protect them as we would our own eyes. We will lead our retinues to their

*place of practice to guard and protect them day and night so that
they will not regress. We will see to it that their families will
forever be free from all calamities and hindrances, that they will
never have any plagues and illnesses, that their wealth and
treasures will be ample, and that they will not be in need."*

There is a great deal of benefit to be gained from this sutra. On its
highest level, practicing according to its teachings will lead to
Buddhahood. On another level, you, your family, and your environment will be protected while you practice. The Buddha has a
two-fold task: to expound teachings guiding bodhisattvas and other
sentient beings in their practice, and to guard those who do practice
from harm and regression. The Buddha need not help directly.
There are Dharma-protecting deities as well as incarnations of
bodhisattvas who can take on this responsibility. Deities will thus
be found not only near those who practice the Dharma but also
wherever there are Buddhist sutras.

Dharma-protecting deities come from the power of the
Buddha, and they can be sensed by accomplished practitioners.
Though a practitioner may not be aware of their presence, they are
nonetheless there. There are times when one's life undergoes a
significant change in direction, and depending on the situation, it
could be the work of a Dharma-protecting deity. You may think
that you came up with a dramatic decision on your own, but there
could have been some influence from outside forces. A Dharma-
protecting deity can act in ways that lead a practitioner, at appropriate times, to a different perspective or a new attitude.

In order to gain the support of these deities, it is important to
have a proper understanding of practice. In my case, I never ask
deities to help me. Nevertheless, I know they are there and that
they are willing to help and support me. Therefore, I have no fear
that my mental environment will be disturbed by outside forces. It
is precisely because I do not ask for anything that the Dharma-
protecting deities help me.

When these deities are invoked, it is important to clarify one's
intentions. If a practitioner is seeking help for the sake of the
Dharma, then there will be no problems, because it is the duty of

these deities to spread the Dharma. However, if the invocation is made for selfish reasons and the request is answered, then the practitioner can expect to have to repay his or her karmic debt.

At this point we reach the end of the sutra. Perhaps it would be best to finish with the verses themselves:

Then Mahabrahma-devaraja, the king of the twenty-eight heavens, the king of Mount Sumeru, and the [four] Lokapalas rose from their seats, prostrated themselves at the feet of the Buddha, circled him three times clockwise and said in unison: "World Honored One! We too will guard and protect those who observe this sutra so that they can live in security and peace without regression."

Then the powerful king of demons, Kumbhanda, and one hundred thousand other demon kings rose from their seats, prostrated themselves at the feet of the Buddha, circled him three times clockwise and said: "World Honored One! We also will guard and protect those who observe this sutra from morning to night so that they will not fall back in their practice. If ghosts and spirits approach within one yojana of their dwelling, we shall pulverize them."

When the Buddha had preached this scripture, all who were in the assembly, including bodhisattvas, devas, nagas, and others of the eight groups with their retinues, as well as the deva kings and Brahma kings, having heard the teaching of the Buddha, were filled with great joy. With faith, they respectfully received and practiced this teaching.

Glossary

A

Amitabha Sutra (*A mi tuo jing* 阿彌陀經): the principle scripture on which the Pure Land practice is based. The practice of recitation of Buddha Amitabha's name is one, if not the most accessible and simplest form of Buddhist practice. Through Amitabha Buddha's vow, any person who sincerely invokes his name and expresses the wish to be born in the Pure Land will be reborn there.

Anuttara-samyak-sambodhi (*a nou duo luo san miao san pu ti* 阿耨多羅三藐三菩提): unexcelled perfect enlightenment of the Buddha.

Arhat (*a luo han* 阿羅漢): "worthy one." In Buddhist tradition, the arhat is thought of as having completed the course of Buddhist practice, and attained liberation, or nirvana. As such, the arhat is no longer subject to, rebirth and death. Arhat is also one of the epithets of the Buddha.

Asamkya (*a seng qi* 阿僧祇): innumerable and infinite.

Asura (*a xiu luo* 阿修羅): one of the type of beings in the six realm of existence. *Asuras* are beings who have the merit to travel to the heavenly realms but are inflicted with a mind of jealousy. They are always jealous of heavenly devas or gods and fight with them.

Avalokitesvara (*Guan shi yin* 觀世音): perhaps the most important bodhisattva in the East Asian Buddhist tradition; he is the embodiment of compassion who hears and responds to the cries of all living beings. Avalokitesvara can be both male and female, but in China, the bodhisattva is usually depicted in the female form.

Avatamsaka Sutra see *Hua-yen Jing*

Avidya (*wu ming* 無明): lit. "unillumined." *Avidya* means fundamental ignorance or darkness. It is usually considered as a fundamental or primal condition of sentient beings, which mistakes illusion as reality. Fundamental ignorance brings about desire and thereby is the essential cause binding sentient beings in cyclic existence experiencing all kinds of suffering. It veils the understanding of the true nature of existence and is the cause for the construct of illusions. The analogy of fundamental ignorance used throughout *The Sutra of Complete Enlightenment* is the flower in the sky.

B

Bhagavan (*Shi zun* 世尊): lit. "World Honored One." One of the ten titles of the Buddha.

Bhikshu, Bhikshuni (*bi qiu* 比丘, *bi qiu ni* 比丘尼): fully ordained Buddhist monk and nun respectively.

Bhumi (*di* 地): the bhumis (ground, regions, or stages) are the last ten stages of the bodhisattva's career on his/her way to full Buddhahood. *See* bodhisattva positions.

Bodhi (*pu ti* 菩提): bodhi can refers to: 1) the principal wisdom that severs all vexations and defilements and realizes nirvana, 2) the phenomenal wisdom that realizes the truth of every conditioned phenemenon that can realized omniscience.

Bodhi-mind (*pu ti xin* 菩提心): the mind of wisdom. A central idea in Mahayana Buddhism; its meaning varies in different contexts: 1) the altruistic mind of a person who aspires to attain Buddhahood for the sake of helping sentient beings, 2) the genuine actualization of enlightenment, awakening to the true nature of reality and the loftiness of Buddhahood, and 3) selfless action. This last meaning is extremely important yet often overlooked. In regards to the first definition, arousing the bodhi-mind is the first step in establishing oneself on the Bodhisattva Path.

Bodhisattva (*pu sa* 菩薩): "enlightened being." The role model in the Mahayana tradition. The bodhisattva is a being who vows to remain in the world of samsara, postponing his/her own full liberation until all other living beings are delivered.

Bodhisattva Positions (*pu sa wei* 菩薩位): anyone who can give rise to the altruistic mind of enlightenment, although still an ordinary person, becomes a bodhisattva and enters into the family of the Buddhas. In the Chinese Buddhist tradition, specifically the Hua Yen tradition, bodhisattva realizations and attainments are divided into 52 positions: Ten Faiths (*shi xin* 十信), Ten Abodes (*shi zhu* 十住), Ten Practices (*shi xing* 十行), Ten Transferences (*shi huei xiang* 十迴向), Ten Grounds (*shi di* 十地), Ultimate Wisdom (*deng jue* 等覺), and Subtle Wisdom (*miao jue* 妙覺). Practitioners at the level of Ten Faith are still considered ordinary people (*fan fu wei* 凡夫位), although there is a division between ordinary people of the "inner circle" (*nei fan* 內凡) and "outer circle" (*wai fan* 外凡). Practitioners of the next thirty positions are considered to have reached sagehood (*xian wei* 賢位). Practitioners at the Ten Grounds and above have reached sainthood (*sheng wei* 聖位).

Another division of Bodhisattva positions is the Path of Seeing (*darsanamarga, jien dao wei* 見道位), the Path of Practice (*bhavanamarga, xiu dao wei* 修道位), and the Path of Attainment (*labhamarga, jiu jing wei* 究竟位). According to the Chinese doctrinal system, when a person perceives self-nature or nature of emptiness (*kung xin* 空性), the person is said to have entered the Path of Seeing and has entered the domain of the ordinary people of the "inner circle" within the Ten Faiths position. Path of Practice begins at the level of the Ten Abodes and ends at the Ten Transferences. The Path of Attainment begins at the first position of the Ten Grounds. A bodhisattva progresses on this path toward complete, perfect Buddhahood through abandoning gross levels of self-grasping to subtler and subtler levels of self-grasping. At the same time, a bodhisattva cultivates merit and benefits living beings until all obstructions to full wisdom of emptiness are realized and omniscience is attained.

Buddha (*fo* 佛): "the awakened one." The historical Buddha is the religious teacher Gautama Sakyamuni, who founded the religion generally known in the West as "Buddhism."

Buddhadharma see Dharma

Buddha-nature (*fo xing* 佛性): the nature or potentiality for Buddhahood; synonym for the nature of emptiness. In is also equivalent to Tathagatagarbha.

C

Causal Ground (*yin di* 因地): another term for Buddha-nature. It is
called ground because it can give rise to all merit and virtue; it is
the potential for Complete Enlightenment. Causal ground can
also refer to the initial generating of the bodhi-mind.

Ch'an (禪): better known in Japanese as "Zen." Ch'an is one of the
main schools of Chinese Buddhism to develop during the Tang
Dynasty (618-907). The designation derives from the Sanskrit
word dhyana, transliterated as *chan-na* 禪那 in Chinese. Ch'an
can mean meditation but it can also mean the heart of Buddhism
— enlightenment.

Cyclic Existence see samsara.

D

Dharani (*tuo luo ni* 陀羅尼, *zhong chi* 總持): dharani derives from the
root word "dhara," which means maintaining, holding, control
or preserving. The literal Chinese translation of this word is
"universal control" or "complete control,". It refers to complete
"maintenance" of wisdom and "control" over evil passions and
influences. The words "complete" and "universal" also bear the
meaning of inclusiveness, because it is the essence of all approaches to the Dharma. Therefore, practicing one dharani
means practicing all approaches to the Dharma. In this sutra,
dharani refer to Complete Enlightenment or Buddha-nature.

Dharma (*fa* 法): dharma has two basic meanings. Dharma with an
upper case "D" means the Buddhist "law" or "teaching." Dharma
with a lower case "d" simply refers to a thing or object, and
physical or mental phenomenon.

Dharmakaya (*fa shen* 法身): Dharma Body. One of the three bodies
of the Buddha — the ultimate body of reality beyond all forms,
attributes, and limits. In the Chinese Buddhist tradition the
expression, "to see the Dharmakaya" means to realize the nature

of emptiness. It is sometimes used as a synonym for Buddha-nature.

Dharma Ending Age (*mo fa shi dai* 末法時代): a period of time when the teaching of the Buddha is weak, and although there may be practitioners, no one is able to gain realization.

Dharmadhatu (*fa jie* 法界): dharma realm, the infinite realms or worlds of reality; it can also be regarded as the ground or nature of all things — the Mind from which all proceeds.

Dhyana (*chan na* 禪那): a term designating certain states of meditative absorption cultivated by Buddhist practitioners as a technique for attaining enlightenment. However, in this sutra dhyana is referring to a practice after enlightenment, in which one solely cultivates the nondual quienscent and still nature of mind. See the chapter on Bodhisattva at Ease In Majestic Virtue for further inquiry.

E

Eight Consciousnesses (*ba shi* 八識): a central idea in the Indian Yogacara (*Yu qie xing pai* 瑜伽行派) or the Consciousness-only school (*vijnaptimatrata, wei shi zong* 唯識宗) of Chinese Buddhism, which divides consciousness into eight modes of operation. Together, these eight modes of operation are divided into three catagories: 1) *vijnana* (*shi* 識), referring to the first five sense consciousnesses (or the "knowing" that arise from contacts between sense faculty and the corresponding sense object) and the sixth sense consciousness, the faculty of mental discrimination (*manovijnana; yi shi* 意識), 2) *manas* (*yi* 意), referring to the seventh ego consciousness (*mo na shi* 末那識), and 3) *citta* (*xin* 心), referring to the eighth consciousness, *alayavijnana*. The first six consciousnesses are named after the sense faculties that serve as their support, 1) eye consciousness, 2) ear consciousness, 3) nose consciousness, 4) tongue consciousness, 5) body consciousness, 6) mind consciousness. The sixth consciousness, our ordinary mind, is characterized by discrinmination and has all dharmas as its object. It utilizes the previous five consciousensses in order to identify, interpret, and define the world. The seventh

consciousenss is the source of the delusion of a separate self, belief
in a self, self-conceit, and self-love; it takes the eighth consciousness as its support and its object of attachment. It can be said to
be the center of these eight consciousnesses. The eight consciousness or (*alayavijnana, a lai ye shi* 阿賴業識) operates as the underlying continuum of the workings of mind and functions as an
underlying projective consciousness on which delusion is ultimately based. It is a kind of a "repository" or "storehouse" that
contains all experiences as karmically-charged seeds, which, under
the proper causes and conditions, ripen as actions of body,
speech, and mind, which in turn creates new seeds. Therefore, the
eighth consciousness is unceasingly conditioned by the previous
seven consciousnesses. When one is thoroughly enlightened, these
consciousnesses become the function of wisdom.

Eighteen Exclusive Attributes of the Buddha (*shi ba bu gong fa*
十八不共法): whether walking, standing, sitting, or lying down, the
physical body of the Buddha is always dignified and recomposed;
a Buddha can never make mistakes in speech or speak inappropri-
ately; a Buddha's mind is always tranquil and luminous; a
Buddha's true form is formless; a Buddha's mind is always in
samadhi, like still water; a Buddha's mind is clear of all thoughts
like a mirror reflecting images without clinging. The Buddha has
an inexhaustible desire to deliver sentient beings, unsurpassable
diligence, inextinguishable mindfulness, inextinguishable Wisdom
of Equality, unending observing Wisdom of Liberation, unending
Mirror-like Wisdom derived from full liberation, all actions of
body, speech and thought are in accordance with wisdom, and the
ability to perceive the past, present and future in accordance with
wisdom.

Eighteen Realms (*shi ba jie* 十八界): theses realms refers to the
domain of the six sense faculties, sense objects, and sense
consciousnesses.

F

Fearless Eye of the Path (*wu wei dao yen* 無畏道眼): perspicacity.
Ability to discern true from false, wholesome from unwholesome, as a result of having realized enlightenment.

Four Kinds of Fearlessness (*si wu wei* 四無畏): the Buddha's ability to bestow fearlessness in the heart/mind of sentient beings: correct wisdom of all Dharmas; exhaustion of all out-flows of wisdom, merit and virtue, as well as extinction of all habitual tendencies; ability to expound remedies to all obstructions and hindrances on the Path; ability to fully explain causes of suffering.

Four Noble Truths (*si shen di* 四勝諦): the four basic principles of Buddhism preached by Buddha in his first sermon: 1) that in the ultimate analysis, life is suffering, 2) that the causes of suffering is desire, 3) that there is a state of peace called nirvana, beyond all suffering and poisons of the mind, and 4) that the way which leads to nirvana includes the practice of morality, concentration, and wisdom.

Four Unhindered Wisdoms (*si wu ai zhi* 四無礙智): four eloquent skills in expounding the Dharma by Buddhas and great bodhisattvas: without hindrance in Dharma — ability to understand the texts and systems of the Dharma; without hindrance in meaning — ability to understand all subtle meanings of the Dharma; without hindrance in eloquent speech — ability to eloquently speak in any dialect; without hindrance in debate — ability to fully present the Dharma eloquently and appropriately to sentient beings.

H

Heart Sutra (*Xin Jing* 心經): one of the most important sutras of Mahayana Buddhism. It is especially significant in Chinese Ch'an and Japanese Zen schools.

Hinayana: a designation for the path of individual liberation within Buddhism. A hinayanist would be anyone in any tradition who practices for self-enlightenment or liberation, regardless of whether he or she practices the Northern or Southern traditions of Buddhism.

Hua-t'ou (話頭): lit. the source of words (before they are uttered), a method used in the Ch'an school to arouse the "doubt sensation" (*yi qing* 疑清). The practitioner meditates on such baffling questions as: "What is Nothingness?" "Where am I?" or "Who is reciting the Buddha's name?" One does not rely on experience, logic, or reasoning. Often, these phrases are taken from kung-ans, at other times, they are spontaneously generated by the practitioner. The term "hua-t'ou" is often used interchangeably with the Japanese useage of "koan."

Hua-yen (*Avatamsaka* 華嚴): lit. "Flower Adornment," one of the most important and influential scholastic schools of Chinese Buddhism to develop during the Tang dynasty (618-907). The fundamental teaching of this school is the equality of all things and the unobstructed interpenetration of and interrelation between absolute reality with all phenomena.

Hua-yen Jing (*Avatamsaka Sutra* 華嚴經): a massive Mahayana Buddhist sutra translated from Sanskrit into Chinese in the fifth century, seventh century, and late eighth century. The sutra became quite popular among Chinese Buddhists, who believed that this sutra was a revelation from the Buddha's enlightenment while still absorbed in the ocean-seal samadhi (*hai yin san mei* 海印三昧) under the bodhi tree. In China, this sutra eventually became the basis of the Hua-yen school. The Ch'an school has always held it in especially high regard.

K

Kalpa (*jie* 劫): an old Indian way of calculating an unimaginably long period of time — an eon. These are of various lengths. The basic kalpa is 13,965 years long. One thousand such kalas constitue a small kalpa (*hinakalpa*; *xiao jie* 小劫). Twenty small kalpas makes a medium kalpa (*antarakalpa*; *zhong jie* 中劫), and four medium kalpas makes a great kalpa (*mahakalpa*; *da jie* 大劫). The creation, continuation, destruction, and emptiness — four phase of a world cycle — is four kalpas.

Karma (*ye* 業): lit. "action." Basically, the law of cause and effect to which all sentient beings indeed, all things, are subject. Karma is broadly construed in Buddhism to include physical, verbal, and mental actions. It is also the cumulative causal situation affecting one's destiny as a result of past acts, thoughts, emotions.

Kung-an (公案): lit. a "public case," as in a law case. A Ch'an method of meditation in which the practitioner energetically and single-mindedly pursues the answer to an enigmatic question either posed by the master, or one that arises spontaneously. The question can be answered only by abandoning logic and reasoning, through directly generating and breaking through the "doubt sensation" under natural causes and conditions. Famous kung-an encounters were recorded and used by masters to test their disciples' understanding, or they served as a catylist for enlightenment. The term "kung-an" is often used interchangeable with "hua-to."

M

Mahayana (*da cheng* 大乘): lit. "great vehicle" whose followers vow to attain Supreme Enlightenment for the sake of delivering all other sentient beings from suffering.

Mani Jewel (*mo ni zhu* 摩尼珠): symbolic of the precious inherent Buddha-nature (*fo xing* 佛性) in all sentient beings.

N

Nirmanakaya: see Transformation Body

Nirvana (*nie pan* 涅槃): total extinction of desire and suffering, the state of liberation through full enlightenment.

No-self (*anatman; wu wo* 無我): the Buddha's central teaching that there is no isolated, self-existing entity that can be grasped as the self; it is merely a conceptual construct from the illusory mind.

P

Paramitas (*bo luo mi* 般羅蜜): "perfections" or ways for transcendance to liberation. The six paramitas are the main practices of Mayayana bodhisatvas: giving (*dana; bu shi* 布施), morality (*sila; chi jie* 持戒), patience (*ksanti; ren ru* 忍辱), diligence (*vira; jing jin* 精進), meditation (*dhyana; chan ding* 禪定), and wisdom (*prajna*; *bo re* 般若). The ten paramitas, practiced by great bodhisattvas above the Ten Grounds, consist of four more additions to the six paramitas: expedient means (*upayakausalya*; *fang bian* 方便), vows (*pranidhana*; *yuan* 願), power (*bala*; *li* 力), and all-knowing wisdom (*jnana*; *zhi* 智).

Platform Sutra (*Tan Jing* 壇經): a scripture attributed to the seventh century Ch'an master, Hui-neng (638-713), who was the Sixth Patriarch in the Ch'an school, and perhaps the most famous of Chinese patriarchs. He was the founder of the southern school of Ch'an, which emphasized sudden enlightenment.

Pratyekabuddha (*bi zhi fo* 辟支佛): a self-enlightened being (*du-jue* 獨覺), one who has attained liberation from all suffering by contemplating dependent origination (*yuan-jue*; 緣覺).

R

Retribution Body (*bao shen* 報身): "sambhogakaya." One of the three bodies of the Buddha: body of beatitude — the form of the Buddha that enjoys the fulfilment of their vows in their Pure Lands.

S

Samadhi (*ding* 定): like dhyana, samadhi also refers to states of meditative absorption, but it is a broader and more generic term than dhyana. Although numerous specific samadhis are mentioned in Buddhist scriptures, the term "samadhi" itself is flexible and not as specific as dhyana. In Mahayana sutras, the term samadhi is inseparable from wisdom.

Samatha (*she mo ta* 奢摩他): a term designating the practice of calming or stilling the mind. However in this sutra *samatha* referrs to a practice after enlightenment, in which a practitioner emphasis the cultivation of the still, mirror-like nature of mind. See the Chapter on Bodhisattva at Ease In Majestic Virtue for further inquiry.

Samapatti (*san mo bo ti* 三摩砵提): a term referring to the four formless states of meditative absorption. However in this sutra *samapatti* refers to a practice after enlightenment, in which a practitioner relies on illusory means of delivering sentient beings to eliminate illusions. See the chapter on Bodhisattva at Ease In Majestic Virtue for further inquiry.

Sambhogakaya: see Retribution Body

Samsara (*lun hui* 輪迴): the relentless cycle of birth and death and suffering in which ordinary, unenlightened sentient beings are deeply entangled. There are three realms within samsara: the desire realm (*yu jie* 欲界), the form realm (*se jie* 色界), and the formless realm (*wu se jie* 無色界).

Samskrta (*wu wei* 無爲): with many nuances, *samskrta* can mean activity, production, contrived effort, conditioned things or any process that results from karma. In this sutra, "practicing with *samskrta*" can mean practicing with attachments.

Sastra (*lun* 論): one of the "three baskets" of the Tripitaka. Sastra is a book of treatise, discource, discussion, or commentary clarifying, or sometimes systematizing, Buddhist philosophical ideas from the sutras.

Sravakas (*shen wen* 聲聞): associated with the Hinayana tradition. Literally "sound-hearer," one who has attained arhatship or at least the first of the four levels of sainthood from having heard the Buddha's teaching.

Srimala Sutra (*Sheng man Jing* 勝鬘經): a Mahayana scripture, it is outstanding for its commentary on the Tathagatagarbha theory and for the teaching that all sentient beings have the potentiality of Buddhahood.

Surangama Sutra (*Leng yen Jing* 楞嚴經): this Mahayana sutra is extremely important in shaping the uniqueness of Chinese Buddhism. It describes twenty-five different perfect penetration samadhis to reach thorough enlightenment, the positive and negative experiences a practitioners may encounter, and fifty different outer-path practices that one can stray into.

Sutras (*jing* 經): generally, scriptures. Specifically, the recorded "open" teachings of the Buddha that can be practiced by anyone. The distinctive mark of a Buddhist sutra is the opening line, "Thus have I heard." This indicates that what follows are the direct teachings of Buddha, as remembered and recorded by his disciples.

T

Tathagata (*Ru lai* 如來): one of the ten epithets of a Buddha, which can means "thus-come" or "thus-gone." The Chinese translation of Tathagata means "thus-come."

Tathagatagarbha (*ru lai zang* 如來藏): womb, or store of the Tathagata — the potentiality of Buddhahood in each sentient being. Another name for Buddha-nature.

Ten Directions (*shi fang* 十方): an expression for all directions: four cardinal directions, four intermediate directions, and the directions above and below.

Ten Titles of the Buddha: Thus-come, Worthy of Offering, Right and Universal Knowledge, Perfect Clarity and Conduct, Well Gone, Understanding the World, Unsurpassable Worthy One, Instructor of People, Teacher of Heavenly and Human Beings, Buddha, the World Honored One.

Ten Powers (*shi li* 十力): the complete knowledge of a Buddha: what is right or wrong in every situation, what is the karma of every being in the past, present and future, all stages of dhyana and samadhi, the powers and dispositions of all beings, the desire and moral direction of every being, the actual condition of every individual in all the different vehicles of practice, the direction and consequence of all teachings, all causes of morality and their good and evil in their realities, i.e. to know all previous lives of sentient beings and their causes for rebirth, to know the future lives of all beings and their entrance to nirvana, the destruction of all illusion of every kind.

Thirty-seven Aids to Enlightenment (*san shi qi dao pin* 三十七道品): the thirty-seven aids to enlightenment are: four foundations of mindfulness (*si nian chu* 四念處), four proper lines of exertion (*si zheng qin* 四正勤), four advance steps to power of ubiquity (*si ru yi zu* 四如意足), five positive capacities (*wu gen* 五根), five forces intensifying the five positive capacities (*wu li* 五力), seven aspects toward enlightenment (*qi jue zhi* 七覺支), the eight noble path (*ba zheng dao* 八正道).

Transformation Body (*hua shen* 化身): Nirmanakaya. One of the three bodies of the Buddha, the form that a Buddha manifests to facilitate the deliverance of sentient beings.

Twenty-five Existences (*er shi wu you* 二十五有): this is a classification of the samsaric realm of existence: the four continents, the four evil destinies, six heavenly realms of desire, the four dhyana stages, the four stages of formlessnesss, the realm beyond conceptualization, and the realm of *anagamin* (*a na han* 阿那含, those arhats who are reborn into the heavens in the realm of form or formless heavens where they will attain nirvana).

Twelve Entrances (*shi er ru* 十二入): six sense faculties and the six sense objects, or "dust."

Two Vehicles (*er cheng* 二乘): vehicles refers to paths or approaches of Dharma practice. The two vehicles refer to the vehicles of sravaka and pratyekabuddha.

V

Vajra (*jin gang* 金鋼): a term that means as indestructible as a diamond and powerful as a thunderbolt.

Vexation (*klesa, fan nao* 煩惱): the innate mechanism to possess and to act, tainted by an attchment to self, which in turn continues the cycle of samsara. Vexations include all kinds of mental states such as joy and resentment, sadness and happiness, as well as greed, hatred, delusion, arrogance, and doubt.

W

Wisdom-eye (*hui yan* 慧眼): that which perceives the true empty nature of all phenomena.

Index

Additional Books by Master Sheng-yen

Getting the Buddha Mind

The Poetry of Enlightenment — Poems by
Ancient Ch'an Masters

Faith in Mind

Ox Herding at Morgan's Bay

Infinite Mirror

The Sword of Wisdom

Zen Wisdom — Knowing and Doing

Dharma Drum — The life and heart of Ch'an practice

Catching a Feather on a Fan

For information about Ch'an Master Sheng-yen and his retreat community in the United States and Taiwan, please contact:

Ch'an Meditation Center
90-56 Corona Avenue
Elmhurst, NY 11373 U.S.A.
Tel: 718/592-6593
Fax: 718/592-0717
E-mail: DDMBAny@aol.com

Dharma Drum Retreat Center
184 Quannacut Road
Pine Bush, NY 12566 U.S.A.
Tel: 914/744-8114

Nung Ch'an Monastery
89, Lane 65, Ta Ye Road
Peitou 11242,
Taipei, Taiwan, R.O.C.
Tel: 8934646
Fax: 8960731
E-mail: iac1586@tpts1.seed.net.tw

If you would like to receive a brochure of books by Dharma Drum Publications, please contact:

Dharma Drum Publications
90-56 Corona Avenue
Elmhurst, NY 11373
Tel: 718/595-0915
Fax: 718/592-0717
Email: DDMBAny@aol.com
URL: http://www.chan1.org

Dharma Drum Publications is a non-profit publisher of books on Buddhism and Ch'an. Our titles are published in appreciation of Buddhism as a living philosophy and with the commitment to preserve and transmit important works and authentic teachings of Buddhist thought and practice. In furtherance of this aim, we publish original commentaries to scriptures and Ch'an discourse records relevant to the growth and understanding of Buddhism in the West.